THE SOCIAL PHILOSOPHY
OF ENGLISH IDEALISM

THE SOCIAL PHILOSOPHY OF ENGLISH IDEALISM

BY

A. J. M. MILNE

Ph.D., B.Sc.(Econ.)

*Lecturer in Social Philosophy
at the Queen's University of Belfast*

LONDON

GEORGE ALLEN & UNWIN LTD

RUSKIN HOUSE   MUSEUM STREET

TO J. J. MILNE

809.91
M65

PRINTED IN GREAT BRITAIN
BY EAST MIDLAND PRINTING CO. LTD
BURY ST. EDMUNDS, SUFFOLK

PREFACE

This book has grown out of work which I first began nearly ten years ago at the London School of Economics. I had been awarded a research grant by the Leon Bequest Committee of the University of London and I should like to express my appreciation to its members for the opportunity which they gave me. From 1952-54 I was in the United States on a Commonwealth Fund Fellowship and if my programme of study was broader than the scope of this book, it nevertheless contributed much which was to prove valuable, particularly in respect of my own philosophical development. This may be a suitable occasion for me to express my appreciation for my two years in America and I would like especially to thank Mr E. K. Wickman and Mr Lancing B. Hammond, who were then officers of the Division of Education of the Commonwealth Fund, for all that they did for me as for other Fellows. I should also like to express my thanks for the facilities which I enjoyed during 1952-53 in the Philosophy Department of the University of California at Berkeley, and during 1953-54 in the School of Historical Studies at the Institute for Advanced Study at Princeton, New Jersey.

When I returned from America the general plan of this book was taking shape in my mind, and working it out occupied me on and off for the next five years. During this period, as well as during the final stages of preparing the book for publication, I have received invaluable help from a number of people. Professor M. J. Oakeshott of the London School of Economics read through the first draft and I would like to thank him for some very helpful comments and suggestions. I am also greatly indebted to Professor W. B. Gallie of the Queen's University, Belfast. He read through two different drafts and, apart from making many valuable suggestions, has been a constant source of friendly encouragement for which I am most grateful. I am most grateful to Mr E. D. Phillips and Mr Philip Thody, both of Queen's; to the former for his many useful suggestions on points of style and expression; to the latter for his Herculean labours over the proofs. I should also like to thank Miss Ann

Greer for her care and trouble in typing the final draft. Last but not least, I must thank my wife both for her general support and for her tolerant indulgence during times when the strain of authorship was making itself rather obviously apparent. Finally, there is an intellectual debt which I should like to acknowledge. It is to the philosophical work of R. G. Collingwood. This has been the chief seminal influence in my thinking while working on this book and, although I never knew Collingwood personally, I should like to put on record my appreciation of what I owe to him.

A. J. M. MILNE

Belfast, August 1961

CONTENTS

NOTE : The numbers in brackets after the quotations in the text
refer to Appendix 1.

The word 'idealism' has a well established meaning in English. It is also the name of a school of philosophy. This book is concerned with the school of philosophy, not with idealism in the ordinary sense. It might be supposed that a clue to the general standpoint of the school could be found in the ordinary meaning of the word but this is not so. As the name of a school of philosophy, 'Idealism' refers to ideas rather than ideals. An Idealist philosopher is not, *qua* philosopher, an idealist in the ordinary sense. This does not mean that he has no concern with ideals. He has; but as a philosopher, not as a devotee.

At the turn of the century Idealism was perhaps the leading school of philosophy in the English-speaking world. Many professional philosophers approached their work in terms of its general standpoint and method. Today the situation is very different. There has occurred during the last two generations what has been described as 'a revolution in philosophy', one consequence of which has been the almost total eclipse of Idealism. Few contemporary philosophers have more than a superficial knowledge of it and fewer still have any interest in it. The general assumption is that it has been discredited by the philosophical revolution. But has it? To raise this question is not to deny that those who made the revolution had something to revolt against. It was largely a revolution against Idealism and there must have been something wrong with Idealism to provoke it. Nor is it to deny that valuable intellectual achievements have resulted from the revolution. But it is to question the assumption that the whole Idealist enterprise was unprofitable, that it was nothing but an unfortunate aberration in the development of modern philosophy. On a more positive note, it is to suggest that, notwithstanding certain defects, there may be something to be said for Idealism.

This book is an attempt to follow up that suggestion. It is a critical study of certain aspects of the work of four Idealist philosophers. It deals mainly with their social philosophy, but some consideration is also given to their metaphysics. By their social philosophy, I mean that part of their work which was concerned with human life in society, in particular their ethics and political theory; by their metaphysics, that part of it which was concerned with first principles, in particular their doctrines about knowledge and reality. It is the thesis of this book that there is a valid and significant form of Idealism to be found in the work of these philosophers, but that they did not succeed in developing it fully and consistently. They came nearest to doing so in their social philosophy and were least successful in their metaphysics. Indeed there are certain defects in their metaphysics which are due to the fact that in this part of their work they drifted away from the Idealist standpoint of their social philosophy. The aim of this book is to contribute to a re-assessment of Idealism by developing this thesis. Such interest as it may have will be largely for philosophers and those interested in philosophy. But perhaps it may not be altogether without interest for students of the social sciences. The social sciences and social philosophy are, or should be, complementary, and it is part of the thesis of this book that there is much of permanent significance in Idealist social philosophy.

Perhaps the most marked difference between English Idealism and contemporary English philosophy is over the nature and scope of philosophy itself. Broadly, the current view is that philosophy is an activity of analysis, the aim of which is intellectual clarification. It does not yield knowledge; for that we must go to the sciences and to history. But according to the English Idealists, philosophy is, or at least can be, something more than merely analysis. It can yield knowledge, and knowledge of a kind which is not to be found in the sciences or history. In the course of this book, I shall argue in support of this conception of philosophy, notwithstanding the fact that the English Idealists sometimes abused it and, especially in their metaphysics, claimed too much for philosophy. But this does not mean that I underrate the value of analysis as it is conceived and practised today. Indeed I do not think there is any fundamental incompatibility between philosophical analysis in the contemporary sense and the form of Idealism which I shall recommend. Their aims are different but need not conflict. There will be disagreement only if it is contended that philosophy must be nothing but analysis, that nothing else is possible. But contemporary philosophers are entitled to demand that a more ambitious conception of philosophy should make good its claims, and I shall do my best in the course of this book to meet that demand.

The four Idealist philosophers with whom this book is concerned are: F. H. Bradley, T. H. Green, Bernard Bosanquet and Josiah Royce. About the first three, little needs to be said by way of introduction. They are generally acknowledged to have been the leading figures of the Idealist movement in British philosophy. One point only calls for a word of explanation. Green was ten years older than Bradley and, when he died in his middle forties, the latter's philosophical career had only just begun. But in this book Bradley's work in social philosophy is discussed before Green's. The reason is that Bradley's major contribution to this field was made at the beginning of his career, while Green's came in the last years of his life. It is moreover an improvement on Bradley's work. From the point of view therefore of both chronological and logical development, it is necessary to discuss Bradley first. Josiah Royce was a contemporary of Bradley and Bosanquet, and like them was a philosophical Idealist. But he was an American, and his inclusion in a book purporting to be about English Idealism may occasion some surprise. The reason is that a study of certain aspects of his work is necessary for the development of the book's main thesis. In addition, a glimpse of the parallel development of Idealism in America is perhaps not without some interest. As regards the word 'English' in the title, my excuse, if I need one, is that by it I mean 'the English-speaking world' rather than England.

I have said that the aim of this book is to contribute to a reassessment of Idealism. This is a philosophical aim, but there is a sense in which it is also historical. Before you can make a critical evaluation of the work of past philosophers, you must know what that work was. This book is, inter alia, a reconstruction and exposition of certain aspects of the philosophy of Bradley, Green, Bosanquet and Royce, and in this sense it is a contribution, for what it is worth, to the history of philosophy. But it is not historical in the broader sense. It is not concerned with the personal biographies of the four philosophers, nor with the effect of their work upon other philosophers or on the general life of their time. Nor again is it concerned with the historical origins of their philosophy. On this last point however a further word may be added. It is well known that the historical origins of English Idealism are to be found in German Idealism, especially in the philosophy of Hegel. It may be thought that some account should first be given of the leading ideas of Hegel's philosophy to prepare the way for an understanding of the English Idealists. Now reference to the work of a predecessor may sometimes be helpful in elucidating some obscurity in the work of a given philosopher. But this is not so in the present case. Indeed I am inclined to think that the boot is on the other foot; certain obscurities in Hegel may be elucidated at least partially through a study of his English successors. In any case, this is a book not about Hegel but about the English Idealists. While they took over certain leading ideas from Hegel, they were not simply restating him. They developed their own philosophy for themselves and it deserves to be considered on its own merits. The question of the relation of English Idealism to the Idealism of Hegel lies outside the scope of this book.

CHAPTER I

THE CONCRETE UNIVERSAL

A : THE ABSTRACT UNIVERSAL

1. The central idea in nineteenth century Idealist philosophy is the notion of the concrete universal. The English Idealists took it over from Hegel and it played a most important part in all their work. In this opening chapter I shall try to give an account of it but some preliminary remarks are necessary first. The notion of the concrete universal is complex and cannot be neatly summed up in a few sentences or even paragraphs. It is bound up with a theory of rational activity and it can be understood only in the light of that theory. Moreover, there is a certain ambiguity about the notion as it was actually developed in the work of the English Idealists. They do not seem altogether to have succeeded in disentangling it from another idea from which, in fact, it is really quite distinct. This is perhaps hardly surprising. The notion of the concrete universal appeared to the English Idealists to be a new and fertile principle in philosophy, the value and significance of which could be appreciated only by putting it to work. In their efforts to explore its implications, it was perhaps inevitable that they should fail to emancipate themselves wholly from different and alien ideas. Later we shall have to pay attention to these ideas and to their consequences in Idealist philosophy. But first we must try to grasp the essentials of the notion of the concrete universal when it is free from ambiguity. In what follows I shall expound the notion as I understand it in my own way. In subsequent chapters I shall try to show that my view is in fact the one to which the English Idealists were committing themselves in their social philosophy, although they did not always appreciate the full implications of this commitment.

One difficulty about the notion of the concrete universal is its name. We are accustomed to think of the universal or general as abstract, and the concrete as particular or perhaps individual. From this point of view, the phrase 'concrete universal' seems equivalent to 'concrete abstraction', a literal contradiction in terms. But are we right in thinking that the universal is always abstract? This is the point at issue. Now it is within the context of rational activity that the notion of the concrete universal is significant. To understand in what way it is significant, we must explore that theory and a large part of this chapter will be devoted to that task. But we must begin with a brief consideration of the abstract universal.

2.   We may gain some understanding of the abstract universal by considering certain elementary features of the notion of a class and the procedure of classification. The notion of a class in its simplest form is the notion of a number of things which are alike in all possessing a certain attribute. Among the books on my shelves, the paper-backs form a class. They are alike in all having the attribute of being bound in paper. This attribute is general or universal in relation to them. But each possesses it in a particular way. Each, that is to say, exhibits a particular instance of the universal. The universal is not something more than or set over against its particular instances. The attribute of being bound in paper is equally present in all the paper bindings of the individual books. It does not exist on its own apart from them. The universal and its particular instances are strictly complementary. From the standpoint of classification, every universal is a universal of particulars* and every particular is the particular instance of a universal. The distinction between them is a distinction between two aspects of an attribute. It is universal in relation to the class of things which have it. It is particular in relation to any one thing which has it.

There is another distinction implied in the notion of a class. This is the distinction between the particular and the individual. They are not the same although our ordinary way of speaking and thinking tends to blur the difference. An individual is what exhibits the particular instance of a universal. The members of a class are always individuals, never merely

* The use of 'particulars' where it is short for 'particular instances' is not to be confused with other well known uses in recent and current philosophy. My reason for adopting it will be apparent in the next para. where I distinguish between 'particular' and 'individual'.

particulars. The members of the class of paper-backs are individual books, not their paper bindings. Classification is a method of identifying individuals. We pick on the particular instance of an attribute exhibited by an individual and identify it as a member of the class of things having that attribute. But identification by classification is a matter of degree. The classification of a book as a paper-back presupposes the prior classification of the individual in question as a book. The priority here is logical not temporal. The two classifications may be made together being fused not in the single judgement: 'This is a paper-backed book.' The point to be noticed here however is that what an individual is identified as depends upon the attribute or attributes which we pick out.

To turn now to the distinction between the abstract and the concrete. From the standpoint of classification, individuals are concrete. They exist as such in their own right. Attributes are abstractions made by us from these concrete existents. The attribute of being bound in paper exists as the attribute of individual books. It exists, that is to say, only in combination with the other attributes which together constitute individual books. When we single it out as a means of identification, we are abstracting it from its context. It follows from this that popular usage to the contrary notwithstanding, the distinction between universal and particular is not synonymous with the distinction between abstract and concrete, at least as far as classification is concerned. Individuals are neither universals nor particulars. They are concrete existents. Attributes may be universal or particular according to which aspect is considered. But in any case they are abstract. As a particular, an attribute is abstracted from its context in one individual. As a universal, it is abstracted from its context in a number of individuals.

It is important not to be misled by the names which we give to individuals. When we classify something as a horse, we are not saying that there is some essence, 'horsiness', which it somehow embodies. We are saying that, in common with a number of other individuals, it exhibits particular instances of certain attributes. The name 'horse' is the name of a certain class of individuals. But we also have a general idea or concept of a horse. This is an intellectual construction made by us out of attributes which we have abstracted from individuals. It might be described as a second order abstraction, being a construction out of abstractions. The name 'horse' thus applies to or denotes an aggregate of individuals. It also represents or connotes an intellectual construction, namely an idea or concept formed by us of a type of individual. Failure to understand this may lead to a wild goose-chase in search of an essence which the members of a class are supposed to embody. It is a wild goose-chase because, within the context of classification, such essences are not realities. The only realities are individuals.

There is another feature of classification to which we must pay attention. A given class may be divided into sub-classes. This division is based upon the different ways in which the universal attribute of a class is exhibited in particular instances. All the books on my shelves are bound but some are bound in paper, the rest in cloth. We have here the relation between a generic attribute and its specific form, a relation which is the basis of the class-sub-class or genus-species relation. The specific forms of a generic attribute are mutually exclusive. Each of my books is either a paper-back or bound in cloth; it cannot be both. The reason for this lies in the nature of the procedure of classification. When we divide a class into sub-classes, when, that is to say, we break down a generic attribute into its specific forms, we are directing attention not merely to the generic attribute but to the different ways in which it appears in particular instances. The aim is to discover the resemblances and differences among these specific instances and to divide up the members of the original class accordingly. If an individual is a member of one sub-class, it is precluded from being a member of another. It is allocated to that sub-class because the particular instance of the generic attribute which it exhibits takes one specific form and not another.

The relation between a generic attribute and its specific forms is a relation between levels of abstraction. The specific form of a generic attribute is possessed not by all but only by some of the individuals possessing the generic attribute. When we move from the specific form and consider the generic attribute, we widen our range and take in a larger number of individuals which we now see to be related to those possessing the specific form. But the higher the level of abstraction, the larger the class which possess an attribute, the less determinate will that attribute be. When a generic attribute is divided into specific forms, we come to know it better by discovering new features of it. When I divide the books on my shelves into paper-backs and cloth-bound, I am taking into account the material in which they are bound and giving more determinateness to the generic attribute which they all possess. Considered as a particular, we have seen, an attribute is an abstraction from one individual, the particular instance of a universal which it exhibits. Considered as a universal, it is an abstraction from a number of individuals, all of which exhibit particular instances of it. We have now seen that, as a universal, it may be either generic or specific. In order to get to know it better, we must inquire if it is generic, into its specific forms. If it is itself a specific form, we must inquire into the generic attribute of which it is a specific form and into the other specific forms of that generic attribute. I dwell on this point, for, from the standpoint of classification, universals are attributes. They are abstract and partake of the relation of generic to specific. We have learned, that is to say, something about universals as abstract within the procedure of classification. They are either generic or specific and we have learned something of the character of this relation. It is important, as we shall see later, in connection with the notion of the concrete universal.

3.   For further insight into the abstract universal we must go to the scientific notion of a law of nature. Scientific laws are regarded as abstract universals and to understand why may help us. I shall therefore say as much but no more than is necessary for this limited purpose. The scientific notion of a law of nature is fundamentally the notion of a uniform relation between events and circumstances. This relation may be summed up in the formula: 'Whenever in a set of circumstances A, event X occurs, event Y will occur.' An elementary example is the following. Whenever the temperature of water under a pressure of one atmosphere falls to 32 deg. F., the water will freeze. It is a law of nature, that is to say, that water will freeze whenever these conditions are present.

A law of nature is universal in the sense that it always holds.

The operative word in the formula is 'whenever'. But there is a hypothetical element in the notion of a law of nature. The formula states that whenever, in certain circumstances, one event happens, another will always happen. It states, that is to say, that if the circumstances are present, one event will always be followed by another. But it makes no pronouncement about whether or not the circumstances are present.

Laws of nature are universal but in what sense are they abstract? The formula states a relation between kinds of circumstances and kinds of events. 'Whenever in circumstances of a certain kind A, an event of a certain kind X occurs, an event of another kind Y will occur.' This presupposes that events and circumstances have already been classified. The concrete fact is the freezing of this water in these circumstances on this occasion. When we interpret it as a particular instance of a universal relation or law of nature, we are ignoring its concrete individuality and concentrating on the way in which it resembles what has happened on other occasions. But the notion of a law of nature goes beyond that of a class. It concentrates attention on how things change and not merely on their given attributes. Classification does not exclude all reference to change. I spoke above of classifying events and this implies the prior recognition of changes in things. But from the standpoint of classification, what is significant is the identification of events as resembling each other or as being different. From the standpoint of laws of nature, what is significant is not just that one event is like another in a certain respect, not just that this change occurring now is like another which occurred previously, although recognition of this resemblance is essential. The focus of attention is rather on the relation between the occurrence of events of one kind or class and those of another. A new dimension is thus added to the perspective afforded by classification.

The concrete is still the individual but the emphasis is now on events, circumstances and occasions, rather than merely the existence of things or entities. A law of nature is abstract in a double sense. It asserts a relation which always holds between a class of circumstances and certain classes of events. This universal relation is abstracted by us from abstractions which we have already made from concrete facts. The freezing of this puddle of water on this road this morning, a concrete fact, exhibits a particular instance of a universal relation between classes of events and a class of circumstances.

In connection with the notion of a class, I drew attention to the relation between a genus and its species, and between a generic attribute and its specific forms. The principle of this relation is applicable to laws of nature. A number of apparently separate laws, each of which relates a different set of circumstances and events, may turn out to be special cases or specific forms of a wider generic law which embraces them all. When this happens, it is always in the context of a development in scientific theory. The discovery of a law of nature always takes place within the framework of a theory in terms of which the manifold variety of things and events in the world are observed, classified, correlated and reduced to order and relative simplicity. The first stage of abstraction, in which individual things and events are classified, is possible only on the basis of a theory which provides a criterion of relevance. I have pointed to the hypothetical element in a law of nature; the universal relation between events in circumstances of a certain kind. The question of what kinds of circumstances there are is a matter for theory. That circumstances of a certain kind are present on a given occasion is an interpretation of concrete fact made on the basis of theory. A development in scientific theory will give rise to new interpretations of concrete situations and to classification of circumstances and events at a higher level of abstraction, so that what were previously thought to be different sets of circumstances and events are now embraced within the framework of a single system. From the perspective of this theoretical system, the various laws discovered at a lower level of abstraction are now seen to be special cases or specific forms of a generic law holding between events and circumstances classified at the higher level of abstraction.

An example of this procedure of scientific advance occurred in the development of classical or Newtonian mechanics. What happened was that a new theoretical system was constructed, in terms of which it was found possible to bring together, within the compass of a single law, a number of separate physical laws concerning different sets of terrestrial and celestial events. These were discovered to be different species of a single genus. Many other examples could be cited from the history of natural science. But my purpose here is confined to elucidating the abstract universal and I am concerned with the notion of a law of nature only in so far as it throws light on this problem. I have tried to indicate the sense in which laws of nature are universal and abstract and to point out the way in which the relation between genus and species is applicable to them. This relation seems to be characteristic of the abstract universal, whether we consider it from the standpoint of classification or the notion of a law of nature. We shall find it a valuable clue to the difference between abstract and concrete universals.

B : THE THEORY OF RATIONAL ACTIVITY

1.   At the beginning of this chapter I said that the notion of the concrete universal is bound up with a theory of rational activity. It is not an empirical theory. It is not, that is to say, an explanation of the occurrence of rational activity in terms of the psychological laws of mental events or of human behaviour. Nor is it a linguistic theory. It is not a theory of the consistent use of the word 'rational' based upon an analysis of its actual usage. What kind of theory then is it? It is a theory of the rationality of rational activity, of what acting rationally is. It is criteriological rather than logical in the technical sense, being an attempt to give an account of a criterion or standard, namely rationality. It starts from the assumption that rational activity is going on and that we have a working practical knowledge of it. It assumes that, for the most part, we try to act rationally. As a theory, its aim is to take what we already have a working knowledge of, and to try to get to know it better.

Let us then begin with our practical working knowledge of rational activity. It is self-conscious, thinking activity; activity in which the agent has at least some idea of what he is trying to do and why he is trying to do it. We may sum up this characteristic by saying that rational activity is activity in which the agent is able to give reasons for what he does. It is tempting to regard this characteristic as the generic attribute possessed by all forms of rational activity. We might then go on to classify the various forms of rational activity on the basis of the different kinds of reasons which are given for them. The problem for the theory of rational activity then becomes the problem of defining a generic attribute in terms of its various specific forms. Let us try this approach. Reflection on our practical working knowledge of rational activity suggests two different kinds of reason for what we do. We do some things simply as the means to ulterior ends; simply, that is to say, for the sake of their consequences. We do other things for their own sake, because in some way they are intrinsically worth doing. Thus it might seem as if the generic attribute of all forms of rational activity, namely that reasons can be given for what is done, may be broken down into two specific attributes or kinds of reason, that of being done as a means to an end, and that of being of intrinsic worth. The genus rational activity, in other words, has two species: activities which are carried out simply as a means, and activities which are carried out for their own sake.

But this approach will not do, as further reflection on our practical working knowledge of rational activity makes clear. The species are not mutually exclusive. We do many things for both kinds of reason at once. A man is digging in his garden. From one point of view his action is a means to an end: he wants to get the bed ready for seeding. But he loves his garden and finds in its care and cultivation a deep personal satisfaction, so that nothing connected with it is merely a chore. Digging the bed is a means to an end, but it is also something more; an integral part of an intrinsically worthwhile activity. Rationality is not a generic attribute. It cannot be divided into mutually exclusive specific forms of rationality. It is therefore not an abstract universal, for the relation of generic to specific is characteristic of the abstract universal. But although not abstract, or at least not abstract in the sense in which attributes and laws of nature are abstract, rationality is a universal. It is in some way present in all forms of rational activity. It is with this universal, a universal whose logical structure is different from that of the universal in classification and natural science, that the theory of rational activity is concerned.

2.   Rational activity is self-conscious thinking activity, activity in which the agent can give reasons for what he does. It is also

self-criticising activity. The rational agent is prepared to reflect upon what he is doing, to criticize it and to revise or modify his conduct accordingly. He is also prepared to listen to criticism from others and to accept it where it seems to him well-grounded. But wherever there is criticism, there are criteria or standards. The theory of rational activity with which the notion of the concrete universal is bound up is in large part a theory of the various kinds of standard implicit in rational activity as we know it in practice, and of the relations between them. We have seen that the relation between activities which are the means to ulterior ends and activities which are worth doing for their own sake, is not the relation between two species of a genus. We shall see in due course that it is the relation between criteria or standards of rationality which is the basis of this distinction, although we shall also see that the notion of activities which are worthwhile for their own sake requires further elucidation.

A course of action carried out as the means to an ulterior end can be criticized on grounds of technical efficiency. Does it enable the end to be attained more successfully than any possible alternative? But it can also be criticized on grounds of economic efficiency. Is it the best way of bringing about the end, having regard to other ends which have also to be brought about, and to a limited amount of resources for attaining them all? These two standards may yield different results. From the technical standpoint, one course of action may be more efficient than another because it enables a given end to be attained more successfully. But from the economic standpoint, it may be the less efficient of the two. It uses up so many resources that the agent is unable to bring about other ends which he regards as equally important. The second course of action, while it does not attain the given end quite so successfully as the first, leaves enough resources available to bring about the other ends.

The difference between technical and economic efficiency is not the difference between the mutually exclusive species of a genus. While the technical standpoint excludes economic considerations, the economic standpoint does not exclude technical considerations. It takes account of them but sees them as subordinate to the problem of allocating limited resources among competing ends. Its perspective is wider than that of the merely technical standpoint. It recognizes that the agent never has just one end to bring about but many, and that his available resources are always limited. The difference between economic and technical efficiency is a difference of kind which is also a difference of degree.* It is rational to aim at technical efficiency but it is more rational to aim at economic efficiency. The two standards constitute different levels of rationality, of which the economic is the higher and the technical the lower. But at the higher level, the lower is not neglected. It is included but in modified and revised form to take account of the wider perspective of the higher level. We have here the model of the relation between criteria or standards of rationality. It is the relation between the different levels in a scale. Its significance will become apparent as we proceed.

3. But rationality is not merely efficiency. That it is something more, is implied in the difference between doing something simply as a means to an ulterior end and doing it for its own sake; a difference which is not that between the species of a genus but which is nevertheless significant. Further consideration of the distinction between ends and means also points to the same conclusion. The distinction can be strictly drawn only if the ends are finite; if, that is to say, they are limited states of affairs which it is possible, at least in principle, completely to bring about. Unless this condition is satisfied, it is impossible clearly to separate the means from the end to which it is the means. Now the decision on a given occasion to try to bring about certain finite ends is made by the rational agent. His ends are not given to him ready-made; he chooses them. Moreover, at the level of economic efficiency, in order to allocate scarce resources between several ends, he must establish an order of priority among them. Upon what principle is he to choose his ends and estimate their relative importance?

To answer this question we must consider what sorts of reasons there are for trying to bring about finite ends. At first sight, it might seem that the bringing about of a finite end is desirable either because it is in its turn the means to a further end, or because its attainment is worthwhile for its own sake. But

* Readers familiar with R. G. Collingwood's *Essay on Philosophical Method* will recognize the source of this idea.

this statement obscures certain points which in the present context are important. A finite end cannot be the means to a further end. Only a course of action can be a means.* But a finite end once it is attained may be a necessary condition for, or a constituent or material component of, some course of action or activity which is itself the means to a further end. Again, the attainment of a finite end is never, strictly speaking, worthwhile for its own sake. But as before, the end once attained may be a necessary condition for, a constituent or material component of, a course of action or activity which is worthwhile for its own sake. In some cases this course of action or activity may be no more than the contemplation of a finite end which has been attained. But in such cases, it is the contemplation and not the attainment of the end which is worthwhile for its own sake. Our statement must therefore be reformulated as follows. The reason for trying to bring about a finite end is that it is a necessary condition for, a constituent or material component of, some course of action or activity which is either the means to a further end, or is worthwhile for its own sake.

An example may help to throw light on the foregoing points. Two men arrange to play a game of tennis. Before they can start the court must have been marked out and the net set up. The marking out of the court and the setting up of the net are the means to an end. But this end is not the game of tennis. It is the existence of a state of affairs which makes the playing of tennis possible, a court properly marked out and a net set up and adjusted to the right height. Playing a game of tennis is not an end to which some other activity is the means. But it is an activity, a necessary condition for which is the attainment of a certain end. The point to notice here is the distinction between a means to an end on the one hand, and a necessary condition for, a constituent or material component of, a course of action or activity, on the other. A means to an end is always some action, course of action or activity. A necessary condition

---

* Ordinary language does not support this point. We ordinarily talk as if things as well as actions are the means to ends. But ordinary language reflects practical not philosophical interests and, although not without philosophical significance, cannot be authoritative where philosophical questions are concerned. It serves well enough for practical purposes but from a theoretical point of view is often ambiguous and elliptical.

for, a constituent or material component of, a course of action or activity is never itself a course of action or activity although it may often be the result of previous action.

I said earlier that the reason for trying to bring about a finite end is that it is a necessary condition for, a constituent or material component of, some course of action or activity which is either the means to a further end, or is worthwhile for its own sake. But where the course of action or activity is the means to a further end, there will always be some other course of action or activity which is worthwhile for its own sake and with reference to which the attainment of the further end is desirable. In the last analysis, the reason for trying to bring about a finite end is that directly or indirectly it has something to contribute to some course of action or activity which is worthwhile for its own sake. There is however a further point to be noticed. Some activities worthwhile for their own sake involve, as an integral part of themselves, the bringing about of certain finite ends. But the actions which are the means to these ends ars not the means of the activities of which they are an integral part. Throwing up the ball to serve in tennis is a means to hitting it over the net. It is not however a means to the playing of tennis but an integral part of the game. Moreover, many activities are at once worthwhile for their own sake and at the same time the means to an end which is a necessary condition for, or in some way contributes to, other activities which are worthwhile for their own sake. A man may play tennis both because he loves the game and for the sake of the exercise, as a means, that is to say, to improving his physical fitness.

Let us now return to our original question. Upon what principles is the rational agent to choose his finite ends and how is he to estimate their relative importance? In the light of the discussion of the last three paragraphs, we can say that he must choose them with reference to the contribution which they can make to courses of action and activities which are worthwhile for their own sake, and that he must estimate their relative importance with reference to the relative importance of these courses of action and activities. But this only points to a re-formulation of our original question. The rational agent must decide what courses of action and activities are worthwhile for their own sake, upon their relative importance, and upon which on any given occasion he is going to embark. Upon what principles is he to make these decisions? Something however has been gained so far as the theory of rational activity is concerned. We have learned that rational activity is not merely a matter of bringing about finite ends as efficiently as possible, but that it is a matter of engaging in courses of action and activities which have been evaluated from the standpoint of their intrinsic worthwhileness and relative importance. We can also see that this standard of the intrinsic worthwhileness and relative importance of courses of action and activities embodies a higher level of rationality than efficiency in either its economic or technical form. This is because questions about efficiency, which are always questions about the choice of means, are subordinate to, and can arise only in the context of, questions about the intrinsic worthwhileness and relative importance of courses of action and activities. Our problem now is to throw further light on this higher level of rationality.

4.   So far we have neglected the rational agent. What is he? He cannot be identified with any one of his courses of action or his activities. Nor is he their total sum or aggregate. But on the other hand, as a rational agent, he is what he does. He cannot be wholly separated from or set over against his activities. The key lies in recognizing that courses of action and activities are not mere sequences of events. Each course of action and each activity is an individual determination of himself by the agent. He is not the sum of his activities but he is the centre from which they originate. Moreover he is equally present in them all. He is the self-conscious unity of which each course of action and each activity is a limited expression. In relation to him, they are fleeting and temporary. In relation to them, he is enduring and permanent. Each course of action and each activity may be described as a temporal and therefore finite microcosm of a non-temporal infinite macrocosm. But in using such language we must not forget that the rational agent is non-temporal only in relation to any one of his courses of action or activities taken singly. He transcends each one of them taken by itself but he is also immanent in each one of them. On the other hand, while he is more than any one of his activities and cannot be identified with their mere aggregate, he

is nothing apart from them. He has his being in and exists through his courses of action and his activities. Take away the possibility of rational activity and you destroy the rational agent.

The doctrine sketched in the last paragraph is in essentials the Idealist doctrine of self-realization.* Most contemporary philosophers know that this doctrine is an integral part of Idealist ethics and social philosophy but few seem to have much idea of what it is about. The central point in the doctrine is that the self of the rational agent is a self which is always in the making. It is being continuously realized in every course of action and every activity of the rational agent. But what sort of self it is that is realized depends in part upon what courses of action and what activities the rational agent engages in, and in part upon the success with which he manages to harmonize them into a coherent way of living. His problem, a problem which is always with him, is to realize himself as fully and effectively as possible in the situation in which he finds himself. He must try to find and develop a way of living which incorporates those activities which summon forth and give expression to his native endowments and capacities. It is these activities and the courses of action which they involve which he finds worthwhile for their own sake. Their relative importance depends upon the strength in him of the various endowments and capacities which they respectively liberate and upon the relative ease or difficulty with which each of them can be incorporated into a coherent way of living.

It follows that on any given occasion the rational agent must decide what courses of action and activities are worthwhile for their own sake, what their relative importance is, and upon which he will embark, with reference to the best self which he can realize in the circumstances. He must make these decisions, that is to say, on the principle of developing the best way of life which is open to him, this being the way of life which will enable him to realize himself most fully in the situation in which he is placed. It follows also that a given course of action may be criticized not only from the standard of efficiency but from the standard of self-realization. Is it a wise course of

* Or self-determinations: Idealist philosophers sometimes use the latter name.

action, having regard to the best way of life open to the agent in the circumstances? Is it an integral part of, or a contribution to, some activity which is itself a contribution to the best achievement of self-realization possible for the agent?

The standard of self-realization, embodies a higher level of rationality than efficiency in either of its forms. Its perspective is wider for it takes account not only of ends and means but also of courses of action and activities which are worthwhile for their own sake. It takes account also of the rational agent and recognizes that rational activity is the activity through which he realizes himself. At the same time, it incorporates within itself the two levels of efficiency. They remain significant as subordinate standards of rationality which are relevant whenever questions about the choice of means for the attainment of finite ends arise. But as we have seen, questions about ends and means are significant in, and can arise only in the context of, questions about courses of action and activities which, directly or indirectly, are worthwhile for their own sake. These latter questions take us beyond the levels of efficiency to the level of self-realization.

5.   But the notion of self-realization as a level of rationality requires further elucidation. Is any course of action or activity which liberates some native endowment or capacity of the rational agent ipso facto worthwhile for its own sake, and therefore to be incorporated, if possible, into his way of life? Are no other considerations relevant? What about the claims of what is called morality? Has the rational agent no responsibilities, no obligations to other people? These considerations may serve to remind us that so far we have been considering the rational agent in isolation. This one-sided point of view must now be corrected. The rational agent does not lead an isolated solitary life. He is a person and not merely an agent. He was born into and has grown up in a community of persons. He was conscious of himself, at least in a rudimentary way, as an individual person and of other persons distinct from himself, before he was able to act rationally. He has realized himself as a rational agent in what, from the outset, has been a social context. He has had to learn to live and act not as an isolated individual but as a member of society.

It follows that a course of action or activity which liberates some native endowment or capacity of the rational agent is not for that reason alone worthwhile for its own sake. It is always relevant to ask whether it is compatible with the agent's social responsibilities. Is it possible for him to engage in it and at the same time fulfil his obligations to other people? This does not mean however that the standard of self-realization has been abandoned. It means only that this standard has been revised. The self which is to be realized in rational activity must be a social self. The way of life in which it is realized must be a social way of life. The roots of morality lie in this social aspect of rational activity. In learning to live and act as a member of his society, the individual agent is realizing himself not merely as a rational but as a moral agent.

But it may be objected that I have gone too far in saying that the self which is to be realized in rational activity must be a social self and that the way of life in which it is realized must be a social way of life. Even if it is granted that in learning to live and act as a member of his society the individual agent is learning to be a moral agent, it does not follow that he can only realize himself as a rational agent by becoming a moral agent. A given agent may be able to realize himself most fully in an immoral way of life, a way of life which, while it liberates his native endowments and capacities most effectively and is to him the most satisfying way of life possible, nevertheless runs counter to the requirements of social discipline and leads him to neglect his social responsibilities. Assuming that he can get away with such a way of life, that he can persuade or hoodwink the other members of his society into thinking that it is not immoral and that he really is a moral agent, is he realizing himself most fully as a rational agent if he pursues it?

To this objection it may be replied that if such a form of self-realization were generally adopted, social life would break down in anarchy. This would result in the destruction of the conditions which make self-realization possible and everyone, including the immoral agent, would suffer. To this reply however it may be further objected that the important question is being begged. The immoral agent not unreasonably assumes that most members of his society will not follow his example. They will not, in any case, know that he is immoral and will continue to act morally, realizing themselves in social ways of living. The point of the objection is that it cannot be maintained that an individual agent can realize himself most fully only in a moral way of life. So far as the individual agent is concerned, the rational and the moral are not necessarily co-extensive. They may sometimes diverge. But there is a further reply to this objection. The individual agent, who expects other people to be moral while he is immoral, is claiming a privileged status for himself, a status for which he can give no rational justification. He is claiming, for no good reason, to be exempt from the responsibilities to which everyone else is liable. It may be conceded that a way of life which is founded on such a claim is not without rationality, for it enables the agent who embraces it to realize himself in a way which to him is very satisfying. But it rests upon an arbitrary assumption, namely the unjustified claim to privileged status, and is therefore less rational than a moral way of life.

I therefore conclude that, so far as its main point is concerned, the objection fails. The rational and the moral are, when properly understood, co-extensive. Full self-realization can be achieved only where the rational agent is also the moral agent. The self which is to be realized must be a social self and the way of life in which it is to be realized must be a social way of life. But this does not mean that the notion of a way of life which is privately satisfying, a way of life which enables the individual agent to liberate his native endowments and capacities and which to him personally may seem the best possible because the most enduringly satisfying, is irrelevant in rational activity. It remains relevant as a subordinate standard within the framework of morality, the framework of morality being the framework of a socially responsible way of life.

We can now see that the notion of self-realization comprises two standards, that of morality and that of private self-satisfaction. Of these, morality embodies the higher level of rationality. Its perspective is wider than that of private self-satisfaction. It takes account of the social aspect of rational activity, of the fact that the rational agent is not an isolated solitary being but a member of a community. It embraces the notion of social responsibility and avoids the arbitrary claim to privileged status, a claim which is tacitly assumed when rationality is confined to private self-satisfaction. But private self-satisfaction finds a place within morality. The two standards of self-realization are not mutually exclusive. The relation between them is that between a higher and a lower level of rationality. It is the same relation as that which holds between economic and technical efficiency. The claims of technical efficiency are not abolished at the higher level of economic efficiency. They survive but in modified form, having been revised in the light of a perspective which takes account of the problem of allocating scarce resources among a number of ends. In like manner, the claims of private self-satisfaction are not abolished at the higher level of morality. They survive but in modified form, having been revised in the light of a perspective which takes account of social responsibility.

6. But the notion of morality itself stands in need of further elucidation. So far we have seen only that its roots lie in the social aspect of rational activity and that it embraces the idea of social responsibility. From the standpoint of the individual agent, morality is something already there. It is embodied in the established rules and customs of his society. This, at least, is how it first presents itself to him. He becomes a moral agent by learning to obey these rules and customs and by learning also to criticize his own and other people's conduct in terms of them. They provide a stable framework within which he grows up as a member of his society. But is morality merely a matter of loyally obeying established rules and customs? These differ in certain respects from society to society. Even within one society, they are not by any means always fully self-consistent. If morality is conceived of as merely obedience to established rules and customs, then there seems to be an arbitrary de facto character about it. The question naturally arises: is the body of rules and customs established in a given society itself moral?

But further reflection on morality shows that in its most developed form it is something more than merely obeying established rules and customs. These are indispensable in the training of the moral agent and after he has become mature they remain useful as working maxims. But they are only working maxims and the moral agent must accept or reject

B

them on his own responsibility. A course of action is not moral because it conforms to an established moral rule but because in the circumstances it is morally the best thing the agent can do. No doubt in most circumstances obeying the established rule will be morally the best thing he can do, but there will be times when this is not so. It is the moral agent's task to decide whether or not he ought to obey the established rule. He cannot make the rule the excuse for his conduct because he is responsible for the decision to obey it. Thus the arbitrary de facto element in morality disappears when it is realized that morality is not merely obeying rules. Morality embraces the idea of social responsibility. It is responsible conduct, conduct in which the agent can accept no authority except his own honest judgement as to where his duty as a social being lies.

But upon what principle is the moral agent to decide where his duty lies if he is not to rely on the prescriptions of established rules and customs? By the time he reaches maturity and becomes fully conscious of himself as a rational and moral agent, he is already involved in a number of social relationships and commitments. He is engaged in some kind of work or occupation, has developed various leisure pursuits and interests, is involved in personal relationships with relatives and friends, and finally is a member of a wider political community. He has become a rational and moral agent, that is to say, through his participation in various spheres of rational activity, each of which is at the same time a social sphere. He cannot be wholly separated from or set over against his activities in these spheres. As a rational and moral agent, he is what he does in his work, in his leisure pursuits, in his personal relations and as a citizen. If he is to act with full moral responsibility in the determination of his day to day conduct, he must have a practical idea of the underlying purpose and general significance of the various spheres in which he is involved. He must see them as different aspects of a social way of life, a way of life which he and other rational agents are together engaged in developing. In the light of such an idea, he must interpret the immediate situation confronting him in his various capacities and work out for himself what his detailed responsibilities are.

A practical idea of the underlying purposes and general significance of the various spheres of rational activity in which he is involved is something which the moral agent can develop for himself only after he has first learned to conduct himself in terms of established rules and customs. He must serve his apprenticeship before he can become a master craftsman. But if he rests content with the prescriptions of prevailing rules and customs, and with received doctrines about the purpose and significance of the various spheres in which he is engaged, he is achieving something less than full moral responsibility. It is only when he is able to subject the received doctrines to the critical scrutiny of his own working knowledge and experience, and, on the basis of that scrutiny, convert established rules and customs into working maxims which he is prepared if necessary to modify or even disregard, that he is in a position to act with full moral responsibility. The morally responsible agent, properly so-called, is the morally autonomous agent, the agent who takes full responsibility for what he does and who determines his conduct in the light of an experienced and well-informed practical understanding of the implicit rationale, the permanent value and worth of the various spheres of rational activity in which he finds himself involved.

But the loyal obedience to established rules and customs is something more than merely a stage in the training of the moral agent properly so-called. It is itself morality, although not morality in its most developed form. Morality, that is to say, involves two standards: that of loyal obedience to established rules and customs, and that of morally responsible conduct proper, conduct in terms of the various spheres of rational activity. These two standards embody two levels of rationality. Morally responsible conduct, conduct in terms of spheres of rational activity, is the higher, obedience to established rules and customs is the lower. At the higher level, the lower is not abolished but is preserved as a subordinate standard. The claims of established rules and customs remain in the form of working maxims at the level of spheres of rational activity. This conception of spheres of rational activity has so far however barely been introduced. It calls in its turn for further elucidation and development. But before attempting that, let us try to recapitulate and sum up our results so far.

7.   In this section we have been engaged in the development

of a theory of rational activity. It is a criteriological not an empirical nor a linguistic theory, the theory of the rationality of rational activity. We have investigated a number of different standards of rationality. We began with efficiency, which turned out to involve two standards, the technical and the economic. We then passed to the notion of courses of action and activities which are worthwhile for their own sake, and thence to the idea of self-realization as a standard of rationality. Here again we found that there were really two standards, that of private self-satisfaction, and that of morality. We then went on to examine morality more closely and resolved it again into two standards, that of obedience to established rules and customs, and that of morally responsible conduct in terms of the responsibilities of spheres of rational activity.

We have also seen that each standard embodies a different level of rationality. We have, that is to say, a scale of levels of rationality. The lowest level is that of technical efficiency. Next above it comes economic efficiency. After economic efficiency comes self-realization conceived of in terms of private self-satisfaction. Above this again comes self-realization in the form of morality in terms of obedience to established rules and customs. Above morality, conceived of as rule-keeping, comes morally responsible conduct in terms of spheres of rational activity. We have further seen that at each level in the scale something is added to our perspective. As we rise in the scale our view of rational activity becomes more comprehensive and coherent. At the lowest level our view is confined to the purely technical problem of how best to bring about a given end. At the level of economic efficiency it is widened to take account of the problem of the best allocation of scarce resources among a number of ends. At the level of private self-satisfaction our view is widened again to take account of courses of action and activities worthwhile for their own sake and of the fact that the rational agent realizes himself in a way of life made up of these courses of action and activities. At the level of morality in terms of rule-keeping, the perspective is widened again to take account of the fact that the rational agent is not an isolated human atom but a social being. At the level of morally responsible conduct in terms of

spheres of rational activity, our view is widened once more to
include the fact that the rational agent, whom we now know
to be identical with the moral agent, is personally responsible
for his conduct and cannot be content with what is merely
established or laid down.

We must not however overlook a genuine sense in which
levels of rationality may be opposed. From the standpoint of
technical efficiency, the claims of economic efficiency may
appear as alien intrusions requiring a sacrifice of purely technical excellence. From the standpoint of economic efficiency,
aesthetic considerations, adduced from the standpoint of
private self-satisfaction, may appear as frivolous and obstruc-
tive. From the standpoint of private self-satisfaction, the claims
of established moral rules and customs may appear as irksome
restraints which interfere with intrinsically worthwhile activities. From the standpoint of established moral rules and customs, morally responsible conduct in terms of spheres of
rational activity may seem deserving of moral censure because
not in accord with those rules. In general, from the standpoint
of a given level of rationality which is below the highest, the
standpoint of the level immediately above it will normally
appear as alien. This is because the standpoint of the lower level
must be modified before it can be harmonized with the wider
perspective of the higher level. The higher level, just because it
takes into account something which is excluded from the perspective of the lower level, is bound to strike a jarring note.
The lower level, so far as it goes, is a standard of rationality,
and it is bound to resent the claims of a different standard
whose point of view it cannot properly appreciate.

The opposition which from the standpoint of a lower level
of rationality exists between itself and the level immediately
above it can be overcome only through a transition to the
standpoint of the higher level. This transition is itself a rational
one, for the higher level takes account of the standpoint of the
lower level. There is a sense in which the higher level achieves
explicitly what the lower level promises but fails to fulfil. Anyone who takes efficiency seriously cannot rest content with
technical efficiency alone. He is likely to find himself driven to
consider the wider question of economic efficiency, for he has
not merely one but many ends to bring about and his re-

sources are limited. The transition from economic efficiency to private self-satisfaction begins when the agent considers the relative priority of his various ends. This will lead him to consider the various courses of action and activities which make up his way of life and the nature and character of that way of life as a whole. The transition from private self-satisfaction to morality at the level of rules and customs will come easily to an agent who is at the same time a social being and who has learned to live and act as a member of a society. It is one which in any case he will find himself obliged to make when he begins to reflect upon the social context of his life. The transition from moral rule-keeping to morally responsible conduct in terms of spheres of rational activity is the most sophisticated of all the transitions. It comes about if and when the moral agent recognizes the arbitrary de facto character of established rules and customs merely as established.

The transition from a lower to a higher level of rationality is thus rational in the sense that if the agent thinks out his situation systematically, trying to take account of all its aspects, he will find himself being led on to the wider perspective of the higher level. But I do not mean that it is an automatic or natural transition in the sense that it invariably happens. What we have been exploring here may be described as the immanent logic of rational activity not its psychology. Rational activity is thinking activity, activity which originates in, and throughout is directed by, ideas. Its immanent logic is the general structure of the leading ideas or categories in terms of which it is realized in practice. Each level in the scale logically implies the one above it in the sense that when we try to think through its implications and ask how it is possible in the world as we know it, we are led beyond it to the level above.

So much then for our discussion so far. The aim of this chapter is to expound the notion of the concrete universal and we have been led into the theory of rational activity because it is bound up with that notion. In the first section we saw something of the scope and significance of the abstract universal. At the beginning of this section we saw that rationality, although in some sense a universal, is not abstract. It is not a generic attribute which can be divided into mutually exclusive specific forms. The relation between the various standards of rationality is the relation between the levels in a scale. The difference between one level and another is a difference at once of kind and degree. It is a difference of kind, because each level is a distinct form of rationality with its own special standpoint. It is a difference of degree, because each level in the scale is a fuller and more adequate form of rationality than those below it. Finally let us try to streamline our terminology. I shall normally hereafter speak simply of the level of ends and means, which should be taken to comprise both economic and technical efficiency. Since every level in the scale above that of ends and means is a level of self-realization, I shall not normally use that term to designate them although I shall of course employ it when the notion of self-realization is itself under discussion. I shall normally speak of 'the level of private self-satisfaction', 'the level of moral rules and customs' and 'the level of spheres of rational activity' or sometimes, in the case of the last named, 'the level of morally responsible conduct'. Too rigid a terminology however is not desirable since the various levels of rationality are not the mutually exclusive species of a genus. I shall therefore extend, amplify or modify mine if and when the context demands it.

C : THE THEORY OF RATIONAL ACTIVITY CONTINUED : SPHERES OF RATIONAL ACTIVITY

1. To return to the conception of spheres of rational activity : the different spheres of work, of leisure, of personal relations and of citizenship, are spheres of morally responsible conduct. They are spheres of self-realization for rational agents who, having become moral agents, recognize that they must determine their conduct for themselves, that it is not enough simply to rely on the prescriptions of established rules and customs, useful though these may be as working maxims. But what is the relation between these different spheres? The moral agent is the self-conscious unity of his various courses of action and activities. He realizes himself in his work, in his leisure pursuits and interests, in his personal relations, and as a citizen, but he remains one and the same person throughout. The different spheres are therefore not separate, self-contained and mutually

exclusive worlds. If they were, then the moral agent could not be one and the same person throughout all his activities. Morally responsible conduct would be schizophrenic conduct. This conclusion is supported by the testimony of common sense. A man cannot divide his life into water-tight compartments. He may distinguish between his work and his leisure, between his responsibilities to his family and his friends, and his responsibilities as a citizen, but these distinctions are not absolute divisions.

How then are the different spheres of rational activity related? To think of them as separate self-contained and mutually exclusive worlds is to think of them as adjacent or contiguous spheres. We shall do better of we think of them not as adjacent or contiguous, but as concentric spheres. We must think, that is to say, of the sphere of leisure as enveloping the sphere of work; of the sphere of personal relations as enveloping the sphere of leisure; and of the sphere of citizenship as enveloping the sphere of personal relations. This involves modifying but not wholly abandoning our ordinary ideas of work, leisure, personal relations and citizenship. We normally think of each of these spheres as a distinct centre of activities, some of which overlap and interpenetrate with those of other centres. But in order to understand their relationship as spheres of rational activity, they must be regarded from another point of view. Each sphere must be considered in turn from the point of view of its adequacy as a way of life for a society of moral agents. It is when they are thought of in this way that they are seen to be related as concentric, not adjacent or continguous, spheres. This way of thinking does not abolish but rather throws fresh light upon our ordinary ideas of work, leisure, personal relations and citizenship.

2. Let us briefly apply this doctrine, beginning with the sphere of work. The essence of work, as a sphere of rational activity, is self-maintenance. It comprises those activities which a society of moral agents must carry out in order to provide and maintain the conditions necessary for its continued existence. A society of moral agents is therefore always a society of workers. But is this all that it is? Is its way of life nothing but self-maintenance, nothing but mere survival? Must

it not also include something worth surviving for? This brings us to leisure. It seems natural, according to our ordinary ideas, to think of work and leisure as opposed to one another. Leisure activities are what we do when we are not working. But there is also a sense in which they are complementary. No man can be a worker all the time. He must have some intervals of rest, recuperation and, at least in some form, recreation. He can be a worker, that is to say, only if he also enjoys some leisure. This might seem to suggest that leisure is part of work because necessary for self-maintenance. It would then follow, not as I contended, that the sphere of leisure envelops the sphere of work, but the other way round. But this would still leave us with the problem of a way of life which was nothing but self-maintenance, which included nothing worth surviving for. Leisure could not be cast for this role since ex hypothesi it is part of work, a mere phase in self-maintenance and not something worth surviving for.

But leisure is something more than merely the rest, recuperation and recreation necessary for work. As a sphere of rational activity, it comprises pursuits and interests which are cultivated not for their survival value but for their own sake. If leisure in the narrower sense of rest, recuperation and recreation is necessary for work, then work in its turn is equally necessary for leisure in the wider sense of pursuits and interests which are cultivated for their own sake. A society of moral agents which cultivates such pursuits and interests must also be a working society, a society which provides and maintains the conditions necessary for its own continued existence. Failure to survive would terminate all leisure pursuits and interests. But the way of life of such a society is something more than mere self-maintenance. It includes, in its leisure pursuits and interests, something worth surviving for.

Thus considered as the way of life for a society of moral agents, the sphere of leisure is more adequate than the sphere of work. It includes the sphere of work but goes beyond it, and at the same time gives it further meaning and significance. The two spheres should therefore be thought of as concentric, with the sphere of leisure enveloping the sphere of work. But this way of thinking does not invalidate our ordinary ideas of work and leisure. We can still think of them as distinct centres of activi-

ties some of which overlap and interpenetrate each other. But
viewed thus, they are not being considered from the standpoint
of their adequacy as ways of life for a society of moral agents.
In thinking of work merely as a distinct centre of activities, we
are ignoring the fact that it is enveloped by the larger sphere
of leisure. But we recognize that there is some overlap between
it and leisure, for we see that it includes certain activities connected with recuperation and recreation. In regarding leisure
merely as a distinct centre of activities, we ignore the fact that
it envelops the lesser sphere of work. We black out, as it were,
that part of it which is filled by the sphere of work. But at the
same time we recognize that there is some overlap, that certain
leisure pursuits and interests, such as for example mountain
climbing, directly give rise to questions of self-maintenance,
and that in none of them is the question of continued existence
ever wholly irrelevant. When we turn to consider work and
leisure as ways of life, and think of them as concentric spheres
of rational activity, we make explicit what was implicit when
we were thinking of them merely as distinct centres of activities.
We were thinking in a deeper more comprehensive way which
takes account of what our ordinary ideas ignore. This does not
mean our ordinary ideas should be given up, that we are wrong
to think of work and leisure merely as distinct centres of activities. For most practical purposes this is the most convenient
way to think of them. We should remember only that in so
thinking our view is incomplete, and that for a full understanding something more is required.

3.   But a way of life consisting only of the concentric spheres
of leisure and work cannot be the way of life of a society of
moral agents. There is nothing social about it, nothing to make
it the way of life of a society. This brings us to the sphere of
personal relations. Its roots lie in the individual moral agent's
social self-consciousness. His consciousness of himself as a
person is at the same time his consciousness of other persons
distinct from himself. He is involved throughout his life in
personal relations with members of his family, with neighbours, with colleagues and with friends. But if these personal
relations are to prosper and not generate hostility and conflict,
there must be mutual consideration and respect. Recognition

of this fact and of the responsibilities which it involves makes personal relations a distinct sphere of rational activity. We ordinarily think of it as cutting across the spheres of leisure and work. Many, but by no means all the activities connected with these spheres involve personal relations. But considered as a way of life for a society of moral agents, it envelops leisure and work. It is the way of life of a society whose members belong to families, and who, in the cultivation of leisure pursuits and interests, and in providing and maintaining the conditions necessary for their own continued existence, treat one another as neighbours, colleagues and friends. This does not mean that no one ever does anything by himself. It means only that what is done in solitude is always subject to and never at the expense of the responsibilities of personal relations. It is in terms of these responsibilities that the members of the society direct their conduct and realize themselves as moral agents.

An adequate way of life for a society of moral agents must include the concentric spheres of personal relations, leisure and work. But is this all that it must include? Such a society would inevitably be no more than a small-scale local community. Its opportunities for corporate organization and for the collective regulation of its affairs would be confined to what could be done through direct personal contact. Its leaders would have to know and be known by each member and their authority would be dependent on personal loyalty. Consideration of these limitations brings us to the sphere of citizenship. Its roots lie in the far reaching consequences of human action. What an individual agent does may affect not only his personal circle but many other people whom he does not and cannot know personally. What they do may affect him. His contact with them is impersonal but none the less real. The essence of citizenship as a sphere of rational activity is the recognition that these impersonal relations give rise to responsibilities no less than do personal relations. In one sense it seems to stand over against the sphere of personal relations as the sphere of public as distinct from that of private life. But there is another sense, for once not unfamiliar to our ordinary way of thinking, in which the sphere of citizenship envelops the sphere of personal relations. Being a citizen does not mean neglecting one's responsibilities to one's family, neighbours, colleagues and friends. It means fulfilling them, but fulfilling them in the light of other responsibilities with which they have to be reconciled and harmonized.

A society of moral agents for whom the sphere of citizenship is a way of life need not be merely a small-scale local community. Its opportunities for corporate organization and for the collective regulation of its affairs, would not be confined to what could be done through direct personal contact. Its leaders would not have to depend upon personal loyalty for their authority. They would be able to rely upon the capacity of the members of the society for recognizing their public responsibilities. In such a society, it would be possible to do something to control the far-reaching consequences of human action, and therefore to mitigate their effects. The capacity of the members for impersonal co-operation also makes possible an increase in division of labour and specialization in the activities connected with providing and maintaining the conditions necessary for the society's continued existence. It also makes possible an expansion in the range of leisure pursuits and interests. In short, considered as the way of life for a society of moral agents, the sphere of citizenship is more adequate than the sphere of personal relations. It does not abolish the latter sphere but envelops it and by virtue of its greater degree of social co-operation, is a richer, fuller and more varied way of life.

At this point our geometrical metaphor of concentric spheres of rational activity has begun to break down. Considered as a way of life for a society of moral agents, the sphere of citizenship envelops the sphere of personal relations. But since within the sphere of citizenship leisure and work are expanded beyond what is possible within the sphere of personal relations alone, we can no longer strictly maintain that the sphere of citizenship envelops the concentric spheres of personal relations, leisure and work. Leisure and work have, as it were, burst through the confines of personal relations. The metaphor is apt so long as we are considering only personal relations, leisure and work as ways of life. It is appropriate also when we are considering only citizenship and personal relations without reference to the spheres of leisure and work. It breaks down when we try to consider all four spheres together from the point of view of their relative adequacy as ways of life. The reason, as we have seen, is that the transition from personal relations to citizenship has repercussions on leisure and work. But all metaphors break down sooner or later. What is required of a given metaphor is that it should be illuminating. We have seen that work, leisure, personal relations and citizenship are not separate, self-contained and mutually exclusive worlds, and that therefore we cannot understand the relations between them by thinking of them as adjacent or contiguous spheres. The value of the metaphor of concentric spheres and the justification for employing it is that, despite its limitations, it enables the relations between work, leisure, personal relations and citizenship as different aspects of morally responsible conduct to be elicited and exhibited.

4. The individual moral agent is always a member of a particular society in a particular place at a particular time. Now this society can never be more than a society of moral agents in the making. Assuming that it has developed beyond the stage of a small-scale local community, its way of life will embrace the spheres of citizenship, personal relations, leisure and work. But by no means all its members will have reached the level of morally responsible conduct in terms of spheres of rational activity. Many will be content to direct their conduct in terms of its established rules and customs. There will be some who have hardly if at all developed beyond the level of private self-satisfaction, and who will disregard the established rules and customs whenever they think it is to their private advantage. Moreover these rules and customs will not be fully self-consistent. Nor will they be wholly free from irrelevancies and anachronisms. They may perpetuate certain institutions and ways of acting which distort the society's corporate organization and impede its management of its public affairs. They may bolster up prejudices which distort personal relations and cut into both work and leisure. Some of the leisure pursuits and interests cultivated by members of the society may seem to have little of intrinsic worth in them. Some of the activities dignified by the name of work will enable individual agents to make a living but make no obvious contribution to providing and maintaining the conditions necessary for the continued

existence of the society as a whole. It is in such a situation, a situation in which there is immorality as well as morality, prejudice as well as enlightenment, vested interests as well as social co-operation, that morally responsible conduct has to be achieved.

We have seen that the rational agent must become a moral agent if his conduct is not to be infected with arbitrariness. He must realize himself in a social way of life, a way of life which allows other rational agents to realize themselves. Now he first becomes a moral agent by learning to obey the established rules and customs of his particular society, and it is in terms of the prescriptions of these rules and customs that he first understands the idea of a social way of life. But at this level of moral development, his capacity for social criticism is limited to breaches of, or departures from, established rules and customs. He is not in a position to assess and evaluate these rules and customs, nor the institutions and ways of acting which they buttress and support. For all that he knows the irrelevancies and anachronisms which they contain, the prejudices which they bolster up, may prevent many members of his society from achieving the rational activity of which they would otherwise be capable. His conduct is still infected by arbitrariness, the arbitrariness of established rules and customs merely as established. He is a member of a society of moral agents in the making and his conduct must contribute to making it more of a society of moral agents not less. This it will do only if it is based on a more adequate understanding of the current institutions and habits of his society. He must think of them not in terms of established rules and customs but in terms of a social way of life made up of the spheres of citizenship, personal relations, leisure and work, and he must try to assess the degree to which they severally assist or impede the achievement of such a way of life.

Morally responsible conduct properly so called is the conduct of an agent who has come to see all this and does his best to act in the light of it. He knows that, as a citizen, he is a member of a society which stretches far beyond the range of his own personal circle, and that this society is corporately organized to deal with matters of public interest. He knows that each member of this society has his own circle of personal relations;

that, among them, a variety of leisure pursuits and interests are cultivated; and that they carry on the business of providing and maintaining the conditions necessary for their own continued existence through a complex system of division of labour and specialization. He has, that is to say, a practical idea of the underlying purpose and general significance of each of the spheres of rational activity which make up the way of life of his society. He knows that to realize himself as a rational and therefore as a moral agent, he must participate constructively in these spheres, and that the way of life which he develops must be a social way of life in which the underlying purpose and general significance of each sphere is duly reflected.

But he also knows that, in the current condition of his society, by no means all its members achieve the full self-realization of which they are capable. He knows that in certain respects its corporate organization is defective and that through ignorance and selfishness some matters of public interest are dealt with inadequately while others are not dealt with at all. He knows that the personal relations of the members of his society are not always characterized by mutual consideration and respect, and that sometimes they involve tension, hostility and conflict. He knows that, among the leisure pursuits and interests currently practised, some are not worth cultivating at all and that the value of others is distorted and exaggerated. He knows that some members of his society manage to provide and maintain the conditions necessary for their continued existence only inadequately and precariously. He knows that, as a result of all these things, many members of his society lead lives which in various ways are marred, cramped or mutilated. In the light of this knowledge he recognizes that his own constructive participation in political and civic activities, in personal relations, in leisure and in work, must include doing whatever he can in the current situation to help others to participate constructively in them too. What he can do in this direction may be much or little, depending upon circumstances. Sometimes it may only be negative: avoiding courses of action which increase the difficulties of other people. But whatever it is, positive or negative, he must do what he can. If he fails, he is developing his own way of life at the expense of other people's opportunities for self-realization, and his conduct is still infected by arbitrariness. Thus he cannot become a morally responsible agent himself without helping to make his society more of a society of moral agents.

In the last section I said that morally responsible conduct in terms of spheres of rational activity embodies a higher level of rationality than morality in terms of established rules and customs. In the present section, after elucidating the conception of spheres of rational activity, I have adduced further reasons to support my contention. But we must not forget that each level in the scale of levels of rationality incorporates those below it as subordinate standards. The morally responsible agent makes use of established rules and customs as working maxims. He will find private self-satisfaction not only in his leisure pursuits and interests but also in his work, his personal relations and his political and civic activities. Questions of ends and means will not be confined to his work. They will arise equally in the activities connected with the other spheres. There is also a sense in which the scale of levels of rationality seems to be continued through the various spheres of rational activity. When they are considered from the point of view of their relative adequacy as ways of life for a society of moral agents, leisure includes work, personal relations includes both leisure and work, and citizenship includes all three. Thus the level of spheres of rational activity breaks down into a number of levels of which the highest is citizenship. But we must remember that a way of life for a society of moral agents must at least embrace personal relations, leisure and work; otherwise there is nothing social about it. Thus it is only the spheres of personal relations and citizenship which can be regarded as further levels in the scale. Leisure and work are intelligible as standards of rationality only within the contexts of personal relations and citizenship. But having acknowledged the limited sense in which the scale of levels of rationality is continued through the spheres of rational activity, it will be as well for the sake of brevity to regard them as constituting one level of rationality, that of morally responsible conduct, or the level of spheres of rational activity.

But does the scale of levels stop at the level of spheres of rational activity? If so, then it follows that the highest form of

rational activity is citizenship. To be a rational agent is to be
a moral agent, and to be a moral agent is to be a good citizen.
But is this all that being a moral agent involves, allowing that
it includes the responsibilities of personal relations? There are
the activities of art and science. They are rational activities, but
can they be thought of simply as connected with work or
leisure? We shall find the Idealist philosophers raising difficulties of this kind and we shall see that there is another level in
the scale above that of spheres of rational activity. But it will
be as well to leave discussion of it and of how the lower levels
are incorporated within it until we come to the works of the
Idealist philosophers. Our development of the theory of
rational activity has for the present gone far enough. We have
what we need for an understanding of the notion of the concrete universal, and in the light of that understanding for
beginning our study of the work of the Idealists.

D : RATIONAL ACTIVITY AND THE CONCRETE UNIVERSAL

1. At the beginning of this chapter I said that the notion of
the concrete universal is significant within the context of
rational activity. Having traced the main lines of the theory of
rational activity in the last two sections, let us see what justification there is for this contention. The universal in rational
activity is rationality. But rationality is not an abstract
universal, for it is not a generic attribute which can be divided
into mutually exclusive specific forms of itself. There are
different standards or forms of rationality, but they are related
not as the mutually exclusive species of a genus but as levels
in a scale of levels. Rationality, that is to say, is a universal the
various forms of which differ in both degree and kind. The difference between one form and another is a difference in the degree
of adequacy with which the universal is embodied. The scale of
levels of rationality is a scale of forms of the universal, each
form being a relatively more adequate achievement of it. Each
form also sums up the whole scale to that point by incorporating within itself all the less adequate forms of the universal.

We came across the idea of the concrete in our examination
of the abstract universal. For classification, the individual

members of a class are concrete realities, while for the scientific inquiry into laws of nature, it is individual natural events which have this character. In these contexts the concrete is taken to be what really exists and really happens, in contradistinction to what we take account of in our classifactory and scientific thought. We do not, in these forms of thought, try to know things and events in their full detail and variety : we confine our attention to certain aspects. We abstract, in other words, from the concrete reality of what exists and what happens. Now within the context of rational activity, it seems natural to take individual courses of action as concrete realities, for rational activity is made up of individual courses of action. But we must be careful here, for it is not the mere fact of a course of action but its rationality which is significant. It is the rationality of an individual course of action which differentiates it from an event or sequence of events. Its reality as a course of action is its rationality. Within the context of rational activity then, individual courses of action are concrete realities, but they are so because they are individual achievements of rationality.

An individual achievement of rationality is always an achievement in terms of one of the levels in the rationality scale. It may be a course of action designed to bring about a certain end. It may be one in the performance of which the agent expects to find pleasure and satisfaction. It may consist in doing something which he regards as his duty because it is prescribed by some established rule or custom. Again, it may be the performance of a course of action which he identifies as his own particular responsibility in the context of his political or civic activities, his personal relations, his leisure pursuits and interests, or his work. You cannot even think of an individual achievement of rationality without thinking of it as an achievement in terms of one of the levels in the scale. Moreover, every individual achievement of rationality is an individual achievement of self-realization by the agent. At the level of ends and means admittedly this is so only implicitly. Considered by itself, it is simply an achievement of efficiency. But there is always a reference beyond the finite end to some course of action or activity, judged to be worthwhile for its own sake, in which the agent realizes himself as a rational agent. There is also one further point which it is important not to overlook. An individual achievement of rationality is always an achievement in a historical situation. It is a course of action performed in a particular set of circumstances at a particular time. How much of an achievement it is must be estimated with reference to this historical situation.

In classification and science, the concrete and individual is set over against the abstract and universal. The former is real: the latter is not, as such, real. But within the context of rational activity, this contrast cannot be maintained. You cannot contrast the individual as the real with the universal as the unreal. Here the individual and the universal together form an indivisible reality. We now have the key to the notion of the concrete universal. In rational activity the universal is rationality. But in rational activity what is real is always an individual achievement of rationality. What is real, that is to say is always an individualized or concrete universal. This is the significance of the notion of the concrete universal. It is the notion of the nature and character of the real in rational activity. Its significance does not extend to classification and natural science. Here, as we have seen, what is real is not an individualized or concrete universal. There is however something suggestive of the notion of the concrete universal. The particular, as distinct from the individual, and the universal are complementary. What we have is always the particular instance of a general attribute and the particular case of a natural law; the paper cover of this book, and the freezing this morning of this pond. But the individuals or concrete realities in classification and science are not the particular instance of universals. They exhibit them but are more than them. This book is something more than its paper cover, this pond something more than the physical state of the water this morning. Nor do the names which we give to these concrete realities refer to universals which they somehow individualize. They stand for intellectual constructions made by us out of the attributes we have abstracted from concrete realities. To sum up: in rational activity the real is an individual achievement of rationality, a concrete universal; in classification and science it is an individual thing or event which is not an achievement of anything.

To know an individual achievement of rationality for what

it is, to know it as a concrete reality, you must criticize and evaluate it. Initially this means criticizing and evaluating it in terms of the level of rationality at which the agent was consciously acting. But for full knowledge, something more is required. Each level of rationality incorporates those below it as subordinate standards. Strictly speaking therefore any level in the scale below the highest is only a subordinate standard of rationality. If the agent is consciously acting at a level below the highest, the question arises: does he understand its status as a subordinate standard? If his course of action is intended as the means to an end, is this end one which in the circumstances he ought to be trying to bring about? What is the activity for which its attainment is a necessary condition? Is this activity connected with his work, his leisure pursuits and interests, his personal relations, or with his civic and political activities? Is it an activity which he ought to be contemplating, in view of his current responsibilities in these spheres? In other words, if an individual achievement of rationality is to be fully known for what it really is, it must be criticized and evaluated in terms of the highest level in the scale, whether or not this was the level at which the agent was consciously acting.

The same point may be made in terms of the doctrine of self-realization. Any course of action is, at least implicitly, an individual achievement of self-realization. Full knowledge of it as a concrete reality is knowledge of it as an achievement of self-realization, and knowledge of it is an achievement of self-realization is knowledge of how good an achievement it is. Having regard to the historical circumstances, is it the best self which the agent could have realized? Is he, in performing this particular course of action, acting as a good citizen, remembering that citizenship as a way of life embraces personal relations, leisure and work, as well as civic and political activities? It follows that there is a sense in which, in considering a course of action in terms of any level of rationality below the highest, we are dealing with an abstraction. We are not considering it in its full context and therefore cannot gain full knowledge of it as an individual achievement of rationality. But in practice we are bound most of the time to deal in such abstractions in order to concentrate our attention on what is immediately relevant. Indeed it is not too much to say that we have a duty to do so whenever, as in many situations, there is no time for leisurely reflection. What is important is not that we should give up considering courses of action in abstraction from their complete context, but that we should acknowledge what we are doing and, when full knowledge is required, be prepared to take account of the complete context.

2. This chapter opened with the statement: 'The central idea in nineteenth century Idealist philosophy is the notion of the concrete universal.' We have just seen how the notion of the concrete universal is significant within the context of rational activity. It is the notion of the nature and character of the real in rational activity. But we have still to see its philosophical significance. What are its implications for the theory of philosophy? Every philosophy implies a theory of itself and Idealism is no exception. We shall find that the question of the nature and scope of philosophy arises at various points in the course of this book. I will now give a provisional statement of the nature and scope of philosophy based on the account which I have already given of the theory of rational activity and the notion of the concrete universal.

It is the business of philosophy to know and expound the rationality implicit in the various standards and values operative in human life. But if this work is to prosper, it must be done on the basis of a correct understanding of the logical structure of rational activity. This is why it is important to differentiate philosophy from classification and natural science. The universal with which it is concerned, namely rationality, is not an abstract universal. The philosopher therefore cannot work in terms of genera and species. His work may be described either as expounding the various standards and values as embodiments of different levels of rationality in a scale, or as articulating the scale in terms of the various standards and values. In fact, he always does both together although the emphasis may be put either on the various standards and values, or, as in this chapter, on the scale of levels. But on whichever side the emphasis is put at the outset, the philosopher will find, if he proceeds far enough, that the other increasingly demands his attention. Thus if the theory of rational activity had been developed further than it was in this chapter, other standards and values would have come into view besides those so far considered, and it would have been necessary to ascertain and exhibit their significance and status within the scale of levels of rationality.

I said earlier that to know an individual achievement of rationality for what it is, to know it as a concrete reality, it is necessary to criticize and evaluate it. Now this work of criticism and evaluation is not philosophy. Philosophy is concerned, not with the morality of this course of action, not the way of life of the citizens of this political community, but with morality and citizenship as such. To know the morality of this course of action, the value of the way of life of the citizen of this political community, is the business not of the philosopher properly so called but of the critic. But it implies philosophy. It implies a theory of the rationality, the individual achievement of which on any given occasion is to be evaluated. But who is this critic? The answer is: the rational agent. The work of criticism is an integral part of rational activity. In the course of articulating and defending his work as a critic, the rational agent may be obliged to make explicit the implicit theory of rationality in terms of which he is working. But he begins to philosophize only when he starts to question that theory and tries to develop it systematically.

But it must be remembered that this is only a provisional definition of philosophy, based on my preceding account of the theory of rational activity and the notion of the concrete universal. Further reflection on that account suggests this definition is not wholly satisfactory. We have seen that within the contexts of classification and natural science concrete reality consists of individual things and events, while within the context of rational activity it consists of individual achievements of rationality. How do these contexts stand to one another? They are contexts of human experience and this suggests that, in order to understand the relation between them, we need a theory of the general character and structure of human experience. The formulation of such a theory has traditionally been the task of philosophy. It involves something more than merely coming to know and expounding the rationality implicit in the various standards and values operative in human life, although the latter work is no doubt a part of it. But having noted this defect in our provisional definition, we may leave further consideration of it until we have seen something of Idealist social philosophy.

CHAPTER II

F. H. BRADLEY'S THEORY OF MORALITY

A : MORALITY AS SELF-REALIZATION

1. F. H. Bradley's *Ethical Studies* appeared in 1876. It was his first book although not his first published work. The aim of the book is to expound and defend a theory of morality. It is to be a philosophical, not a psychological or sociological theory. Bradley, that is to say, is concerned with morality as a rational activity and sets himself the task of investigating its rationality. Now in the last chapter, I have argued that rationality is not a generic attribute which can be divided into mutually exclusive specific forms. There are distinct forms of rationality but the relation between them is that of levels in a scale of levels, each one of which sums up and embodies those below it. Morality is rational activity at a level above those of efficiency and private self-satisfaction. According to this doctrine, the development of a theory of morality and the development of a theory of rational activity are not two different enterprises but one and the same. The theory of morality when it is fully worked out, is also the theory of rational activity.

Bradley accepts this doctrine and makes it the foundation of his work in *Ethical Studies*. But he does not explicitly expound it in advance of his main inquiry. It is only as that inquiry develops that its character and method gradually emerge. In this chapter, I shall trace the main lines of Bradley's argument and will try to show how it is based on the notion of the concrete universal and the theory of rational activity with which that notion is linked. The book marks the beginning of the Idealist epoch in English philosophy for it was the first major attempt to make the notion of the concrete universal the basis of a philosophical theory. But the attempt, as I shall also try to show, is not wholly successful. Bradley raises a problem which he is only partially able to solve. The problem is one which, as we shall see, is important in the subsequent development of Idealism. One further point may be noted at the outset. In *Ethical Studies* Bradley is anxious to avoid what he regards as questions of metaphysics, as distinct from moral philosophy. But he finds himself unable to keep wholly within his self-imposed limits. Metaphysical questions break through towards the end of his argument and have an important bearing upon his conclusions.

Bradley takes as his point of departure the practical moral experience of every-day life. Morality is a going concern, something with which in practice we are all familiar, and the business of moral philosophy is to understand it. The way to this understanding lies in developing the implications of common sense notions of morality and revising these notions in the light of what analysis and criticism reveals. A philosophical theory of morality must explain our ordinary common sense notions but it must not explain them away. Its task is to make them intelligible by transforming them into systematic theory. In Essay I of *Ethical Studies*, Bradley argues that the key notions of ordinary morality are those of responsibility and accountability. He maintains that these notions presuppose the principle of self-sameness or enduring personal identity. 'Now the first condition of my guiltiness or of my becoming the subject of moral imputation,' he writes, 'is my self sameness. I must be throughout one identical person.' And he continues; 'If when we say "I did it", the "I" is not to be the one "I" distinct from all other I's, or if the one "I" here is not the same with the "I" whose act the deed was, then there can be no question whatever that the ordinary notion of responsibility disappears.'[1]*

In Bradley's view, no theory which explicitly or implicitly denies the principle of self-sameness can claim to be a theory of morality. Such a theory does not make morality intelligible: it simply denies that there is such a thing. Two rival doctrines of considerable contemporary influence, both of which claim to be theories of morality, are convicted by Bradley on this ground. They are the doctrines of 'Free Will' and 'Necessity'. According to him, the 'Free Will' doctrine maintains that every action is the result of an absolutely undetermined and abso-

* All references are in Appendix I, pp. 315-319.

lutely unpredictable decision. 'You are free,' he writes, 'because there is no reason which will account for your particular acts, because no one in the world, not even yourself, can possibly say what you will or will not do next. You are accountable, in short, because you are a wholly unaccountable creature.'[2] The enduring personal identity of the self is dissolved into a chaos of anarchic actions. Morality gives way to caprice.

The flaw in the doctrine of 'Necessity' or 'Determinism', according to Bradley, lies in the psychology on which it professes to rest. 'Without personal identity,' he writes, 'responsibility is sheer nonsense, and to the psychology of our Determinists, personal identity with identity in general, is a word without a vestige of meaning.'[3] According to this psychology as Bradley understands it, the mind is nothing but a collection of sensations held together by the laws of association. This seems to him to lead to the conclusion that 'the mind itself is but a fiction of the mind'[4], and upon this he comments; 'The only thing which it is hard to understand is this; that we ourselves who apprehend the illusion, are ourselves the illusion which is apprehended.'[5]

2.   In Essay 2 of *Ethical Studies* Bradley says that the end or purpose in morality is self-realization. A full defence of this thesis would, in his view, involve entering the arena of metaphysics and this he is not prepared to do. 'How can it be proved that self-realization is the end?' he asks, and answers, 'There is only one way to do that. This is to know what we mean when we say "self" and "realize" and "end", and to know that is to have something like a system of metaphysics, and to say it will be to exhibit that system.'[1] Then after confessing that he has no such system to exhibit, he continues; 'All that we can do is partially to explain it and try to render it plausible. It is a formula which our succeeding essays will in some way fill up and which we shall try to recommend to the reader beforehand.'[2]

We have already encountered the conception of self-realization or self-determination in the last chapter. The rational agent is not something different from or set over against his activities, nor is he merely their aggregate. He is the self-conscious unity of his various activities, each one of which is a limited determination of himself. Bradley is making essentially the same point but is entering the discussion at the level of morality. Although there is a purpose or end in morality, he maintains that morality is not merely a means to an end lying beyond itself. It is an activity which must be pursued for its own sake, which is worth while on its own account. It is rational activity, that is to say, at a level above that of efficiency. Bradley thinks that ordinary moral experience bears out this view. 'Let us first go to the moral consciousness, and see what that tells us about its end.' He writes: 'Morality implies an end in itself: we take that for granted. Something is to be done, a good is to be realized. But that result is, by itself, not morality: morality differs from art, in that it can not make the act a mere means to the result. Yet there is a means. There is not only something to be done, but something to be done by me—I must do the act, must realize the end. Morality implies both the something to be done, and the doing of it by me; and if you consider them as end and means, you can not separate the end and the means. If you chose to change the position of end and means, and say my doing is the end, and the "to be done" is the means, you would not violate the moral consciousness; for the truth is that means and end are not applicable here.'[3]

Morality is a way of acting in which the self or personal identity of the moral agent is realized. Bradley expresses this in a series of rhetorical questions. 'Are we not forced to look on the self as a whole, which is not merely the sum of its parts, nor yet some other particular beside them?' he writes: 'And must we not say that to realize self is always to realize a whole, and that the question in morals is to find the true whole, realizing which will practically realize the true self?'[4] The reference to 'the true self' and 'the true whole' makes it clear that, for Bradley, the merely satisfying is not as such the moral. It is a matter of the self which in some sense ought to be realized, as distinct from that which we happen to want to realize.

In support of his thesis, Bradley turns once more to practical experience. 'And, if we turn to life,' he writes, 'we see that no man has disconnected particular ends; he looks beyond the moment, beyond this or that circumstance or position; his ends are subordinated to wider ends; each situation is seen (consciously or unconsciously) as part of a broader situation, and in this or that act he is aiming at and realizing some larger whole, which is not real in any particular act as such, and yet is realized in the body of acts which carry it out.'[5] And he sums up by saying; 'What I am saying is that, if the life of the normal man be inspected, and the ends he has in view (as exhibited in his acts) be considered, they will, roughly speaking, be embraced in one main end or whole of ends.'[6]

Bradley's use of the word 'whole' must not be misinterpreted. He does not mean by it, a closed system. The self which is to be realized in morality is an infinite whole. By 'infinite' in this connection, Bradley does not mean a mere undifferentiated blank. The true infinite in his view 'is the unity of finite and infinite'.[7] And he says that; 'the finite is relative to something else, the infinite is self-related'.[8] I take Bradley to mean that the self is an infinite whole in the sense of being the self-conscious unity of its individual actions. Each individual action is a limited or finite determination of the self but the self is always something more than any one of its individual actions taken separately and something more also than the mere aggregate of these separate actions.

Summing up Bradley's argument so far; he has made the point that the theory of morality must be the theory of the rationality of a certain way of acting or which comes to the same thing, of the self which is realized in that way of acting. It must make explicit what it is that we are implicitly trying to do in our practical activity as moral agents. Bradley's main task thus still lies before him. So far, he has only established the requirements which the theory of morality must satisfy. But this limited result is not without significance for it provides a criterion on the basis of which certain theories can be eliminated at once. Unless a theory gives an account of the rationality of a way of acting, it cannot be a theory of morality at all. In Essays 3 and 4 of *Ethical Studies* Bradley rejects two well-know theories on this ground. They are; Hedonism or 'Pleasure for pleasure's sake' the leading exponent of which, according to Bradley, is John Stuart Mill, and 'Duty for duty's sake' a theory which Bradley takes to be an important constituent of Kant's moral philosophy although he is careful to say that he does not wish his account of it to be taken as a full statement of Kant's ethical theory. I shall not, however, attempt to summarize his criticism of these two theories but will pass straight on to Essay 5, where he begins the positive task of expounding his own theory of morality.

B : THE SOCIAL SELF

1. Essay 5 of *Ethical Studies* has the somewhat forbidding title of; 'My Station and its duties'. It is the best known essay in the book and is not infrequently read on its own apart from the other essays. Many have regarded it as expressing Bradley's full and complete view of morality. In fact, it is only a step in the development of his theory of morality, albeit an important one. In Essay 6, the argument of Essay 5 is criticized and revised in several important respects. Moreover it is difficult to see how anyone who had not grasped the essentials of the arguments of the first two essays of the book, could understand Essay 5. The key to the first two essays lies in the theory of rational activity and anyone who lacks this key is unlikely to understand what Bradley is trying to do in Essay 5.

Bradley has set himself the problem of giving an account of the moral self, the self which it is the activity of morality to realize. In Essay 5, he offers a provisional solution. The moral self is the social self. To be moral is to be a good member of one's society, loyally discharging the various responsibilities which membership involves. Thus conceived, morality is a way of acting which embraces the moral agent's whole life. 'We have found self-realization, duty and happiness in one,' he writes, 'yes, we have found ourselves when we have found our station and its duties, our function as an organ in the social organism.'[1] This phrase 'an organ in the social organism' needs elucidation. We may notice, however, at the outset that in identifying the moral self with the social self, Bradley is following the main lines of the theory of rational activity according to which the roots of morality are to be found in the social context of all human life.

He explicitly rejects the atomistic doctrine according to which society is nothing but an aggregate of separate, independent individuals whose nature and character is unaffected by their social relations. 'We say that, out of theory, no such individual men exist,' he writes, 'and we will try to show from fact that, in fact, what we call an individual man is what he is because of and by virtue of community, and that communities are thus not mere names but something real, and can be regarded, if we mean to keep to facts, only as the one in the many.'[2] He proceeds to illustrate. 'Let us take a man, an Englishman as he is now, and try to point out that, apart from what he has in common with others, apart from his sameness with others, he is not an Englishman—nor a man at all; that if you take him as something by himself, he is not what he is.'[3] And he continues; 'What we mean to say is that he is what he is because he is a born and educated social being, and a member of an individual social organism, that if you make abstraction from all this which is the same in him as in others, what you have left is not an Englishman nor a man, but some, I know not what, residuum which never has existed by itself and does not so exist.'[4]

According to Bradley, the moral agent is a member of many social groups ranging from the family to the state and including intermediate associations such as the occupational group and the local community. Each is a field for self-realization. To be a moral agent, according to the doctrine of 'My Station and its duties' is to fulfil one's responsibilities in these various fields. The state is regarded as the widest community in terms of which the claims of other social groups are to be interpreted and harmonized. The social self, that is to say, is the self of the good citizen, a conception which includes within itself other forms of social activity. To live morally is to live socially, and to live socially is to live civically or politically. For the purpose of his discussion, Bradley limits the state to the nation-state but does not rule out the possibility of an international political community. 'Leaving out of sight the question of a society wider than the state,' he writes, 'we must say that a man's life with its moral duties, is in the main filled up by his station in that system of wholes which the state is, and this, partly by its laws and institutions, and still more by its spirit, gives him the life which he does live, and ought to live.'[5]

'My Station and its duties' satisfies Bradley's criterion of a theory of morality; it is the account of a way of acting. When he says that communities must be regarded as 'the one in the many', his point is that a community is a way of acting achieved by rational agents. They are the many, but they are also one in that they are not a mere aggregate but constitute a systematic unity. Nor is the rational agent anything apart from his membership of communities. Living and acting socially however involves living and acting politically. Social life must be within the framework of an organized political community so that its various forms with their several demands can be harmonized. Thus rational activity, the rational agent's determination of himself, turns out to be the activity of citizenship, an activity which includes all other forms of social activity. The activity of citizenship, rational activity at its most developed, is then identified with morality. Such is the doctrine of 'My Station and its duties.'

We have already seen that Bradley draws an analogy between a society and an organism. No doubt he found it useful in order to bring out the fact that a society is a way of acting achieved by the co-operation of its members and that apart from society, the individual moral agent is nothing at all. But it may be objected that this analogy is as misleading as it is helpful for there is a sense in which a society is fundamentally different from an organism. The members of a society are self-conscious; they know themselves to be members and fulfil their functions in the light of this knowledge. The organs in an organism are not self-conscious and do not know that they are organs. They fulfil their functions blindly and automatically. A society lives in the thought and volition of its members; the life of an organism is a complex process of natural events. In *Ethical Studies*, Bradley seems to be aware of the limits of his analogy and does not think that a society is literally an organism. The following passage shows that he is fully alive to the fundamental role of thought and volition in the life of a society. 'It is quite clear that a nation is not public-spirited unless the members of it are public-spirited, that is, feel the good of the public as a personal matter or have it at their hearts. The point here is that you cannot have the moral world unless it is willed, that to be willed it must be willed by persons, and that these persons must not only have the moral world as the content of their wills but must also in some way be aware of themselves as willing this content."[6] But in spite of this passage, we shall see in a later chapter of this book that Bradley is in fact not altogether clear in his mind about the limits of the organic analogy. He seems to have thought that while they are different things, a society and an organism are alike in structure. So far as the argument of *Ethical Studies* is concerned, however, this point need not trouble us. It will be important when we come to the notion of the concrete universal which he explicitly formulated in his logic and metaphysics and we shall consider it in that connection.

2.   According to the theory of rational activity expounded in the last chapter, the highest level of rationality is embodied in the sphere of citizenship. From what we have seen of it so far, 'My Station and its duties' appears to endorse this conclusion. But in my account of the theory of rational activity, an important point was the distinction between morality at the level of rule and custom and morality at the higher level of responsible conduct or spheres of rational activity. Now in Essay 5, Bradley does not draw this distinction. The passage just quoted, where emphasis is laid upon the thought and volition of self-conscious moral agents, suggests that 'My Station' is intended to be an account of morality at the level of spheres of rational activity. But elsewhere in Essay 5, it is the objective character of the morality of 'My Station' which is stressed. The moral agent's duties are defined for him by the rules and customs of the institutions of his society. They are there, waiting for him to carry out, irrespective of his personal desires and feelings. He must, if he is to be moral, fulfil them loyally and conscientiously. This objective element in Bradley's view is one of the strongest points in favour of 'My Station' for it is here in complete harmony with ordinary common sense notions.

When we come to Essay 6, where Bradley criticizes 'My Station', it becomes clear that what Bradley had in mind in that doctrine is something along the lines of morality at the level of rule and custom rather than the level of spheres of rational activity. But the distinction which he draws is in certain respects different from that given in my account in the last chapter. The nature of this difference is significant and we shall have to return to it later. But for the present, we shall do best to regard 'My Station' as an account of morality at the level of rule and custom, recognizing that in expounding it, Bradley tries to show the roots of rules and customs in the various spheres of rational activity which make up the life of a society. After expounding it, he devotes some space in Essay 5 to discussing an objection which he thinks is likely to be made against it and which he believes to be ill-founded. The objection is one which is liable to be made against any theory which finds the roots of morality in the social context of human life. Bradley's attempt to meet it is not without interest in the light of issues which we shall have to discuss in later chapters.

The objection is that if, as in 'My Station', the moral self is identified with the social self, then morality becomes purely relative. There is not one morality but a large number, each being the morality of a particular society in a particular place at a particular time. No one morality can be said to be better than another for there is no independent standard according to which they can be judged. This conflicts with our ordinary notions of morality according to which the moral is in some sense absolute and universal and not merely relative and particular. Bradley thinks that this objection rests on a confusion. In one sense, morality is relative. What a man's duty is on a given occasion, depends upon who he is, where and when he is living, what his activities are and with whom he is in contact. But it is also absolute in the sense that whatever a man's duty is, it is absolutely binding upon him. He must do it, whether it is pleasant or painful, profitable or unprofitable from the standpoint of his personal self-interest. Morality is not relative in the sense of depending upon private interest, whim or inclination and it is an important part of the doctrine of 'My Station' to emphasize this point. In so far as the objection fails to appreciate these different senses of 'relative', it is ill-founded.

But this does not dispose of the main charge that according to 'My Station' every society has its own morality and that there is no independent standard by which they can be evaluated and judged. But in Bradley's view, the fact that morality is relative to the life of a given society at a given time and place, does not rule out the possibility that it is also something more. On a teleological interpretation of human history, the various social moralities of different times and places appear

C

as successive approximations in the stages of a gradual development of a universal human morality which will be achieved
when different societies are united together into the harmonious life of one universal human society.

Bradley thinks that this teleological interpretation of human
history is in accord with the general theory of evolution. 'The
process of evolution,' he writes, 'is the humanizing of the bestial
foundation of man's nature by carrying out in it the true idea
of man, in other words by realizing man as an infinite whole.
This realization is possible only by the individual's living as a
member in a higher life, and this higher life is slowly developed
in a series of stages. Starting from and on the basis of animal
nature, humanity has worked itself out by gradual advances of
specification and systematization and any other progress would
in the world we know be impossible.'[1] If human history is a
process of this kind, then different social moralities might be
compared from the standpoint of the level of human achievement which they make possible and how far they further the
development of wider human co-operation.

Bradley clearly has some sympathy for the teleological interpretation of history, but he does not commit himself to it. He
insists, however, that even if it is false, 'My Station' although as
he says 'grievously curtailed' is still a tenable theory of
morality. The ordinary unreflecting notion of a universal
morality is dependent for its truth upon the truth of a teleological interpretation of the above kind and 'My Station' in no
way precludes such an interpretation. But it does not depend
upon the truth of such an interpretation, and if, after all,
morality is only the morality of particular societies in particular conditions of time and place, then 'My Station' is still a
tenable theory of that morality. 'We have rejected teleology
but have not yet embraced Individualism.' Bradley writes; 'We
still believe that the universal self is more than a collection or
an idea, that it is reality, and that, apart from it, individuals
are fictions of theory. We have still the fact of one self par-
ticularized in its many members, and the right and duty of
gaining self-realization through the real universal is still as
certain as the impossibility of gaining it otherwise.'[3] We are
still entitled, that is to say, to identify the moral self with the
social self and to regard a society as a way of acting realized

in the co-operative activity of self-conscious rational agents who simultaneously realize themselves in so acting. In abandoning the teleological interpretation of history, we are not forced to accept the doctrine of social atomism.

3. Bradley ends Essay 5 with a brief account of certain objections which he thinks 'My Station' can not meet. In Essay 6, he develops them in detail and on the basis of the criticism which they imply, proceeds to revise and expand his theory of morality. 'My Station' is not wholly abandoned but is taken up and included in a wider theory. Before turning to that theory, let us see briefly what the objections to 'My Station' are. Bradley argues that the social self does not exhaust the content of the moral self. Morality is something more than being a good citizen, although the latter is an important part of it. 'It is first an error to suppose,' he writes, 'that in what is called human life, there remains any region which has not been moralized. Whatever has been brought under the control of the will, it is not too much to say, has been brought into the sphere of morality.'[1] Morality, that is to say, is co-extensive with rational activity and with self-realization. No form of rational activity is exempt from the claims of morality. But if there are some kinds of rational activity which are not intrinsically social, morality cannot be identical with citizenship. It must include these non-social activities which fall outside the sphere of citizenship.

At first it may seem as if the doctrine that there are non-social forms of rational activity cuts right across Bradley's earlier arguments and indeed the theory of rational activity sketched in the last chapter. Bradley's point, however, is that there are certain forms of rational activity which can be performed by individual moral agents working on their own. The activities he has in mind are art and science. He does not mean that the artist and scientist are non-social beings. He is not going back, that is to say, on the basic position of 'My Station', that it is only by living as a member of a society that a rational agent can determine himself. Art and science are activities which can be engaged in only by social beings, by men and women who are members of societies. His point is that in engaging in art and science these men and women are not further determining themselves as members of their societies although they are further determining themselves as rational agents. Moreover in this rational, non-social self-realization, they are still within the sphere of morality.

From the standpoint of the theory of rational activity, it may seem as if Bradley is maintaining that art and science are cases of worthwhile, satisfying ways of acting: forms of self-realization which, however, must be subjected to criticism and revision in the light of the higher level of rationality embodied in morality. The worthwhile or satisfying is a level of rationality which is not, as such, social. But this is not Bradley's point. If art and science were cases of rational activity at the level of the satisfying, they would be subject to the claims of social morality. They would come within the sphere of citizenship, having to be modified and amended in order to contribute to that sphere. They would be co-ordinate with forms of enjoyment, with recreation and so forth, which are properly regarded as subordinate to the claims of citizenship and there would be no ground for objecting to 'My Station.' But Bradley is arguing that art and science are themselves ways of being moral although they are not ways of being a good citizen. He is suggesting that morality is a sphere of rational activity at a level of rationality above that of citizenship. It includes citizenship but also embraces other activities such as art and science which make their appearance for the first time at this new and higher level of rationality. This at least is how his doctrine appears when it is interpreted in terms of the theory of rational activity. He does not explicitly formulate it in these terms, for the theory of rational activity remains implicit in his argument, but, as we shall see, the general drift of his remarks bears out this interpretation.

He expresses his view that art and science are ways of being moral, positive achievements of morality by saying: 'It is the moral duty of the artist or inquirer to lead the life of one and a moral offence when he fails to do so.'[2] He then makes it clear that in his opinion, this way of being moral is not a social way of acting, not a contribution to citizenship. "But on the other hand,' he writes, 'it is impossible without violent straining of the facts to turn these virtues into social virtues or duties to my neighbour.'[3] Elaborating this assertion, he continues: 'The end

they aim at is a single end of their own, the content of which
does not necessarily involve the good of other men. This we
can see from supposing the opposite. If that were true, then it
would not be the duty of the inquirer, as such, simply to inquire, or of the artist, as such, simply to produce the best work
of art, but each would have to consider ends falling outside his
science or art and would have no right to treat these latter as
ends in themselves.'[4] The moral self then is something more
than the merely social self and 'My Station' is inadequate as a
theory of morality. We must now turn to the wider theory
which Bradley offers in its place.

C : THE IDEAL SELF

1. The central thesis of the revised theory of morality developed by Bradley in Essay 6, is that the moral self is an ideal
self. To the question : what is the content of this ideal self, he
answers: 'We can at once gather that the good self is the self
which realizes a) a social, b) a non-social ideal; the self which
first does, second does not, directly and immediately involve
relations to others.'[1] The sphere of morality, that is to say, includes the social self of 'My Station' but it also includes the
non-social activities of art and science. Bradley argues that:
'The first and most important contribution comes from what
we have called "My Station and its duties".'[2] And he maintains
that: 'The basis and foundation of the ideal self is the self
which is true to "My Station and its duties".'[3] But non-social
forms of self-realization must not be overlooked, and the conception of the moral self as an ideal self allows for their
inclusion.

But why does Bradley call his revised conception of the
moral self an ideal self? His intention is to contrast it with
the social self of 'My Station'. He maintains that : 'If we investigate our good self, we find something besides, claims beyond
what the world expects of us, a will for good beyond what we
see to be realized anywhere. The good in "My Station and its
duties" was visibly realized in the world and it was mostly
possible to act up to that real ideal. But this good beyond is
only an ideal, for it is not wholly realized in the world we see;
and do what we may, we cannot find it realized in ourselves.

It is what we strive for and in a manner do gain, but never attain to and never possess.'[4] He tells us what he is referring to : 'The perfect types of zeal and purity, honour and love which figured and presented in our own situation and circumstances and thereby unconsciously specialized, become the guides of our conduct and law of our being,'[5]; and these, he says: 'are social ideals; they directly involve relations to other men and, if you remove others, you immediately make the practice of these virtues impossible.'[6]

Bradley's point here seems to be that reflection on our practical moral experience tells us that morality is something more than merely doing what is expected of us. To be moral is to achieve something more than mere social respectability. 'My Station' with its emphasis on established social institutions fails to bring out this ideal element. Morality involves living up to the spirit, not merely the letter of one's responsibilities, and this spirit eludes formal embodiment in social institutions. This is why Bradley speaks of the 'social ideal' as part of the content of the ideal self. It includes the social self of 'My Station' but also something more which is still social but which the former omits. Within the Ideal self, that is to say, all that is sound in 'My Station' is preserved, but its limitations are off-set. It remains a valuable conception, being the basis of moral education and training, and there is a sense in which the moral agent, in living up to the social ideal, remains true to 'My Station'; but without the conception of the moral self as an ideal self, a vital element in social morality is excluded. As for the non-social activities of art and science, these are embraced under the head of the non-social ideal, the other element in the content of the ideal self. They are ideals, because they involve standards which are never in practice more than imperfectly achieved. Being an artist or a scientist is never merely a matter of observing aesthetic and scientific conventions. There is always an element of creative originality, of aesthetic and intellectual autonomy which cannot be reduced to rule and convention.

From the standpoint of the theory of rational activity, Bradley is maintaining that there is a level of morality above the sphere of citizenship. His revised theory of morality appears as a further development in the theory of rational activity. We can now also see that although he did not, in expounding 'My Station', distinguish between morality at the level of rule and custom and morality at the level of responsible conduct or spheres of rational activity, he is apparently taking account of it in the distinction between the social self of 'My Station' and the ideal self of morality at the higher level. The explicit recognition of a social ideal within the ideal self, as well as the non-social activities of art and science, suggests that this sphere of ideal morality may be analysed into a scale of spheres along the lines of the theory of rational activity. The ideal social self, that is to say, may be seen as consisting of a scale of spheres of social ideals, the highest of which is that of ideal citizenship. The sphere of morality then appears as the highest, including within itself and summing up the scale of ideal social spheres as well as embracing the non-social rational activities of art and science. I am suggesting, in other words, that if we interpret Bradley's distinction between the ideal self and the social self of 'My Station' along the lines of my distinction between morality at the level of rule and custom and morality at the level of responsible conduct, Bradley's revised theory of morality can in principle be incorporated within the theory of rational activity. But is Bradley's conception of ideal morality really the same as my notion of morally responsible conduct? Does he mean by 'ideal' what I mean by rationality at the level of spheres of rational activity? The two notions clearly have much in common, but as we shall see later, they are not identical, and the difference is significant.

2.   But the conception of the moral self as an ideal self needs further elucidation. How are the different elements which make up its content related to each other? Upon what principle is the moral self to be realized? Bradley recognizes that more needs to be said. 'Our result at present is as follows:' he writes: 'morality is co-extensive with self-realization as the affirmation of the self which is one with the ideal. And the content of this self is furnished: a) by the objective world of "My Station and its duties": b) by the ideal of social, and c) of non-social perfection. And now we have to do with the question: how do these spheres stand to one another?'[1] It should be noted that Bradley is using the term 'spheres' in this passage

in an ordinary colloquial sense and not in the special sense which I gave to it in developing the theory of rational activity. In asking how they stand to one another, he is in effect asking whether they are to be regarded as merely contiguous or as concentric. As I have already pointed out, his earlier argument suggests that he thinks of 'My Station' and the social ideal as concentric spheres, the former falling within the latter, but here he is simply posing the question.

But although he poses this question, Bradley's answer is unsatisfactory; indeed in one sense, as we shall see, he provides no answer at all. He begins by drawing attention to a fact of ordinary moral experience. The moral agent sometimes finds himself in a situation in which there is a clash between the different responsibilities arising out of the various activities in which he is engaged. In such cases, there is a genuine moral problem. Bradley insists that there can only be a moral problem when the clash is between different moral responsibilities, not when it is between a moral responsibility and a personal desire or inclination. 'The first point to which we must call attention,' he writes, 'is that all these are cases of colliding duties: in none of them is there a contest between the claims of morality and something else not morality. In the moral sphere, such a contest is impossible and meaningless.'[2] He continues with an example. 'We have in all of them, a contest between moral duties which are taken to exclude one another: e.g. my duty as artist on the one hand and father of a family on the other, and so on.'[3]

Bradley insists that moral problems are essentially practical problems and as such, fall outside the domain of moral philosophy. 'And the second point on which we desire to insist with emphasis,' he writes, 'is that cases of the collision of duties are not scientific but practical questions. Moral science has nothing whatever to do with the settlement of them: that would belong, did such a thing exist, to the moral art. The difficulties of collisions are not scientific problems; they arise from the complexity of individual cases and this can be dealt with solely by practical insight, not by abstract conceptions and discursive reasonings.'[4] A sympathetic man of the world may be able to give useful practical advice, but 'the man of mere theory is, in the practical sphere, a useless and dangerous pedant'.[5] It follows. in Bradley's view, that the failure to discharge some recognized social duty is not necessarily a moral failure. It may be for the sake of contributing to some ideal that the omission has occurred and we are not entitled morally to condemn it on the abstract ground that a rule has been broken. 'So when the service of the ideal is appealed to,' he writes, 'in justification of neglect and breaches of law, we say that the claim is valid in itself, the abstract right is undeniable, the case is a case of collision and the question of moral justification is a question of particular fact.'[6]

Now we need not quarrel with Bradley's point that moral problems are essentially practical, but we must not lose sight of the question which gave rise to the whole discussion. That was: how do the various elements of the ideal self stand to one another? How, in other words, are the various spheres which Bradley has himself distinguished, related? Are they contiguous or concentric? This is a theoretical question, a question which it is the proper business of the theory of morality to answer. Bradley recognizes that something is required of him on this point. 'And now in particular,' he writes, 'the relation of the two ideal spheres to the real sphere is precisely what subsists inside the real sphere between its own elements.'[7] The relation, that is to say, of the social ideal and art and science to 'My Station' is precisely the same as the relation between the different elements which make up the social self of 'My Station'. It is a relation of the same kind as that which holds between family, occupation and local community.

Now this will not do as an answer to the question with which Bradley is faced at the present stage of his argument. The relation between the various elements of the ideal self must be an ideal relation. It must, that is to say, be a relation exhibiting a rational structure according to which the elements are harmonized. Unless it is a relation of this kind, the conception of the moral self as an ideal self, as a whole or system collapses. But the relation between the elements of the social self of 'My Station' which we are told is the model, is not an ideal relation. It is a relation articulated in the actual rules and customs of the institutions of a given society. On Bradley's own argument, to find the rational structure of the social self, we must go not to 'My Station' but to the social ideal. But we are then still left with the problem of the relation between the two ideals, the social ideal and the non-social ideal comprising the activities of art and science. We need, that is to say, an account of the rational structure of the ideal self and it is the business of the theory of morality, according to Bradley's own conception of it, to meet this need. His theory breaks down at the crucial point in its development.

Possibly this failure may have been concealed from Bradley himself through his pre-occupation with the practical character of moral problems. There is much wisdom and insight in his remarks on this latter point. Moral problems arise for a rational agent who has achieved a level of rationality above that of mere rule and custom. There can therefore be no rule or formula for their solution, and the theory of morality cannot be made the major premise of a moral syllogism in which particular duties are inferred. A moral rule may be made to serve this purpose, but we are concerned with a level beyond that of rule and custom. Moral problems are personal: they cannot be delegated, and the moral agent must solve them for himself. In all this, Bradley is summing up and articulating the verdict of mature moral experience. But moral problems are rational problems. They arise within the context of rational activity and demand a rational solution. The fact that they are practical does not mean that they are outside the range of rational inquiry. The moral agent in solving them must not act capriciously. His solution, if it is genuinely moral, must embody some principle. Moreover, it is not exempt from criticism, even though this may be hazardous in the case of other people's decisions, since knowledge and appreciation of some one else's situation can never be more than partial. While we may agree that the theory of morality cannot provide a formula for the solution of moral problems, it does not follow from this that it cannot give an account of the principles upon which such problems should be solved. In emphasizing the practical character of moral problems, Bradley has not justified his failure to give an account of the rational structure of the ideal self.

3.   I will take up later the question of why Bradley fails to give a proper answer to this question which, if his theory is to

be adequate, he ought to face and meet. First we must follow the main lines of his subsequent discussion. Having stated his revised theory of morality which is to make good the deficiencies of 'My Station', he proceeds to criticize it. But in his criticism, he gives no sign of being aware that his account of the ideal self is incomplete, that as it stands, it is not an intelligible conception, since no account is given of the rational structure which must relate the various elements. There is something else which troubles him, and we must try to see what it is, since it leads to a further step in his attempt to develop a theory of morality.

It is, however, by no means an easy task to disentangle and elicit Bradley's argument in the last part of *Ethical Studies*. The impression grows in the reader that Bradley is himself wearied by the tortuous path down which his argument has led him. The vigour and freshness which were so marked a feature of the earlier essays has deserted him; the style becomes heavy and oppressive and the exposition is clouded by much obscurity. There is moreover a long digression into psychology, which begins in the latter part of Essay 6, and to which the whole of Essay 7 is devoted. It is only in the eighth and concluding essay that he returns to his main task and endeavours to complete the development of his theory of morality. The psychological excursion is by no means without interest, and it includes a penetrating analysis and criticism of the doctrine of psychological hedonism which is well worth careful study on its own account. An exposition of it would, however, carry me away from the main theme of the present chapter, and I shall confine myself to what is directly relevant to Bradley's theory of morality. I will conclude this section with a brief statement of Bradley's own criticism of his revised theory of morality; and in the next, I will turn to his attempt in the eighth essay to provide a solution.

Bradley is troubled by what seems to him to be an inherent defect in morality itself. The conception of the moral self as an ideal self brings out the character of this defect. It is that in the last analysis, morality is an activity which is inconsistent with itself. Rational activity, the activity of self-realization, cannot therefore be identified with morality. It must be something more than merely morality. 'Morality implies knowledge of what the "ought" means,' Bradley writes, 'and the "ought" implies contradiction and moral contradiction.'[1] His point, as I understand it, seems to be that the activity of morality implies that what ought to be, the ideal self, must be a mere ideal and not real, while what is real must be non-moral and even immoral. 'So we see,' he writes, 'morality is negative; the non-moral and the immoral must exist as a condition of it since the moral is what it is only in asserting itself against its opposite.'[2]

Bradley is not maintaining that morality consists in merely abolishing the non-moral and immoral. It is not mere asceticism. 'But morality is not merely negative:' he goes on: 'it is a great mistake to suppose that the immoral is there already and that morality consists simply in making it not to be. The good will is not that which merely destroys the natural or the immoral: it does indeed destroy them as such but this by itself is not morality. It is when it destroys them by its own assertion, and destroys them by transforming the energy contained in them, that the will is moral.'[3] In these passages, Bradley does not seem to distinguish between the merely non-moral and the immoral. I will return to this point later, but for the moment let us concentrate on grasping the essentials of the difficulty about morality which he is trying to articulate. Morality presupposes the reality of the unmoralized, purely animal, side of human nature. But what is to be achieved in morality is the realization of a completely moralized self in which no traces of the merely natural remain. This moral self is an ideal, something which ought to be, but which on any given occasion is not real. The inconsistency in morality lies in the fact that this ideal, completely moralized self can never be achieved, for the attempt to realize it can be made only so long as the unmoralized animal self is real. Morality, that is to say, is the attempt to achieve a way of acting which in the nature of the case can never be achieved. A necessary condition of the attempt is that it should never be successful. The would-be moral agent is embarking on a hopeless enterprise. He will never succeed in realizing himself as a moral agent because there must always remain as part of himself, an intrinsically unmoralized element.

The conclusion to which Bradley comes as a result of this criticism is that: 'Morality is an endless process and therefore a self-contradiction: and being such, it does not remain standing in itself but feels the impulse to transcend its existing reality.'[4] Summing up what he believes to be the inherent defect of morality, he continues: 'It is a demand for what cannot be. Not only is nothing good but the good will, but also nothing is to be real so far as willed but the good, and yet the reality is not wholly good. Neither in me nor in the world is what ought to be, what is, and what is, what ought to be.'[5] This conclusion leads Bradley to the final step in his argument. The rational activity of self-realization must be something more than merely morality. The theory of morality must include some account of what this something more is. It must, that is to say, having exposed the inherent defect of morality as such, go on to a revised theory of the rational activity of self-realization in which the inherent defect of morality as such, is shown to be overcome. This is the task to which Bradley addresses himself in the eighth and concluding essay of *Ethical Studies* and we may postpone comment on his criticism of morality until we have seen how he accomplishes it.

D : MORALITY AND RELIGION

1. In Essay 8, Bradley maintains that the inherent defect which he believes himself to have located in morality is made good in religion. 'Reflection on morality leads us beyond it,' he writes: 'It leads us in short to see the necessity of a religious point of view.'[1] He then continues: 'What it tells us is that morality is imperfect and imperfect in such a way as implies a higher which is religion. Morality issues in religion.'[2] Bradley then says that he will try to make good this assertion. 'Our object,' he writes, 'is to show that as a matter of fact religion does give us what morality does not give, and our method is simply as far as our purpose requires, to point out the facts of the religious consciousness without drawing conclusions to the right or left, without trying to go below the surface or doing anything in this connection beyond what is wanted for morality.'[3] We are to be offered, that is to say, as much but no more of the theory of religion as is needed to complete the theory of morality, and the method to be followed is to interrogate ordinary religious experience without raising deeper metaphysical issues.

The first thing which we learn from religious experience, according to Bradley, is that: 'Religion is essentially a doing, and a doing which is moral. It implies a realizing, and a realizing of the good self.'[4] So far religion and morality appear similar but there is a fundamental difference. 'Religion is more than mere morality.' Bradley writes: 'In the religious consciousness we find a belief, however vague and indistinct, in an object, a not-myself, an object further which is real. An ideal which is not real and which is only in our heads, cannot be the object of religion.'[5] A few pages further on, expanding his account of the religious object, he writes: 'Its positive character is that it is real and further, on examining what we find in the religious consciousness, we discover that it is the ideal self considered as idealized and real. The ideal self which in morality is to be, here truly is.'[6]

Bradley then proceeds to draw a parallel between the religious object and the objects pursued in art and science. 'With religion, we may here compare science and art,' he writes: 'The artist and poet, however obscurely, do believe that beauty where it is is not seen, yet somehow and somewhere is and is real, though not as a mere idea in people's heads nor yet as anything in the visible world. And science, however dimly, starts from and rests upon the perception that, even against appearances, reason not only ought to be but really is.'[7] The artist and the scientist presuppose the reality of the object which they pursue in their respective activities. In like manner, the religious man presupposes the reality of the religious object. Bradley continues: 'In the very essence of the religious consciousness, we find the relation of our will to the real ideal self. We find ourselves as this or that will, against the object as the real ideal will which is not ourselves and which stands to us in such a way that, though real, it is to be realized because it is all and the whole reality.'[8]

As I understand it, the central thought which Bradley is trying to express in his account of the religious object is as follows. For religion, the ultimate reality of the world is spiritual. The perceptible world of nature, the world of human society and social institutions, are appearances rather than realities. They are media through which we achieve a partial experience of reality, but they are not ultimately real in their own right. We must, that is to say, make a Copernican revolution in our ordinary way of thinking for which reality is equated with the perceptible and the tangible, and locate it in the spiritual. This spiritual reality is the ideal self of morality which from the religious point of view is no longer a mere ideal. What from the standpoint of morality is only an ideal in contrast with the reality of human society, from the point of view of religion is real while society is only an appearance. We ourselves become real only to the extent that we are able to spiritualize ourselves, to live a genuinely religious life in which we try to embody in ourselves the ideal self which we now know to be the ultimate reality. The ideal self, from the point of view of religion, is already there. It does not depend on us for its reality. It is we who are dependent on it and we emerge from the transience and finitude of the merely natural life only by realizing in ourselves, albeit incompletely, something of the character of the ideal. This, as I understand Bradley, is the account of the religious object vouchsafed by religious experience.

The following passage bears out this interpretation of Bradley's account of the religious object. 'We find in the religious consciousness,' he writes: 'the ideal self as the complete reality and we have besides its claim upon us. Both elements and their relation are given in one and the same consciousness. We are given as this will which because this will, is to realize the real ideal. The real ideal is given as the will which is wholly real and therefore to be realized in us.'⁹ Bradley interprets the conception of religious faith in terms of his account of the religious object. 'Faith then is the recognition of my true self in the religious object,' he writes, 'and the identification of that both in judgement and will, the determination to negate the self opposed to the object by making the whole self one with what it really is.'¹⁰

2.   Having given an account of the religious object, Bradley next argues that, in content, religion and morality are the same. He returns to his first point, that religion is essentially practical. 'It means doing something which is a duty:' he writes: 'apart from duties, there is no duty and as all moral duties are also religious, so all religious duties are also moral.

In order to be, religion must do. Its practice is the realization of the ideal in me and in the world. Separate religion from the real world and you will find it has nothing left it to do.'[1] He then goes on: 'The practical content which religion carries out comes from the state, society, art and science, but the whole of this sphere is the world of morality and all our duties there are moral duties.'[2] It follows that since the content of religion and morality is the same, particular duties may clash in religion just as they do in morality but there can never be a conflict between religion and morality as such. 'And if this is so,' he continues, 'then this religious duty may collide with that religious duty just as one moral duty may be contrary to another. But that religion as such should be in collision with morality as such, is out of the question.'[3]

But although in content, religion and morality are the same, the fundamental difference between them remains. It is a difference of attitude, a difference both of belief and of feeling. 'So far religion and morality are the same,' Bradley continues, 'though, as we have seen, they are also different. The main difference is that in morality what only is to be, in religion somehow and somewhere really is, and what we are to do is done. Whether it is thought of as what is done now or what will be done hereafter, makes in this respect no practical difference.'[4] According to Bradley, this difference is not merely theoretical, it is of practical importance. The religious man faces his responsibilities in a spirit of confidence which is denied to one who is merely moral. "The importance for practice of this religious point of view,' Bradley goes on, 'is that what is to be done is approached not with the knowledge of a doubtful success, but with the perfect certainty of already accomplished victory.'[5]

So much for the last step in Bradley's argument: ignoring for the moment the fact that we have still not been given any account of the rational structure of the ideal self, let us try to interpret it from the standpoint of the theory of rational activity. He has already argued in his revised theory of morality according to which the moral self is an ideal self, that morality is a sphere of rational activity at a level of rationality above that of citizenship. It sums up and includes all that is embraced by the sphere of citizenship but includes also the non-social activities of art and science which fall outside the sphere of citizenship. But there remains a difficulty. Morality as the activity of realizing the ideal self suffers from an internal inconsistency. The ideal remains only an ideal and, in the nature of the case, cannot be fully realized. An unmoralized element in the self must remain as a condition of the attempt to be moral being made at all. The highest sphere of rational activity, the sphere within which citizenship and the non-social activities of art and science are embraced, the sphere which is to be the basis of a coherent way of life, cannot after all be identified with morality. It must be something more than merely the moral sphere. Bradley argues that it is the sphere of religion.

Religion is a total way of living and acting. It is the all-embracing sphere of rational activity in which all the lesser spheres are summed up and included. Its distinctive character comes from the attitude of mind and heart which it requires from those who are to achieve it. The Copernican revolution which it involves in ordinary secular ways of thought, enables the internal inconsistency of morality to be overcome. It preserves all the positive achievements of morality but is freed from its limitations. Moreover, it makes room for an activity which cannot properly be included within any other sphere of rational activity except religion, the activity of church membership. To locate this activity within the sphere of citizenship or within that of purely ideal morality, would fail to do justice to the character and rationale of churches. This at least seems a legitimate inference to draw from Bradley's general account of religion. In fact, his remarks about churches and about religious ritual, creeds and theology are only subsidiary to his main discussion. From the drift of his remarks, it appears that he regards churches primarily as institutions for moral training and discipline and he makes it clear that he is concerned only with the religious attitude of mind and not with particular creeds and dogmas. This is in keeping with his object of going no further into the theory of religion than is necessary to complete the development of his theory of morality. This, he believes to be accomplished, when he has shown from the facts of ordinary religious experience, that the inherent defect of morality is made good in religion, that religion in principle provides an all-embracing sphere for the rational activity of self-realization.

3.   I return now to the question of why Bradley fails to give an account of the rational structure of the ideal self in his revised theory of morality. This omission is not remedied in the last step of his argument in which he attempts to find in religion a cure for what he believes to be an inherent defect in morality as such. The ideal self from the standpoint of religion is to be regarded as already real, but we are still not told what its rational structure is. We do not really know what it is that from the standpoint of religion is already real. We can form no coherent idea of the religious object, for we do not know how the various elements, which are said to compose it, are related to one another. The ideal self is not a whole or system : it is not really on Bradley's view a self at all. It is only an aggregate of different elements which are not related in a system on any intelligible principle. Why is Bradley unaware of this gap in his argument; that at a crucial stage in the development of his theory of morality he has failed to answer a question of fundamental importance?

The reason is that although the notion of the concrete universal, together with the theory of rational activity, form the basis of his work, his understanding of them is imperfect. He has failed, that is to say, to work out all the implications of the ideas with which he is working and to appreciate their full significance. He sees that rationality is something more than either efficiency or the merely satisfying. He sees that it is coextensive with morality and that the roots of morality are social. He recognizes that the rational agent is not something separate from and set over against his individual actions but that rational activity is the activity of rational self-determination. He recognizes also that to be a rational agent and to be a moral agent is really the same thing. Up to this point, he has a clear grasp of the scale of levels of rationality. He understands, that is to say, that rationality is not a generic attribute, that it cannot be divided into mutually exclusive specific forms and that the various forms which it takes are related in an ascending scale of levels, each of which includes and sums up those below it. He has followed through and understood the development of the scale up to the level of morality but here his intellectual grip begins to slacken. He is not clear about the further development of the scale and the reason lies in his inability properly to distinguish between morality at the level of rule and custom and morality at the level of spheres of rational activity. This inability in turn is due to a failure to understand the conception of spheres of rational activity.

In section B of this chapter, I suggested that we should interpret 'My Station and its duties' as an account by Bradley of morality at the level of rule and custom. On this basis, it was possible to go on in Section 3 to give a provisional interpretation of his revised theory as an account of morality at the level of spheres of rational activity. But in fact Bradley is not clear in his own mind whether 'My Station' is an account of morality at the level of rule and custom or an account of citizenship in terms of morality at the level of spheres of rational activity. He oscillates between the two without grasping the difference between them. He fails to see that to act rationally as a responsible citizen is to have passed beyond the level of mere obedience to rule and custom to a higher level of rationality at which these rules and customs are subject to criticism and not merely accepted as given.

Bradley seems to have recognized that spheres of rational activity must be thought of as concentric and not merely contiguous. He certainly thinks of the state as embracing the other social spheres and the sphere of religion as embracing all the rest. There are indications that he thought of the ideal social self as summing up and including the social self of 'My Station' although his remarks about the former are so fragmentary that it is difficult to be certain on this point. But in spite of this recognition, his understanding of the conception of spheres of rational activity seems to have been hazy, indeed he seems never really to have systematically thought it out. That a sphere of rational activity is constituted by the idea of a rational way of living and acting, that it therefore claims to be self-consistent and complete and is open to criticism on these criteria, is something which he does not seem to have properly grasped. He seems to have thought that what constitutes citizenship a sphere is the body of rules and customs of a given society and, as we have seen, he has no real answer to the question : what constitutes the unity, i.e. the rational structure of the ideal self.

It follows that we cannot regard Bradley's revised theory of morality in which it is conceived as the activity of realizing the ideal self, as equivalent to morality at the level of spheres of rational activity. It expresses his intuitive recognition that morality is something more than obedience to rule and custom and also, a point of some importance, that art and science are rational activities which cannot properly be included within the sphere of citizenship. But he is unable to articulate this recognition into a systematic theory and what purports to be a revised theory must be regarded as a penetrating but, as it stands, undeveloped insight. What then are we to make of Bradley's view that morality as such is inherently defective? According to him, morality presupposes the permanent reality of an unmoralized element in human nature from which it follows that the ideal self can never be fully realized and must remain, in the last analysis, a mere ideal. The way out lies through the Copernican revolution involved in the religious standpoint for which the Ideal self is already real and the natural self is only an appearance.

Now Bradley does not seem to realize that within the context of rational activity there is a sense in which the Copernican revolution is already accomplished. Within the context of rational activity, the real is not the natural but the rational. The concrete reality of an individual action is the rationality which it achieves. To know what it really is, we must evaluate it as an achievement of rationality. We may agree with Bradley that the natural is the basis of the rational and the moral in the sense that without the natural, the rational and moral would be impossible. But this does not mean, at least within the context of rational activity, that the natural is to be regarded as real on its own account apart from its function within that context. What is real, that is to say, is rational activity and whatever enters into it is to that extent also real. In this sense, the Copernican revolution is already accomplished and we do not have to go to religion for it. But Bradley does not see this because his understanding of rational activity is imperfect.

It may be objected that, although within the context of rational activity, the real is the rational, the question remains whether what is real within this context is ultimately real? It may be said on Bradley's behalf that he has tried to raise this question and that I am being less than fair to him in saying that the Copernican revolution which he believed to be necessary is already accomplished within the context of rational activity, that I am simply begging the question. But in reply, I must point out that it is Bradley who wishes to exclude metaphysical questions from the theory of morality and that he is therefore not entitled to smuggle them in surreptitiously under the pretext of developing that theory. If the question of the ultimate reality of rational activity and *a fortiori* of morality is to be raised, then it should be done openly and we must subject the whole conception of reality to a critical examination. My point is that Bradley need not have overstepped his self-imposed limits in developing the theory of morality and the fact that he does so without apparently being aware of the fact is a further indication that his understanding of his own principles is imperfect.

I do not wish, however, to beg the metaphysical question and in later chapters we shall have to return to it. In particular, we shall have to see how Bradley himself handles it at a more mature stage in his philosophical career. Setting it aside for the present as irrelevant to the main argument of *Ethical Studies*, my chief criticism of the theory developed in that book is that it breaks down at a crucial stage because it fails to answer a question which, on the logic of its own argument, it ought to answer. We are given no account of the rational structure of the ideal self. But this does not detract from the significance of *Ethical Studies* as a pioneering achievement in which Bradley blazed a trail which others were to follow. Although unsatisfactory, the conception of the ideal self is highly suggestive. In drawing attention to art and science as rational activities, it poses a problem for the theory of rational activity. Do they properly fall within a sphere at a level of rationality higher than that of citizenship and, if so, what is the character and rationale of that sphere? As we shall see in the next chapter, T. H. Green takes up this problem and tries in his theory of morality to provide a solution.

I will end this chapter with a brief reference to a point touched on in section C. There I drew attention to the fact that

Bradley does not appear to distinguish between the merely non-moral and the immoral. In discussing what he believes to be the inherent defect of morality as such, he lumps them together, but in fact he is perfectly well aware that they are not the same. By the non-moral, he means the merely natural or animal. His view of the immoral appears in the course of his psychological discussion, especially in Essay 7, which has the title of 'Selfishness and the Bad Self.' Bradley's account is somewhat involved and no short excerpt will do it justice. Briefly, he seems to regard immorality as the conscious abandonment of responsibility. The bad self is the anarchic self, the self which is no self at all because lacking any principle of organization. The immoral man knowingly sets about the impossible task of realizing this bad self for the sake of the immediate satisfaction to be gained and heedless of the outcome. Later we shall have to take up the question of immorality again and I will say no more about it here. My purpose in mentioning it has been only to show that, in spite of his somewhat loose language at least as it appears in passages which I have quoted, Bradley does not deny the significance of the common sense distinction between what is merely non-moral and what is immoral or morally bad.

CHAPTER III

T. H. GREEN'S THEORY OF
MORALITY

A : THOUGHT AND EXPERIENCE

1. T. H. Green, who was ten years older than Bradley, was born in 1836. He died prematurely in 1882 when Bradley still had the greater part of his philosophical career ahead of him. But Green's most important works in social philosophy, *Prolegomena to Ethics* and *Lectures on the Principles of Political Obligation*, may fairly be regarded as the sequel to *Ethical Studies*. They were the fruit of the years immediately preceding his death and were published posthumously. The first is devoted to the exposition and defence of a theory of morality while the second is concerned with questions of political philosophy, but they are not strictly separable. The argument of the second presupposes that of the first and is a continuation and development of it. They should be regarded as the two halves of a single work in which an attempt is made to set forth and work out a single point of view. In this chapter and the next I shall try to state the essentials of that point of view and to elucidate it.

Bradley in *Ethical Studies* did his best to confine himself to the theory of morality without raising metaphysical questions. Green's approach in *Prolegomena to Ethics* is different. It is a central thesis of his philosophy, as of all Idealism, that man cannot come to know himself as a rational agent by means of natural science. But while Bradley in *Ethical Studies* was content to base his work on this thesis without trying to justify it,* Green thinks that it must be explained and defended. The past achievements of natural science make plausible the idea of a science of man which would include the subject-matter tradi-

* Except implicitly through his criticism of the doctrine of necessity. See Chapter II, section A, sub-section 1 of this book.

tionally assigned to moral philosophy. Is there really anything for moral philosophy to do when the scope and significance of psychology and anthropology has been properly understood? Green thinks that this question must be faced at the outset before moral philosophy begins. If, as he believes, there is work for it to do, this must be because the perspective of natural science is of such a kind as to exclude knowledge of rational activity. The first task to which he addresses himself is therefore to show that this is so.

Green thinks that the limitations of a natural science of man can be most readily appreciated in the case of knowledge rather than morality. 'As the first charm of accounting for what has previously seemed the mystery of our moral nature passes away,' he writes, 'and the spirit of criticism returns, we cannot but inquire whether a being, which was merely the result of natural forces, could form a theory of those forces as explaining himself.'[1] He then continues: 'Can the knowledge of nature be itself a part or product of nature in the sense of nature in which it is said to be an object of knowledge? This is our first question. If it is answered in the negative, we shall at least have satisfied ourselves that man, in the respect of the function called knowledge, is not merely a child of nature.'[2] The task which Green has set himself falls into two parts. First, he has to show that his questions must be answered in the negative, that man as a cognitive agent is not merely natural. Then he must show that this is true also of man as a moral agent.

In order to carry out the first part of his task, Green finds it necessary to raise those metaphysical questions which Bradley in *Ethical Studies* was anxious to avoid. He undertakes an examination of the place of the world of nature within human experience and of the scope and significance of human knowledge. In the course of this examination he develops a theory of the general character and structure of human experience against the background of which he interprets both human knowledge and the world of nature. I shall not try to follow his argument in detail in this chapter but will attempt to summarize the essentials of his theory of human experience. This theory is important not only for the understanding of Green but also of Idealist philosophy generally. It embodies a point of view which to some extent all Idealists share although they differ about some of its implications. Moreover it involves issues which, as we shall see later, cannot be ignored in any attempt to criticize and assess Idealist social philosophy.

2.   According to Green, the characteristic thing about human experience is that it is thinking experience. It is an error in his view to suppose that there is anything in human experience which is given ready-made without having been categorized and interpreted by thought. What we experience is always something already within a framework of thought. This is so even in the case of our experience of sensation. 'For a sensation can only form an object of experience,' Green writes, 'in being determined by an intelligent subject which distinguishes it from itself and contemplates it in relation to other sensations. So that to suppose a primary datum or matter of the individual's experience wholly void of intellectual determination is to suppose such experience to begin with what could not belong to, or be an object of, experience at all.'[1] Green's point is that we become conscious of our sensations by attending to them and to attend is always to identify in however provisional and rudimentary a way. What is attended to is never a mere 'this', it is always something located within some framework of thought. To be conscious of a sensation is already to have identified it as a sensation of a particular kind and so to have begun to think.

This is not to say that we can choose what sensations we are going to have. 'It certainly does not depend on ourselves,' Green writes, 'on any effort which we can suppose it rests with our will to exert or withhold, whether sensations shall occur to us in this or that order, this or that degree of intensity.'[2] But although the activity of attention through which we become conscious of our sensations is only partly under our control in the sense that we cannot help becoming conscious of many sensations which force themselves into our consciousness, this does not mean that sensations are given in human experience apart from the work of thought. Green continues: 'But the question is whether the relation of time between one sensation and another, or the relation between a sensation and other possible modes of itself which is implied in its having a degree, could exist if there were not a subject for which the several sensations, or modes of the same sensation, were equally present and equally distinguished from itself?'[3] We have the experience of sensation which we do, according to Green, only because we are thinking subjects. Our experience is never of bare atomic sensations but always of identified sensations and this is possible because our experience is self-conscious thinking experience.

As with sensation, so with other levels of experience : to be conscious of an individual object is to have identified it however provisionally and tentatively as an object of a certain kind. It may even be only as a problem calling for further identification. We have no experience of self-contained isolated individuals but always of objects which are in some way related. According to Green, this experience of related objects is possible only through the activity of thought. 'If there is such a thing as an experience of related objects,' he writes, 'there must be operative in consciousness a unifying principle which not only presents related objects to itself, but at once renders them objects and unites them in relation to each other by this act of presentation and which is single throughout the experience.'[4] His point is that the common sense world of physical objects is not given ready-made to human experience. It is articulated and developed within experience through the work of thought. The same is true of the world of natural events investigated by science. We are conscious of natural events only because we think and, apart from the work of thought, there would be no world of natural events for science to investigate.

This doctrine about nature may at first seem rather strange. We ordinarily think of our experience as occurring within the world of nature. Green seems to be saying that we should think of the world of nature as occurring within our experience. Such an idea however loses much of its strangeness if we take Green's point to be that what we call the world of nature is an interpretation which we make of an aspect of our experience. What the world of nature is in itself, what lies behind the things which happen to us, the events of which we are conscious, we do not know. It may be objected, however, that, stated in this form, Green's doctrine is of little significance. No one would deny it. But for him it is significant because it

reveals the fundamental part played by thought in human experience and enables us to see that, as thinking subjects, we
are something more than merely natural. He insists that what
he has called 'the unifying principle', which makes possible
our consciousness of related objects and events, is distinct from,
and cannot be reduced to the related objects and events of which
we are conscious. 'No one and no number of a series of related
events,' he writes, 'can be the consciousness of the series as
related.'[5]

Green also insists that his doctrine does not mean that we
must abandon our ordinary ideas about objectivity and fact.
'Objects do not cease to be objective, facts do not cease to be
unalterable,' he writes, 'because we find that a consciousness
which we cannot alter or escape from, beyond which we cannot place ourselves, for which many things indeed are external
to each other but to which nothing can be external, is the
medium through which they exist for us: or because we can
analyse in some elementary way what it must have done in
order to these things being there for us.'[6] What his doctrine
does mean is that we must revise our ideas about the character
and structure of our experience. 'It is not the conception of
fact,' he continues, 'but the conception of the consciousness for
which the facts exist that is affected by such analysis.'[7] We
must give up, that is to say, the notion that there is anything
in human experience which is given ready-made without
having been categorized and interpreted by thought.

But we must also revise our ordinary ideas about the world
of nature and about the scope and limits of scientific knowledge. This, for Green, is the most important result of his
doctrine. Summing up his theory of the general character and
structure of human experience, he writes: 'The purpose of this
long discussion has been to arrive at some conclusion in regard
to the relation between man and nature, a conclusion which
must be arrived at before we can be sure that any theory of
ethics in the distinctive sense of the term is other than wasted
labour. If by "nature" we mean the objects of possible experience, the connected order of knowable facts or phenomena,
and this is what our men of science mean by it when they
trace the natural genesis of human character, then nature
implies something other than itself as the condition of being

what it is.'[8] What it implies is the work of thought. If, that is to say, we are to follow scientific usage, we must mean by 'nature' not an independent reality given ready-made to human experience, but a world which is articulated and developed within human experience by the work of thought, a world which is forever in the making in the sense of progressively becoming continually further articulated and further developed.

Continuing the summary of his argument, Green says of the activity of thought or, as he calls it, the unifying principle in consciousness: 'We are further entitled to say of it negatively that the relations by which, through its action, phenomena are determined, are not relations of it, not relations by which it is itself determined. They arise out of its presence to phenomena, or the presence of phenomena to it, but the very condition of their thus arising is that the unifying consciousness which constitutes them should not itself be one of the objects so related.'[9] It is the activity of thought, that is to say, which makes possible our experience of related objects and events. Thought cannot itself therefore be one of the objects or events the experience of which is made possible by its own activity. Natural science is limited in its perspective to related objects and events. If man is therefore to know himself as a thinker and cognitive agent, he must do so by methods other than those of natural science. Such, in brief, is the argument by which Green carries out the first part of the preliminary task which he set himself in *Prolegomena to Ethics*, the task of showing that a philosophical as distinct from a scientific theory of morality is necessary.

3. The account given in the preceding paragraphs of Green's theory of human experience, although accurate enough so far as it goes, is incomplete. There is something else which must be added. But it may be helpful, before completing the account, briefly to consider certain objections to which the theory as stated so far may seem liable. It may be said that Green, in arguing that man cannot know himself as a thinker and cognitive agent through the methods of natural science, fails to take account of empirical psychology. Granted that a man's consciousness of related events on a given occasion is distinct from and cannot be reduced to the events of which he

is conscious, it does not follow from this that his consciousness and thought cannot be empirically studied by someone else. There is nothing in principle, it may be said, to prevent an empirical study of thought so long as the thought which does the studying is distinct from the thought which is studied. Intelligence tests are a case in point. On the basis of the inform- ation gained by such tests, it may be possible to correlate the capacity to perform certain intellectual operations with cer- tain other factors such as social and economic status, emotional dispositions, and even biological characteristics. In short, Green has not made out a convincing case that man cannot know himself as a thinker and cognitive agent through the methods of natural science.

When Green wrote *Prolegomena to Ethics*, empirical psy- chology was in its infancy, but its subsequent development does not invalidate the main point of his argument. This is that when thought is studied empirically it loses its distinctive character as thought and becomes merely one class of events among others. Its character as self-conscious, self-criticizing activity is excluded from the perspective of natural science which takes account only of events. This is not to deny the significance of intelligence tests, nor the possibility of correlat- ing ability in the performance of certain standardized intellec- tual operations with other factors. But such an investigation presupposes a theory of what intelligence is and of the nature and significance of the intellectual operations which are to be tested. This theory is not an empirical theory. The psychologist must bring it with him to his empirical work. He must already know what intelligence is, that is to say, before he can study its empirical manifestations. Green's central point therefore remains. Man cannot know himself as an intelligent, thinking and cognitive agent through the methods of natural science although this does not mean that the empirical manifestation of intelligence cannot be studied by such methods.

But even if Green is right about the limitations of natural science, exception may be taken to his insistence on the central role of thought in human experience. The new-born human infant, it may be objected, experiences but does not think. But in Green's view, the infant embarks on human experience only when it begins to think. In calling it 'human' we are saying that it has this capacity although it has not yet begun to develop it. We are conscious of it as a new-born infant but it has only the most primitive and rudimentary consciousness of itself. Its experience at this stage is only at a sub-human level. It rises to the human level through becoming conscious of itself as a person, a process which involves learning to recognize other persons and, in an elementary way, to communicate with them. This development of social self-consciousness is a development of the capacity to think. To insist on the central role of thought in human experience is not to deny that there is a level of experience at which the role of thought is not central. Nor is it to deny that human experience presupposes and is developed out of this level. It is to deny only that such a level is itself a level of human experience properly so-called.

4. But we have still to see how Green completes his theory of the general character and structure of human experience. In his view further development is required to take account of an important aspect of knowledge which has hitherto been neglected. If there is to be knowledge, according to Green, knowing must make no difference to what is known. The facts of which we have knowledge must be the same, whether we have knowledge of them or not. 'But we cannot suppose,' Green writes, 'that those relations of fact or objects of consciousness which constitute any piece of knowledge of which a man becomes master, first come into being when he attains that knowledge.'[1] But according to the theory which Green has been developing, there is nothing in human experience which is given ready-made prior to, and independent of, the work of thought. It follows from this theory that what we have knowledge of is always something categorized and identified within a framework of thought, never something as it is in itself apart from all thought. How can this be reconciled with the doctrine that knowing must make no difference to what is known? How can what we have knowledge of be the same whether we have knowledge of it or not, if it is not something as it is in itself but only something as it is for thought? This is the problem with which Green believes he must now deal.

He solves it by arguing that, although 'those relations of fact or objects of consciousness which constitute any piece of knowledge' must be independent of our thought, they are not independent of all thought. 'They must exist,' he writes, 'as part of an eternal universe and that a spiritual universe, a universe of consciousness, during all the changes of the individual's attitude towards them.'[2] The facts of which we have knowledge are thus the same, whether we have knowledge of them or not. But they are not independent of all thought. They are part of the system of thought of an eternal consciousness. In our human experience we are participating in this eternal consciousness. What we come to know on any given occasion is some fragment of what it knows already. It is by incorporating into his theory of human experience this doctrine of an eternal consciousness, that Green believes he can reconcile it with his conviction that, so far as human knowledge is concerned, knowing must make no difference to what is known.

Green's doctrine of an eternal consciousness is reminiscent of Bradley's doctrine of the real-ideal self of religion in *Ethical Studies*. Starting from the side of knowledge rather than that of morality, he seems to have arrived at a similar conclusion. But does he really need this doctrine to complete his theory of the general character and structure of human experience? Is the problem, which it is introduced to solve, a real one? He thought that it was, because of his conviction that knowing must make no difference to what is known. Now there are really two points involved in this conviction, although, as we shall see, Green does not seem to have realized it. The first is that for there to be knowledge, there must be something which is already there and which is independent of knowledge. The second is that, in our knowledge, what we know is always this independent reality or some part of it as it is in itself apart from our cognitive activity. These two points are separate. Accepting the first does not commit you to accepting the second. Granted that there is something which is already there which is independent of knowledge, it remains an open question whether, in our knowledge, what we know is this independent reality or some part of it as it is in itself, or whether in coming to know it we alter, modify or in some way transform it.

Now a fact is always independent of the particular occasion on which it was discovered, and of the particular person by whom it was discovered. It might have been discovered by someone else on some other occasion. The same fact can be discovered by different persons separately and at different times. This public character of facts no doubt implies that there is something already there which is independent of knowledge. But it does not imply that what we know when we know a fact is this independent reality or any part of it as it is in itself. What is required for facts to have a public character is not that they should be the same, whether or not they are known, but only that they should be the same for all who know them. That in coming to know facts, we should alter, modify, or in some way transform what is already there, is quite compatible with the public character of facts.

Green's theory of the general character and structure of human experience commits him to holding that to know a fact is to know something, not as it is in itself apart from thought, but as it is for thought. But since the public character of facts does not necessitate knowledge of anything as it is in itself apart from thought, there is no problem. But if there is no problem, the need for the doctrine of an eternal consciousness disappears. Green does not seem to have examined his conviction that knowing must make no difference to what is known very carefully. Had he done so, he might have seen that it involves two points, and that accepting the first does not commit him to accepting the second. Had he seen this, he would have realized that there is no problem of reconciling his theory of human experience with the public character of facts, and consequently no need for the doctrine of an eternal consciousness.

All this, however, is not to deny that there may be other reasons for incorporating a doctrine of an eternal consciousness into a theory of the general character and structure of human experience. We shall return to this topic in Chapter VIII of this book. At present my point is only that, in *Prolegomena to Ethics*, Green does not make out a case for the doctrine. It is not needed to complete the theory which he has been developing. Whether that theory is wholly adequate even without the doctrine of an eternal consciousness is another topic which for the moment we must defer. We shall see in a moment that it is adequate for Green's main purpose, the development of a theory of morality. So far as that theory is concerned, the doctrine of an eternal consciousness is of no real significance. The substance of the theory can be stated without it and I shall therefore make no further reference to it in my discussion of Green's social philosophy.

5. In order to complete the preliminary task which he has set himself in *Prolegomena to Ethics*, Green must show that the limits of the perspective of natural science prevent man from knowing himself not merely as a cognitive but also as a moral agent. The way for this has however already been prepared by his account of the central role of thought in human experience. Just as it is thought which makes possible our perceptual experience of a world of related objects, so it is thought which makes possible our practical experience as rational agents. It is because we are self-conscious thinking subjects that we can know what we want on any given occasion, and take steps to get it. After reminding the reader of the work of thought in perception, Green writes: 'In like manner, the transition from mere want to consciousness of a wanted object, from the impulse to satisfy the want to an effort of realization of the idea of the wanted object, implies the presence of the want to a subject which distinguishes itself from it and is constant throughout the successive stages of the want.'[1]

Since it is thought which makes possible our practical experience as rational agents no less than our perceptual and cognitive experience, and since natural science excludes thought from its perspective, it follows that we cannot gain adequate knowledge of ourselves as rational agents through the methods of natural science. Now morality arises within the context of our practical experience as rational agents. Only rational agents can be moral agents. It therefore follows that a merely scientific theory of morality is inadequate. There is work for moral philosophy to do which cannot be handed over to one of the natural sciences. This, in brief, is how Green completes the second part of his preliminary task. Man is a moral agent only because he is a thinker and an adequate theory of morality must do justice to the central role of thought in human experience. It must, in Green's view, be a philosophical theory, since it is a distinctive mark of philosophy to be concerned with the nature and significance of thought. His theory

D

of the character and structure of human experience is by implication a theory of the standpoint and method of philosophy. He does not, at this stage, formulate an explicit theory of philosophy. But, as we shall see later, his view gradually emerges in the course of his argument.

The passage quoted above, in which Green speaks of 'the consciousness of a wanted object' and of 'an effort of realization of the idea of the wanted object', suggests that what he has in mind is rational activity at the level of ends and means. From the way in which he continues, however, it is clear that his conception of rational activity is not confined to the level of ends and means. 'At the same time,' he writes, 'as the refecting subject transverses the series of wants which it distinguishes from itself while it presents their fulfilling as its object, there arises the idea of a satisfaction on the whole, an idea never realizable but striving to realize itself in the attainment of a greater command over means to the satisfaction of particular wants.'[2] This reference to 'a satisfaction on the whole' suggests that Green is thinking of rational activity at the level of private self-satisfaction, a level which includes that of ends and means. In fact, as we shall see, his conception of rational activity is substantially along the lines of the theory sketched in Chapter I of this book, although he expresses it in somewhat different terms. For him, as for Bradley, the theory of rational activity and the theory of morality are not two different things but one and the same.

6. There are some further points in Green's theory of human experience which it may be useful to touch on briefly before turning to his theory of morality. He distinguishes, as we have seen, between our perceptual and cognitive experience on the one hand, and our practical experience as rational agents on the other. But this does not mean that he thinks of them as separate compartments. For him the cognitive and the practical are interdependent throughout human experience. Cognition is bound up with rational activity from the beginning. 'So soon as any desire has become more than an indefinite yearning for we know not what,' he writes, 'so soon as it is really a desire for some object of which we are conscious, it necessarily involves an employment of the understanding upon those con-

ditions of the real world which make the difference so to speak between the object as desired and its realization.'[1] Cognition in its turn has a practical side. Desire and volition are always involved. 'In all exercise of the understanding,' Green writes, 'desire is at work. The result of any process of cognition is desired throughout it. No man learns to know anything without desiring to know it.'[2]

In Green's view our practical experience as rational agents is always at the same time cognitive and perceptual experience. But this does not mean that he is equating human experience with the experience of rational agents. The new-born human infant embarks on human experience properly so-called only when it begins to think. But it becomes conscious of itself as a person, and of other persons with whom it communicates, before it is able to act rationally. There is a level of human experience, that is to say, which is not yet the experience of rational agents but which is nevertheless properly called human because thought has already begun to play its central role. It is, in a rudimentary way, a level of cognitive and practical experience. It is cognitive in that it involves identification and recognition. It is practical in that it involves attention and communication. Moreover, its cognitive side and its practical side are interdependent. Attention is practical and identification is cognitive. But attention and identification are inseparable. One always identifies, however tentatively and provisionally, what one attends to.

But while it is necessary to take account of this lower level, it is no less important to recognize that, for the most part, human experience is the experience of rational agents. In so far as it is the experience of rational agents, its structure is the structure of rational activity. Each level of rationality is a level of human experience and this experience is always cognitive and perceptual, and for that matter also aesthetic, as well as practical. Green does not develop this point explicitly but it is implicit in his general doctrine. It has a bearing on the problem noticed at the end of Chapter I of this book. This was the problem of reconciling our idea of the concrete within the contexts of classification and natural science with our idea of it within the context of rational activity.

For classification and science individual things and events

are concrete realities. We regard them as really existing and really happening, whether or not we take account of them in our classificatory and scientific thought. But, according to Green's theory of human experience, setting aside his doctrine of the eternal consciousness, we have no knowledge of independent realities as they are in themselves. We know only that the individual things and events with which we deal in classification and science, exist and happen within the context of our experience as rational agents. What they are in themselves, apart from this context, we do not and cannot know. It follows that the concrete in classification and science is not individual things and events as such, but our individual experience of things and events, experiences which we have as rational agents engaged in the work of classification and science. Now our individual experience as rational agents is always an individual achievement of rationality. Each level of rationality is a level of human experience, and the concrete in human experience, in so far as it is the experience of rational agents, is coextensive with the concrete in rational activity. It is not merely practical but cognitive, perceptual and aesthetic as well. There are not really two ideas of the concrete, one within the contexts of classification and science, and one within the context of rational activity. There is only one, the idea of the concrete within the context of rational activity. It is the merit of Green's theory of human experience that it enables us to see this. It also enables us to see how the provisional definition of philosophy given in Chapter I may be brought into line with its traditional task. In so far as human experience is the experience of rational agents, the task of formulating a theory of its general character and structure, and the task of coming to know and expound the rationality implicit in the standards and values operative in human life, are complementary tasks. The one necessarily leads on to the other. But we shall return to these topics in a later chapter, and it is time now to consider Green's theory of morality.

B : RATIONAL ACTIVITY AND MORALITY

1.   Green develops his theory of morality in three stages. The first is devoted to an analysis and discussion of rational activity

or, as he calls it, 'deliberate action', without any specific reference to morality. In the second, the question of morality is taken up and the central thesis of the theory is expounded. In the third, the question of the relation of the theory of morality to moral practice is raised, and the theory is itself further developed and elucidated. The core of the first stage is in his account of motives. 'The motive in every imputable action,' he writes, 'for which the agent is conscious on reflection that he is answerable, is the desire for personal good in some form or other, and however much the idea of what the personal good for the time is, may be affected by the pressure of animal want, this want is no more a part or component of the desire than is the sensation of light or colour which I receive in looking at this written line, a component part of my perception in reading it.'[1]

The desire for personal good is not like the desire to satisfy some bodily appetite such as hunger or sex. Nor is it the aggregate or compound of such desires any more than the meaning of a written line is the aggregate or component of the coloured marks on the paper. But the use of the term 'desire' in this context is rather misleading. In another passage Green says of a motive: 'It is constituted by an act of self-consciousness which is not a natural event, an act in which the agent presents to himself a certain idea of himself, of himself doing or himself enjoying, as an idea of which the realization forms for the time his good.'[2] Green's point is that an action properly so-called is always the outcome of a decision. It is never merely the response to a stimulus. A motive is simply the idea of an action which a man has decided to try to do. But the decision to do one action rather than another is always made in the light of what he thinks in the circumstances will be for his personal good. The desire for personal good, that is to say, is the ground of every decision. The purpose of action is to achieve the agent's personal good in the particular circumstances in which he finds himself.

It might seem at first as if Green is simply propounding a form of psychological egotism. But this interpretation is premature. We must first see how the notion of personal good is developed. According to Green, a motive embraces both the idea of an action and the reason for which it is to be done. The reason is never merely that the action is the means to an end lying beyond it. It is that, in the situation confronting the agent, his personal good requires him to do the action. The notion of personal good, that is to say, includes both ends and means. The key to the notion lies in Green's reference to the agent's idea 'of himself doing or himself enjoying'. What he has in mind is the idea of the agent's personal self-realization through some course of action or activity. Whether the agent is right, whether the activity is really worthwhile, are further questions. Green's point is that this is what the agent is implicitly doing when he decides to try to do a given action although he probably will not present the matter to himself explicitly in such a way.

I said that Green's use of the term 'desire' is somewhat misleading. In the second stage of his exposition, where he is directly concerned with morality, he continues to use it. 'Regarding the good generically as that which satisfies desire,' he writes, 'but considering the objects we desire to be by no means necessarily pleasures, we shall naturally distinguish the moral good as that which satisfies the desire of a moral agent or that in which a moral agent can find the satisfaction of himself which he necessarily seeks. The true good we shall understand in the same way. It is the end in which the effort of a moral agent can really find rest.'[3] This passage is likely to be misunderstood unless it is interpreted in the light of the special sense which Green gives to the term 'desire' in his account of motives.

What he has in mind in saying that the good generically is 'that which satisfies desire' seems to be the following. Anything which satisfies a desire arising out of a bodily appetite or psychological need is to that extent good. But it must be further assessed from the wider standpoint of the rational agent's desire for personal good. Something which satisfies an immediately felt desire may be an obstacle to the rational agent's self-realization. It may prevent him from participating effectively in some worthwhile activity. It is therefore not good from this wider standpoint. In saying that the good generically is that which satisfies desire, Green is not saying that only those things which satisfy desires in the ordinary sense of the term are good. This interpretation is borne out by the following passage where Green writes: 'For an agent merely capable of seeking the satisfaction of successive desires without capacity for conceiving a satisfaction of himself as other than the satisfaction of any particular desire, and in consequence without capacity for conceiving anything as good permanently or on the whole, there could be no possibility of judging that any desire should or should not be gratified. No such judgement can be formed of any desire unless the desire is considered with reference to a good other than such as passes with the satisfaction of a desire.'[4]

In this passage Green is using the term 'desire' in its ordinary sense and pointing out that the criticism and control of desires presupposes a standard which is not that of the immediate satisfaction of desires as they arise. The standard is that of the agent's permanent good, or his good on the whole. Why then does Green introduce his special sense of the term 'desire'? Why does he choose to define the good as that which satisfies desire when he is himself using the term in two different senses? If he has been misunderstood, it may be said, it is largely his own fault for adopting so confusing a terminology. One reason is that, throughout the development of his own theory of morality, Green has in mind the ethical theory of Utilitarianism, especially that of J. S. Mill. His theory is intended to be a criticism of Utilitarianism but at the same time to do justice to it. This is why, having stated that the good generically is that which satisfies desire, he adds the qualification; 'but considering the objects we desire to be my no means necessarily pleasures . . .' He is trying to meet the Utilitarians half way, agreeing that what satisfies the desire for a pleasure is so far good, but at the same time insisting that many other things are also good.

But another reason is to be found in the structure of Green's theory. Although he speaks of 'the good generically', it is not his intention to apply the categories of genus and species to ethics. He does not regard the good as consisting of two mutually exclusive species, the members of one being those things which satisfy desires arising out of bodily appetites and psychological needs, and of the other those things which satisfy the desire for personal good. On the contrary, as we have seen, in his view the distinction between the satisfaction of desires in the ordinary sense and the satisfaction of the desire for personal good, is a distinction between two levels of goodness or value in a scale of levels. Of these, the satisfaction of the desire for personal good is the higher and it includes the lower within itself although transformed and modified by the inclusion. In saying that the good generically is what satisfies desire, Green is stating what he regards as the minimum characteristic of goodness. This characteristic remains at higher levels but appears in altered form in the light of the new standards introduced at these levels.

Green, that is to say, is expounding the theory of rational activity sketched in Chapter I of this book, but is expressing it in a different terminology. The effect is to place the emphasis on a different aspect but not substantially to alter the theory. Rational activity is seen as the activity of satisfying desire and the different levels of rationality are seen as different levels of desire with correspondingly different levels of satisfaction. Since each level of rationality is a level of purposive activity and since all purposive activity involves the desire to execute the relevant purpose, there is nothing fundamentally wrong in Green's way of putting the matter. His terminology has the drawback that it involves a somewhat unusual use of the term 'desire' with a consequent risk of ambiguity, but he may well have thought the risk worthwhile in order to bring out the relation between Utilitarian ethical theory and his theory of morality. The relation between levels of rationality or levels of purposive activity is of such a kind that no terminology used to express it can be wholly free from the risk of misinterpretation. Whether Green's choice is the one most likely to minimize the risk may be doubted, but what is important is not the particular terminology he has adopted but the essence of the doctrine which he is trying to express.

2. In the passage quoted where Green says that the good generically is that which satisfies desire, it will be recalled that he continues: 'we shall naturally distinguish the moral good as that which satisfies the desire of a moral agent or that in which a moral agent can find the satisfaction of himself which he necessarily seeks'. He then tells us that the true good 'is the end in which the effort of a moral agent can really find rest'.

We must not be misled by the use of the term 'end' here. He means the way of acting in which a moral agent can realize himself. Having in the first stage of his exposition given an account of rational activity at the level of private self-satisfaction or, in his terminology, the level of satisfying the desire for personal good, Green is now addressing himself to the task of giving an account of rational activity at the level of morality. In his terminology, this is the level of satisfying the desire of the moral agent. It includes the lower levels within itself. The personal good of the rational agent, that is to say, when it is properly understood, is the moral good. To be a fully rational agent is to be a moral agent. This is the central thesis which Green develops in the second stage of his exposition.

He develops it by working out the implications of his conception of personal good. 'Our ultimate standard of worth is an ideal of personal worth' he writes. 'All other values are relative to values for, of, or in a person. To speak of any progress or improvement or development of a nation or society or mankind except as relative to some greater worth of persons is to use words without meaning.'[1] But while insisting that individual personality is the ultimate standard of value, Green also insists that the individual person is not an atom. He is always a member of a community of persons. 'Without society no persons,' he writes, 'this is as true as without persons, without self-objectifying agents, there could be no such society as we know.'[2] He goes on to say that: 'only through society is anyone enabled to give that effect to the idea of himself as the object of his actions, to the idea of a possible better state of himself, without which the idea would remain like that of space to a man who had neither the sense of sight nor touch. Some practical recognition of personality by another, of an "I" by a "thou" and a "thou" by an "I", is necessary to any practical consciousness of it as can express itself in act.'[3]

In another passage, Green says that: 'social life is to personality what language is to thought. Language presupposes thought as a capacity but in us the capacity of thought is only actualized in language. So human society presupposes persons in capacity, subjects each capable of conceiving himself and the bettering of his life as an end to himself. But it is only in the intercourse of men, each recognized by each as an end not merely a means, and thus as having reciprocal claims, that the capacity is actualized and we really live as persons.'[4] Thus the rational agent's personal good when it is properly understood is a social good. The self which he realizes must be a social self and the ways of acting through which he realizes it must be ways of acting which are consistent with life in society.

It is this social aspect of rational activity which gives rise to morality. 'Thus we conclude,' Green writes, 'that in the earliest stages of human consciousness in which the idea of a true or permanent good could lead anyone to call in question the good of an immediately attractive pleasure, it was already an idea of a social good, of a good not private to the man himself but good for him as the member of a community.'[5] The rational agent, that is to say, in becoming conscious of himself as an individual person also becomes conscious of himself as a member of a community and of the responsibilities which this involves. In becoming a self-conscious rational agent, he is at the same time becoming a moral agent with obligations to others. His personal good, when it is properly understood, is a social or common good. Thus in his own terminology, Green develops the theory of rational activity sketched in Chapter I of this book.

3. So far Green has developed his theory of morality along fundamentally the same lines as Bradley in the early stages of *Ethical Studies*. They agree in distinguishing between rational activity at the level of ends and means, at the level of private self-satisfaction and at the level of morality. They agree also in recognizing that, above the level of ends and means, rational activity is the activity of self-realization and that it is from the social aspect of rational activity that morality arises. But Bradley sees the problem of the theory of morality as being that of eliciting and expounding the nature of the self which is to be realized in morality. While this self is necessarily social, it may also be something more. Green, on the other hand, sees the problem as being that of deciding what the ultimate community is, of which the moral agent is a member. He differs from Bradley in rejecting the idea that the moral self can ever be more than a social self and sets himself the task of eliciting and expounding the nature of the moral social self. Bradley, we

saw in the last chapter, fails to distinguish clearly between morality at the level of rule and custom and morally responsible conduct at the level of spheres of rational activity. He is aware that in some sense there is a distinction but fails to grasp its real import. Green on the other hand in principle understands this distinction. He does not expound it in detail but rather takes it in his stride.

He argues that the ultimate moral community is co-extensive with mankind. 'Given the idea of a common good and self-determined participators in it,' he writes, 'the idea implied as we have seen in the most primitive human society, the tendency of the idea in the minds of all capable of it is to include as participators in the good, all who have dealings with each other and who can communicate as "I" and "thou". With growing means of intercourse and the progress of reflection, the theory of a universal human fellowship is its natural outcome.'[1] There is, in Green's view, no justification for restricting the moral community to any group less than mankind. This does not mean that the claims of limited communities, of family, neighbourhood and nation, may be ignored in favour of a vague loyalty to humanity in the abstract. It means that these responsibilities must be interpreted and evaluated in the light of a wider responsibility to take account of the interests of all human beings who may be affected by the activities of these limited communities. No course of action is morally defensible however worthwhile in itself, if its achievement is possible only at the cost of riding roughshod over the opportunities for rational living of other human beings.

In another passage Green writes: 'Whenever and wherever then, the interest in a social good has come to carry with it any distinct idea of social merit, of qualities which make the good member of the family, or good tribesman or good citizen, we have the beginning of that education of the conscience of which the end is the conviction that the only true good is to be good. This process is properly complementary to that previously analysed, of which the end was described as the conviction that the true good is good for all men and good for them all in virtue of their same nature and capacity. The one process is complementary to the other because the only good in which there can be no competition of interests, the only good which

is really common to all who may pursue it, is that which consists in the universal will to be good, in the settled disposition
in each man's heart to make the most and best of humanity in
his own person and in the persons of others.'[2]

Readers familiar with the ethical writings of Kant will
recognize their influence in this passage. But Green is not
merely restating Kant. He has tried in his theory of morality
to incorporate what he believes to be of permanent value in
Kant's doctrine and he clearly has much sympathy for the
general spirit of his work. But he is fully alive to Kant's limitations and has tried in his own theory to go beyond them. The
'education of the conscience' from the idea of 'qualities which
make the good member of the family or the good tribesman
or good citizen' to 'the conviction that the only true good is to
be good' is in principle the transition from morality at the level
of rule and custom to morality at the level of spheres of
rational activity. It is a development of the moral agent's self-
consciousness in the course of which he gradually becomes
aware that he alone is responsible for his life, that there is
ultimately no authority to which he can turn except his own
honest judgement of the demands of the situation facing him
and that in the last analysis what matters is that he should
meet these with integrity and intelligence. But as his self-consciousness develops, the moral agent passes from the idea of a
limited common good to 'the conviction that the true good is
good for all men'. He gradually becomes aware, that is to say,
that he is not only a worker, a member of a family and a
citizen, but a human being and that his responsibilities extend
to all human beings whether or not they are members of his
own nation.

Bradley, as we saw in the last chapter, indicates in the latter
part of *Ethical Studies* that there is a level of rational activity
above that of citizenship. But owing to his failure to grasp the
essentials of the theory of rational activity beyond the level of
private self-satisfaction and especially to be clear about the
distinction between morality at the level of rule and custom
and morality at the level of spheres of rational activity, he is
unable to give an account of the defining characteristics of this
highest level. Green is here doing the same thing, and since
his understanding of the theory of rational activity is deeper

and goes further than Bradley's, he is more successful. In arguing that the ultimate moral community is co-extensive with mankind, he is characterizing and delineating a level of rational activity higher than that of citizenship. It is the level of human achievement as such. It incorporates within itself but also goes beyond the various spheres of work and leisure, personal relations and citizenship. Like each of these spheres, it has its own distinctive activities. Of these, the most obvious are creative art in all its forms and the systematic pursuit of knowledge exemplified in natural science, historical research and scholarship and philosophy. But it also includes all the activities of lower levels modified and partially transformed by their new context. Its characteristic principle upon which all these activities are harmonized is that of the self-consistent development of human capacities. This is the thought which Green is expressing when he says that: 'the only good in which there can be no competition of interests, the only good which is really common to all who may pursue it, is that which consists in the universal will to be good, in the settled disposition in each man's heart to make the most and best of humanity in his own person and in the persons of others.'

From the standpoint of self-realization, Green is arguing that the self which the rational agent ought to realize, the self to the realization of which he is implicity committed, is the human self. He must, if he is to be fully rational, try to be not merely a good worker, family-man, neighbour and citizen, but a good human being. While he cannot be a good human being unless he is a good worker, family-man, neighbour and citizen, he must interpret and evaluate his responsibilities in these spheres from the standpoint of the contribution he can make in his situation to the development of human capacities. But the development of human capacities must be self-consistent. There is no genuine human achievement when development in one direction is carried out at the expense of frustrating it in another. The human self to the realization of which the rational agent is implicitly committed is therefore a social self. His ultimate responsibility is to the community of mankind, the community which is dedicated to the self-consistent development of human capacities. It is in the light of this ultimate responsibility that he must interpret and evaluate the other claims upon him.

One way of expressing the essence of Green's doctrine is to say that genuine human achievement is non-competitive in the sense that, to borrow Bosanquet's phrase, 'it is not diminished by being shared'. The ultimate standard of rationality is the standard of genuine human achievement, for rational activity is the activity of a plurality of agents and it can only be fully realized on a non-competitive basis. But it must not be forgotten that rationality is a matter of degree. We are concerned here only with the highest level in the scale of levels. Green is in no sense denying that, for most practical purposes, we have to be content with something less than the ultimate standard. At least in one sense this is so, for it is clear that as he understands it we rarely, if ever, find genuine human achievement unalloyed by imperfections. But there is a sense also in which the ultimate standard is always within reach. To understand what this is, however, and to see how Green elaborates and fills out his theory of morality we must pass to the third stage of his exposition.

C : MORAL THEORY AND MORAL PRACTICE

1. According to Bradley, the philosophical theory of morality has nothing to contribute to the practical solution of moral problems. Green agrees that it is not the task of the moral philosopher to act as an authority in such matters. No one except the moral agent whose problem it is can solve a moral problem. But he differs from Bradley in thinking that the theory of morality is still not without relevance. In the third stage of his exposition, he places the question of the relation between the theory of morality and moral practice in the centre of his discussion, and endeavours, through a systematic examination of it, further to elucidate and develop his own theory. 'In considering whether our theory of the good and of goodness,' he writes, 'can be of use in helping us to decide what ought to be done and whether we are doing it, it is important to bear in mind the two senses, the fuller and the more restricted, in which the question "what ought to be done?" may be asked. It may either mean, and this is the

narrower sense in which the question may be asked, "what ought an action to be as determined in its nature by its effects?' or it may be asked with the fuller meaning: "what ought the action to be with reference to the state of mind and character which it represents?" "[1]

Green then goes on to say that: 'The former is the sense in which the question is asked when it is not one of a self-examining conscience but of perplexity between different directions in which duty seems to call. The latter is the sense in which a man asks it when he is comparing his practice with his ideal.'[2] Green then explains why the former sense is narrower and the latter fuller. 'We reckon the latter sense the fuller,' he writes, 'because a man cannot properly decide whether, in respect of character and motives, he is acting as he ought, without considering the effects of the course of action he is pursuing as compared with the effects of other courses of action which it is open to him to pursue, while he can compare the value of one set of effects with another without considering the nature of the motives which might prompt him to the adoption of the several courses of action leading to the several effects. Thus whereas the question in the latter sense includes the question as asked in the former sense, the question can be dealt with in the former sense without raising it in the latter.'[3]

The narrower sense of Green's question, in which 'it is not one of a self-examining conscience but of perplexity between different directions in which duty seems to call', is strictly practical. It concerns the particular ends which the moral agent ought to try to bring about in a given situation and the means which ought to be used for the purpose. It must be answered by estimating the foreseeable consequences of alternative courses of action and evaluating them. The standard by which they are to be evaluated is that of morality, but the nature of this standard does not come within the narrower sense of the question. It is assumed that a man is trying to act morally, that he has a working idea of how he ought to live and act, and the problem is how best to implement this idea in detail in the situation in which he is placed. The fuller sense of the question in which a man 'is comparing his practice with his ideal' and trying to decide 'whether, in respect of his character and motives, he is acting as he ought', raises the problem of the nature of the moral standard itself. In order to know whether he is living up to his ideal, he must know what that ideal is. In order to know whether, in respect of character and motives, he is acting as he ought, he must know what character and motives he ought to have. He must, that is to say, have a theory of morality if he is to be able to criticize his own conduct. Moreover, the particular theory which he has is not without practical significance. It will be reflected in the standard which he employs in answering the question in the narrower sense. The question in the fuller sense is not itself a theoretical question, not a question about the nature of morality, but it clearly implies the answer to such a question. A man who reflects critically upon his own conduct can hardly avoid asking himself not only whether he is living as he ought but how he ought to try to live.

Green proceeds to contrast his own theory of morality with that of Utilitarianism in order to illustrate his point that the theory of morality is not without practical significance. 'To the Utilitarian,' he writes, 'the virtuous character is good simply as a means to an end quite different from itself, namely a maximum of possible pleasure. An action is good, or has moral value, or is one which ought to be done, upon the same ground. If two actions done by different men are alike in their production of pleasure, they are alike in moral value, though the doer of one is a virtuous character and the doer of the other not so.'[4] By the 'virtuous character' Green means the morally conscientious character, the man who is genuinely trying to act morally for the sake of so acting. According to Utilitarianism, such a character is of no intrinsic moral value. 'In our view,' Green continues, 'the virtuous character is good not as a means to a "summum bonum" other than itself but as in principle identical with the "summum bonum"; accordingly, if two actions could be alike in their moral effects, as they very well may be in production of pleasure, but represent the one a more virtuous the other a less virtuous character, they would still be quite different in moral value. The one would be more, the other less of a good, according to the kind of character which they severally represent.'[5]

Green admits that: 'It is only an action done by himself that a man has the means of estimating in relation to the character represented by it. Actions done by others, if similar outwardly or in effect, can only be referred to similar states of character.'[6] But he then goes on: 'When from the nature of the case, however, a consideration of effects can alone enter in to the moral valuation of an act, the effects to be considered according to our view will be different from those of which the Utilitarian according to his principles would take account. They will be effects not in the way of producing pleasure but in the way of contributing to that perfection of mankind of which the essence is a good will on the part of all persons. These are the effects which in our view an action must in fact tend to produce if it is one which ought to be done according to the most limited sense of that phrase, just as these are the effects for the sake of which it must be done if it is done as it ought to be done.'[7]

For Utilitarianism, the question 'what ought to be done?' is significant only in the narrower of the two senses distinguished by Green. The standard in terms of which the effects of alternative courses of action are to be evaluated is different from that which is derived from Green's theory. Hence it follows that a man may well act differently in a given situation, according to whether his standard is derived from Utilitarianism or Green's theory of morality. His moral appraisal of the actions of others will also differ. But the difference between Utilitarianism and Green's theory is a philosophical difference. Broadly it is the difference between a theory which conceives rational activity solely at the level of ends and means, whose only standard of rationality is efficiency, and a theory based on a more far-reaching conception of rational activity which distinguishes other levels of rationality beyond that of ends and means, and other standards besides that of efficiency. Hence it follows that the philosophical theory of morality is not irrelevant to moral practice.

2. The difference between Green's theory of morality and that of Utilitariansm is not as to whether it is the motive or the effects of an action which constitute its morality. Green is not contending in opposition to Utilitarianism that the motive is everything and the effects nothing. He agrees that the effects are always relevant. But he insists that, from the point of view

of moral evaluation, the motive and the effects are interdependent, the latter cannot really be good if the former is bad. 'For it is only to our limited vision,' he writes, 'that there can seem to be such a thing as good effects of an action that is bad in respect of the will which it represents and that in consequence the question becomes possible whether the morality of an action is determined by its motives or its consequences. There is no real reason to doubt that the good or evil in the motive of an action is exactly measured by the good or evil of its consequences as rightly estimated: estimated i.e. in their bearing on the production of a good will or the perfecting of mankind. The contrary only appears to be the case on account of the limited view which we take of both action and consequences.'[1]

He then proceeds to illustrate: 'We notice, for instance, that selfish motives lead an able man to head a movement of political reform which has beneficent consequences. Here, we say, is an action bad in itself according to the morality of the good will but which has good effects. Is it to be judged according to its motive or according to its effects? But, in fact, if we look a little more closely, we shall find that the selfish political leader was himself much more of an instrument than an originating cause, and that his action was but a trifling element in the sum or series of action which yielded the political movement. The good in the effects of the movement will really correspond to the degree of good will which has been exerted in bringing it about, and the effects of any selfishness in its promoters will appear in some limitation of the good which it brings to society.'[2]

According to Green, the proper standard by which a movement of political reform ought to be evaluated is that of citizenship. The aims of the movement must not be divorced from the way in which it is conducted. How far is the movement, taking account of both its aims and its methods, an achievement of citizenship? In the present situation, is the pursuit of these aims by these methods likely to contribute to the welfare of the political community? If so, then the good citizen has a duty to do what he can to assist the movement. To the extent that those who participate in the movement are animated by these motives and play their part in it with integrity and intelligence, the movement is an achievement of citizenship. This is what

Green has in mind when he says that 'the good in the effects of the movement will really correspond to the degree of good will which has been exerted in bringing it about.' The selfish political leader who takes part from motives of private self-interest, contributes nothing to this achievement. He may be useful as a means although his value in this respect must be weighed against the corrupting influence which he may exert upon the movement.

In evaluating a political movement as an achievement of citizenship, the success which it has in bringing about its special aims, the particular legislative and administrative changes which it advocates, is by no means irrelevant. But it is not the only, nor the most important consideration. The movement may fail to realize its special objectives and still be a valuable achievement of citizenship. Citizenship is not the means to an end lying beyond itself but a sphere of rational activity, a way of living and acting, and what is of ultimate importance is that, in the situation in which they find themselves, people should try to live and act as citizens. This does not mean that questions of particular ends and means should be regarded as unimportant. It means only that the achievement of a way of living and acting is something more than the achievement of efficiency in the bringing about of particular ends although efficiency remains a necessary ingredient. A man cannot be a good citizen without being efficient in his particular actions but he can be efficient in his particular actions without being a good citizen. If a political movement fails to achieve its special aims through a lack of efficiency on the part of those engaged in it, it is at best only a feeble achievement of citizenship. But if it fails not from lack of efficiency in the details of its work, but because the forces opposed to it are too strong, the failure does not in itself detract from it as an achievement of citizenship. The attempt may have been worth making even though success in terms of particular results was problematical from the outset.

In considering whether he ought to assist a movement of political reform, the citizen is in effect asking the question: what ought to be done? in the fuller of the two senses distinguished by Green. He is asking himself whether, in assisting the movement, he is doing what, as a citizen, he ought to do.

The question presupposes a conception of what citizenship is. We are here brought back to the relation of philosophy to practice. In Green's view, the theory of citizenship is a part only of the theory of morality, albeit a most important part. The ultimate moral community is not the state but mankind. A full theory of citizenship, that is to say, involves interpreting it in terms of the higher level of self-consistent human achievement. As we shall see in the next chapter, this is what Green tries to do in his political philosophy. The point to notice here, however, is that a citizen's practical conduct may be affected by the theory of citizenship in terms of which he puts practical questions to himself.

But there is, in Green's example of the selfish political leader, something which appears to be inconsistent with his previous argument. Earlier he said that 'it is only an action done by himself that a man has the means of estimating in relation to the character represented by it'. Now he speaks of our noticing that 'selfish motives lead an able man to head a movement of political reform'. But if it is only in the case of our own actions that we can estimate integrity, how can we tell that the motives are selfish? Indeed it is hard to see how we are ever justified in estimating the moral character of others. But we do form such estimates and they are not arbitrary. We base them on our knowledge of the conduct of the person concerned in situations in which loyalty and responsibility are called for. It is improbable that Green intended to deny this and we must therefore not take his first statement too literally. His point may be interpreted as being that it is only where we have full and detailed knowledge of conduct that we are in a position to form an estimate of moral character. We are in a better position to do this in the case of ourselves than in the case of others and it is only where we are intimately acquainted with someone else that we should be prepared to risk a judgement as to his integrity. The less we know about a man's habitual conduct, the more cautious we should be in forming definite conclusions about his moral character.

3.   Although Green thinks that the theory of morality is not without practical significance, he is fully alive to its limitations. 'Any value,' he writes, 'which a true moral theory may

have for the direction of conduct depends upon its being applied and interpreted by a mind which the ideal as a practical principle already actuates.'[1] The theory of morality, that is to say, can be of help only to a man who is already trying to be moral. Even here, the value is indirect. 'And it will be as well at once to admit,' Green continues, 'that the value must be rather negative than positive, rather in the way of deliverance from the moral anarchy which an apparent conflict between duties equally imperative may bring about: or of providing a safeguard against the pretext which, in a speculative age, some inadequate and misapplied theory may afford to our selfishness; than in the way of pointing out duties previously ignored.'[2]

According to Bradley, the problem posed by 'the apparent conflict between duties equally imperative' is strictly practical. Theory has nothing to contribute to its solution. But in Green's view such a problem can arise only for a moral agent who has got beyond the level of rule and custom and is trying to think out his conduct for himself. It is the process of thought which has given rise to the problem and the solution must be sought not by abandoning the process but by carrying it further. According to Green, 'No good will come of this unless under the direction of a genuine interest in the perfecting of man.'[3] But he thinks that: 'Given this interest, it is only through philosophy that it can be made independent of the conflicting because inadequate formulae in which duties are presented to it, and saved from distraction between rival authorities of which the injunctions seem at once absolute and irreconcilable because their origin is not understood.'[4]

A little later, after saying that the function of bringing home their duties to men is that of the preacher rather than the philosopher, Green continues: 'Speculatively, there is much for the philosopher to do in examining how that ordering of life has arisen to which these duties are relative. What is the history of their recognition? What is the rationale of them? What is the most correct expression for the practical ideas which underly them?'[5] In another passage, speaking of the work of the moral philosopher, he writes: 'As a moral philosopher, he analyses human conduct, the motives which it expresses, the spiritual endowments implied in it, the history of thought, habit and institutions, through which it has come to be what it is.'[6]

Green's point is that, for the moral agent who has got beyond the level of rule and custom, duties are not given ready-made. He must decide them for himself, and in order to do this he must have some understanding of the nature and significance of the various spheres of rational activity within which his immediate responsibilities arise. He is committed to a process of thought which, if its implications are fully developed, will lead him into philosophy. Green is not, however, saying that it will normally be necessary for the implications of the process to be fully developed. He is not maintaining that a man can achieve morally responsible conduct only if he first 'analyses human conduct, the motives which it expresses, the spiritual endowments implied in it, the history of thought, habit and institutions through which it has come to be what it is'. Ordinarily, it will be enough if the process of thought is carried to the point where the moral agent feels that he has a practical understanding of what he is responsible for, without troubling himself about its ultimate meaning within the framework of human experience. But there may be occasions, such as 'an apparent conflict between duties equally imperative' when the process must be carried further and the moral agent may find himself driven into 'examining how that ordering of life has arisen to which these duties are relative', and asking: 'what is the rationale of them? What is the most correct expression of the practical ideas which underly them?'

Nor is it Green's view that philosophy should only be undertaken when practical problems seem to demand it. It should be cultivated in the same spirit as scientific research or creative art, for its own sake as a valuable human achievement. His point is that there will be times when it will join hands with practice and that the union will be better effected when there is a vigorous tradition of philosophical thought already going on. The moral agent who asks the question: 'what ought to be done?' in the fuller sense, who asks himself whether he is living and acting as he ought, and who is thus led to wonder how he ought to live and act, will be the beneficiary of such a tradition. He will be less likely to fall a victim to what Green, probably having Utilitarianism in mind, calls 'some inadequate and misapplied theory'.

Bradley in *Ethical Studies* was unable to establish an intelligible connection between the practical thought of the moral agent in determining his conduct and the theoretical thought of the moral philosopher. He failed to see that the moral agent is committed to a process of thought which, when its implications are fully developed, leads to moral philosophy. This failure was due to his inadequate grasp of the theory of rational activity. Green, having a deeper understanding of that theory, is able to make the connection. For him, the highest level of rational activity is that of self-consistent or non-competitive human achievement. At this level all the subordinate levels of rationality find a place. It is a social level but the relevant society is not confined to any limited group. It is co-extensive with mankind. This human community is the ultimate moral community. The moral agent can realize himself fully only by living and acting as a member of it. Final 'deliverance from the moral anarchy which an apparent conflict between duties equally imperative may bring about' can be found only by interpreting immediate responsibilities in the light of the deeper responsibility to the ultimate moral community. But this interpretation, if it is to be adequate, involves thinking out the nature and significance of the ultimate moral community, and it is here that practical thought about moral problems passes into moral philosophy.

Green is not however maintaining that the moral agent who supplements his practical thought by moral philosophy will thereby be relieved from all problems of conduct. He may still be in doubt about what to do on a given occasion owing to uncertainty about the probable outcome of different courses of action which seem to be open to him, an uncertainty which he has no means of removing. His problem is technical rather than strictly moral but it is still a problem of conduct. Green's point is that where the problem is strictly moral, where it is a case of doubt as to which of two loyalties ought to be respected, the theory of morality may be of practical significance. It must also be remembered that Green is not maintaining that the nature and significance of the ultimate moral community can be understood in isolation, without reference to the more immediate responsibilities of family, neighbourhood and nation. On the contrary, it is an integral part of his doctrine that it is only through an understanding of these limited communities that an understanding of the ultimate moral community is possible. A man can be a good human being only by being a good family man, neighbour and citizen. The theory of the highest level of rational activity must also be the theory of the spheres which it incorporates. Hence it is to Green's political philosophy that we must go for a fuller understanding of his moral philosophy.

4. To end this chapter, I will say something about Green's conception of freedom. It is an aspect of his general theory of morality and a brief consideration of his doctrine may serve as an introduction to his political philosophy. There is some reference to freedom in *Prolegomena* but Green's view is most systematically expounded in an essay entitled 'The different senses of freedom'. It seems to have been composed at the same time as *Prolegomena* and was posthumously published as an introduction to his *Principles of Political Obligation*. Early in the essay, Green writes: 'As to the sense given to freedom, it must of course be admitted that every usage of the term to express anything but a social and political relation of one man to others involves a metaphor.'[1]

Explaining the necessity of this metaphorical sense, Green writes: 'Reflecting on their inner life, i.e. their life as viewed from within, men apply to it the terms with which they are familiar as expressing their relations to each other. In virtue of that power of self-distinction and self-objectification, which he expresses whenever he says "I", a man can set over against himself his whole nature or any of its elements and apply, to the relation thus established in thought, the term borrowed from relations of outward life.'[2] Green thinks that this metaphorical use of terms can be misleading. The problem of the freedom of the will is, he thinks, a misconceived problem arising out of the inappropriate use of a metaphor drawn from the relations of social life and the natural world. The point, according to Green is that the will is the man as a self-determining agent. It is not something like a body in space which can be acted on by another body. As Green puts it: 'A man in willing is necessarily free since willing constitutes freedom.'[3] What is self-determining, in other words, cannot be the product of something else acting upon it.

Thus, according to Green, while it makes sense to talk of a man being unfree in that he is interfered with and restrained by others in his attempts to execute his own decisions, it does not make sense to speak of him as not being free in making his decisions. A decision, by its nature, must be free. A man may make a decision while being exposed to strong inducements one way or the other, but he alone remains responsible for the decision. A decision, as distinct from the attempt to implement it, cannot be restrained or interfered with. Thus rational activity, the activity of self-determination, is necessarily free activity. But there is another sense in which it is possible to speak significantly of decisions which are not free, or of rational activity which is not free. After speaking of a man as being free in the attempt to realize objects of his own choice, Green goes on:

'But in another sense he is not free because the objects to which his acts are directed are objects in which, according to the law of his being, satisfaction of himself is not to be found. His will to arrive at self-satisfaction not being adjusted to the law which determines where this self-satisfaction is to be found, he may be considered in the condition of a bondsman who is carrying out the will of another, not his own. From this bondage, he emerges into real freedom, not by overcoming the law of his being, not by getting the better of its necessity, every fancied effort to do so is but a new exhibition of its necessity, but by making its fulfilment the object of his will, by seeking the satisfaction of himself in objects in which he believes that it should be found and seeking it in them because he believes that it should be found in them.'[4]

In this passage, Green is arguing that there is a sense in which real freedom can be found only in morally responsible conduct. The man whose actions are directed towards objects 'in which, according to the law of his being, satisfaction of himself is not to be found' is trying to realize himself as a rational agent without becoming a moral agent. He is trying to develop a satisfying way of living and acting without taking account of his responsibilities as a social being. We may consider him as being 'in the condition of a bondsman who is carrying out the will of another not his own' because he is not fully in control of his conduct. He remains in the last resort subject to the caprice of his own private inclinations. By contrast, the man who is capable of morally responsible conduct is free from this subjection. He is able to discipline his private inclinations for the sake of meeting his social responsibilities and is thus in control of his conduct in a way in which the other is not.

What Green has in mind may perhaps be summarized as follows. Rational activity is determined by decisions. A decision is a choice between alternatives and every decision is free in the sense that on any given occasion a different choice might have been made from that which was made. Hence rational activity is free. But this is not the end of the matter. There are different levels of rationality and there is a sense in which these may be regarded as different levels of freedom. The rational agent who moves from a lower to a higher level of rationality is moving from a less to a more adequate way of thinking about human conduct and its situation. He is expanding his horizon and learning to understand and take account of what previously had either been ignored or merely accepted uncomprehendingly. He is putting himself in a position to make better informed decisions than before and so to increase his control over himself and his conduct.

Thus in moving from the level of mere private satisfaction to that of morality, the rational agent is freeing himself from a way of thinking which confines him to the circle of his own private inclinations and for which the responsibilities of social life appear only as alien restraints. He is entering upon a way of thinking which will enable him to criticize and, where necessary, discipline his private inclinations instead of being subject to them, and which will enable him to see the responsibilities of social living as responsibilities which belong to him. Equally, in moving from morality at the level of rule and custom to morally responsible conduct at the level of spheres of rational activity, he is freeing himself from the limitations of an uncritical acceptance of established authority, and is entering a way of thinking in terms of which he can understand the nature and ground of rules and customs, and make them his servant rather than his master. Such, in brief, seems to be the central thought underlying Green's essay. There is, however, one further point which, although Green does not deal with it explicitly, is implicit in his doctrine. It concerns the distinction between the amoral and the immoral. The amoral man is unable to reach the level of morality and is less free than the moral man, being subject to the caprice of his private inclinations. But the immoral man is capable of morality and is as free as the moral man. His immorality lies in his knowing disregard of his responsibilities. He decides to do what he knows he ought not to do and need not do. He is the rational agent who deliberately renounces the highest level of rationality of which he is capable and it is for this reason that he is censured. The amoral man must not be censured for he is not capable of morality.

CHAPTER IV

T. H. GREEN'S POLITICAL
PHILOSOPHY

A : RIGHTS AND OBLIGATIONS

1. For Green's political philosophy we must go to his *Principles of Political Obligation*. This book, which was posthumously published, consists of the text of a course of lectures given by Green at Oxford in 1881. The lectures were a sequel to an earlier course on ethics in which some of the main ideas of *Prolegomena to Ethics* were expounded. Green announces his intention at the beginning of the first lecture. 'My plan will be:' he writes: 'a) to state in outline what I consider the true function of law to be, this being at the same time the true ground of our moral duty to obey the law; and throughout I shall distinguish moral duties from legal obligations: b) to examine the chief doctrines of political obligation that have been current in modern Europe and, by criticizing them, to bring out more clearly the main points of a truer doctrine: c) to consider in detail the chief rights and obligations enforced in civilized states, inquiring what is their justification, what is the ground for respecting them on the principles stated.'[1]

This plan has been formulated in the light of the theory of morality developed in *Prolegomena*. When Green speaks of 'the true function of law' and of 'the true ground of our moral duty to obey the law' it is the rationality of law as a human achievement and the rational basis of the duty to obey it that he has in mind. When he speaks of 'bringing out more clearly the main lines of a truer doctrine of political obligation' he has in mind the nature and significance of citizenship as a sphere of rational activity and of the responsibilities to which it gives rise. The plan is not so much an application of the theory of morality worked out in *Prolegomena* as a further development of that theory. To be moral is to be a good human being and this is something more than merely being a good citizen. But on the other side it is not something less than being a good citizen. An important part of the theory of morality must be the theory of citizenship as a rational human achievement. In this chapter, I shall try to show how Green develops this idea and will follow him in the main lines though not the full details of his plan.

2. We may begin with Green's proposal to distinguish moral duties from legal obligations. Legal obligations are those which arise out of the provisions of a given code of law and which, if necessary, the government will enforce by the use of its coercive power. But moral duties, just because they are moral, cannot be enforced. 'The question sometimes put,' Green writes, 'whether moral duties should be enforced by law, is really an unmeaning one, for they simply cannot be enforced. They are duties to act, it is true, and an act can be enforced. But they are duties to act with certain dispositions and from certain motives and these cannot be enforced.'[1] Moral duties, that is to say, belong to a rational agent as a social being. They are the particular actions which on a given occasion he must do in order to play his part as a member of a society. But they must be done freely and voluntarily, because the rational agent recognizes them as his responsibility in the situation: otherwise he is not contributing to his society and fails to realize himself as a social being. The man who does an action not because it is his duty but for the sake of avoiding punishment or social censure is not playing his part as a member of his society. His action is rational but at a level below that of morality. He may be achieving a way of acting which is satisfying to him as a private individual but he is not realizing himself as a moral and therefore as a social agent.

But although moral duties cannot as such be legally enforced, one and the same action may be both a moral duty and a legal obligation. The distinction between them is not that between the mutually exclusive species of a genus. Green puts this by saying: 'There is a moral duty in regard to obligations but there can be no obligations in regard to moral duty.'[2] Normally it will be the moral duty of the citizen to discharge his legal obliga-

tions. But it is not the fact that, if necessary, they will be enforced by the government which makes their discharge a moral
duty. Citizenship is something more than merely obeying the
law. The law is concerned with what in the last resort can be
enforced by coercive power and is therefore confined to the
external or physical side of action. As Green puts it: 'Only outward acts then can be matter of legal obligation.'[3]

But what actions ought to be made legally obligatory? 'The
answer to this question,' Green writes, 'arises out of the above
consideration of the means which law employs to obtain the
fulfilment of obligations, combined with the view of law as
relative to a moral end, i.e. the formation of a society of persons
acting from a certain disposition, from interest in the society
as such.'[4] In speaking of law 'as relative to a moral end' Green's
point is that the function and scope of law must be interpreted
from the standpoint of rational activity at the level of morality. Ultimately this means from the standpoint of the highest
level of rational activity, that of self-consistent human achievement. Giving a provisional answer to his question, he writes:
'Those acts only should be matter of legal injunction or pro-
hibition of which the performance or omission, irrespectively
of the motive from which it proceeds, is so necessary to the
existence of a society, in which the moral end stated can be
realized, that it is better for them to be done or omitted from
that unworthy motive, which consists in fear or hope of legal
consequences, than not to be done at all.'[5]

This answer indicates that, according to Green, it is the
proper function of law to compel those who would not otherwise do so to conform to certain minimum standards. These
are the standards which must be observed if the members of a
society are to have the chance of achieving the higher levels of
rationality of which they may be capable. These higher levels
must be achieved freely and voluntarily but the law can and
should be used to prevent those who are capable of them from
being pulled down to the level of the minority who are incapable of any sustained achievement of morality at all. These
latter will be a minority for if they become a majority, rational
social life will disintegrate into anarchy. Compulsion is thus
used only against those who are incapable even of the minimum level of morality. There is no question of trying to en-

force moral duties. All those capable of morality will obey freely and voluntarily as a moral duty. But for a fuller answer, we must go to Green's theory of rights. It is to this theory that the major part of the first lecture is devoted after the initial distinction of moral duties from legal obligations has been made.

3.   Green rejects the doctrine of natural rights or the 'Rights of Man' in its traditional form, although he does not deny that there is some significance in the idea. 'Natural rights,' he says, 'so far as there are such things, are themselves relative to the moral end to which perfect law is relative.'[1] The traditional doctrine gives no moral justification for the rights which it asserts. They are simply laid down and it is supposed to be the task of law to enforce them. But in Green's view : 'A law is not good because it enforces natural rights but because it contributes to the realization of a certain end. We only discover what rights are natural by considering what powers must be secured to a man in order to the attainment of this end. These powers perfect law will secure to their full extent. Thus the consideration of what rights are natural in the only legitimate sense, and the consideration what laws are justifiable, form one and the same process, each presupposing a conception of the moral vocation of man.'[2]

Green's point is that the idea of rights is an aspect of the idea of law. A given system of law, together with the rights which it secures, should be subjected to criticism. But the standard of criticism is not some alleged body of natural rights which are supposed to be already there prior to all inquiry. It is the standard of morality, ultimately the standard of self-consistent human achievement. In criticizing a given system of law, we must ask : how effectively does it contribute to self-consistent human achievement in the particular circumstances in which it operates? In considering how it can be improved, we are led to consider what rights people have in the sense of morally justified claims to have certain powers secured to them by the law, or, to put the matter from the other side, what actions they are morally entitled to have made legally obligatory? To have a natural right is to have a morally justified claim to have certain powers secured by law whether or not the law at the time actually secures them. In this sense and no other, according to Green, the phrase 'natural right' is significant. Therefore to inquire what rights are natural and what actions ought to be made legally obligatory is one and the same inquiry.

Having contrasted it with the traditional doctrine of natural rights, Green proceeds to develop his own theory further. 'The doctrine here asserted,' he writes, 'that all rights are relative to moral ends or duties, must not be confused with the ordinary statement that every right implies a duty or that rights and duties are correlative. This is of course true in the sense that possession of a right by any person both implies an obligation on the part of someone else and is conditional upon the recognition of certain obligations on the part of the person possessing it.'[3] This ordinary view, it may be noted in passing, does not support the traditional doctrine of natural rights in which little or no emphasis is placed on obligations. Green, however, has another point in mind. 'But what is meant,' he continues, 'is something different: viz that the claim or right of the individual to have certain powers secured to him by society and the counter-claim of society to exercise certain powers over the individual alike rest upon the fact that these powers are necessary to the fulfilment of man's vocation, to an effectual self-devotion to the work of developing the perfect character in himself and others.'[4]

It is thus as a moral agent and therefore as a member of a society that a man has rights. On the other side, it is as the corporate organization of a group of moral agents that society has rights, that it is morally justified in claiming the power to regulate the conduct of its members in certain respects. It is this social basis of rights which underlies the ordinary view that the possession of a right 'is conditional upon the recognition of certain obligations on the part of the person possessing it'. Green sums up the social character of rights when he says: 'No one therefore can have a right except a) as a member of a society, and b) of a society in which some common good is recognized by the members of the society as their own ideal good, as that which should be for each of them. The capacity for being determined by a good so recognized is what constitutes personality in the ethical sense.'[5]

Green's second point, that the society must be one in which

the members recognize a common good, is significant. It is re-stated in another passage where he writes : 'There can be no right without a consciousness of common interests on the part of members of a society. Without this, there might be certain powers on the part of individuals but no recognition of these powers by others as powers of which they allow the exercise nor any claim to such recognition. And without this recogni-tion or claim to recognition there can be no right.'[6] Green is here saying that, without the consciousness of common in-terests among the members of a society, there would be no basis upon which they could agree that the exercise of certain powers should be allowed. Nor would there be any basis upon which the claim could be made that the exercise of a certain power, at present forbidden, ought to be allowed. There can be rights, that is to say, only in a society where there is funda-mental agreement.

It might be objected that, while as a matter of fact unless there is fundamental agreement within a society, the rights of its members are not likely to be secured, still this makes no difference to the rights themselves. If certain claims are morally justified, then whether or not the members of a given society agree that they are makes no difference. But in Green's view, this is another form of the fallacy of the traditional doctrine of the 'Rights of Man'. The root of the fallacy lies in the assumption that rights are independent realities which are somehow already there independently of any social situation. But for Green what is real is the level of rationality embodied in a given social situation. Where this falls below the level of morality, where the people concerned fail to recognize any common good in terms of which they can agree upon the regu-lation of their conduct, the notion of rights becomes irrele-vant. An example of such a situation (which could hardly have occurred to Green) is where two different racial groups within a population come into conflict. Within each group, the level of morality will be reached, there will be genuine social relations and rights will be a reality. But, between them, there will be no genuine social relations, no achievement of morality and no rights. The situation represents a moral failure on the part of the members of both groups and it can be improved only when they can achieve some consciousness of common interests on

E

the basis of which they can develop genuine social relations. Unless and until they can make this improvement and raise their inter-communal relations to the level of morality, the question of mutual rights and obligations between them cannot arise.

Thus, for Green, the existence of a system of law which effectively secures certain rights to the members of a society is an indication that among them there is a widespread achievement of rationality at the level of morality. This is not however to say that the system of law cannot be improved. There may be rights which are overlooked or which are very imperfectly secured to certain groups. There may be vested interests which prevent whole classes from enjoying many of their rights. There is an indication only that a minimum level of morality has been generally reached. Nor does the mere possession of rights of itself guarantee the achievement of higher levels of rationality. It merely provides conditions under which these higher levels may be achieved. This is the thought which Green has in mind in the following passage in which he sums up the moral basis of rights and at the same time their limitations. 'Only through the possession of rights,' he says, 'can the power of the individual freely to make a common good his own have reality given to it. Rights are what may be called the negative realization of this power, i.e. they realize it in the sense of providing for its free exercise, of securing the treatment of one man by another as equally free with himself. But they do not realize it positively because their possession does not imply that, in any active way, the individual makes a common good his own.'[7]

B : THE THEORY OF THE STATE

1.   After the first lecture, Green turns his attention to the second stage of his plan : the critical examination of the chief theories of political obligation current in modern Europe and the development of a truer doctrine. He devotes five lectures to reviewing and commenting upon the political philosophies of Spinoza, Hobbes, Locke, Rousseau and the analytical jurisprudence of John Austin. Summing up his criticisms, he writes : 'Looking back on the political theories which we have dis-

cussed, we may see that they all start by putting the question to be dealt with in the same way and that their errors are very much due to the way in which they put it.'[1] Describing their way of putting the question, he goes on: 'They look only to the supreme coercive power on the one side and to individuals to whom natural rights are ascribed on the other, and ask: what is the nature and origin of the right of that supreme coercive power as against these natural rights of individuals?'[2]

Green then states what he thinks is wrong with this way of putting the question. 'The power which regulates our conduct in political society,' he writes, 'is conceived in too abstract a way on the one side, and on the other are set over against it as the subjects which it controls, individuals invested with all the moral attributes and rights of humanity. But in truth it is only as members of a society, as recognizing common interests and objects, that individuals come to have these attributes and rights, and the power, which in a political society they have to obey, is derived from the development and systemization of those institutions for the regulation of a common life without which they would have no rights at all.'[3] It is not because they make use of the notion of rights that Green objects to the way in which these theories formulate their questions. In his view, the notion of rights is of fundamental importance in the theory of the state. 'The state then presupposes rights and rights of individuals,' he says: 'It is a form which society takes in order to maintain them.'[4] What he objects to is the way in which rights are conceived, a way which takes no real account of their moral and social basis.

In the following passage he sums up the essentials of his own view of the state in which he thinks the real character of rights is recognized. 'A state,' he writes, 'presupposes other forms of community with the rights which arise out of them and only exists as sustaining, securing and completing them. In order to make a state, there must have been families of which the members recognized rights in each other, recognized in each other powers capable of direction by reference to a common good. There must further have been intercourse between families, or between tribes that have grown out of families, of which each in the same sense recognized rights in the others.'[5] What he has in mind is that, when a political community is

formed, there is a transition on the part of at least the leaders
of local communities from the sphere of personal relations to
that of citizenship. They must already have achieved morality
not merely at the lower level of rule and custom but at the
higher level of spheres of rational activity. They move into the
sphere of citizenship when, having been carried beyond the
confines of their various local communities by the increasing
range and complexity of their activities, they become conscious of common interests which they all share and of the
need to regulate their conduct for the sake of maintaining and
developing them.

Only when this transition has been accomplished, only when
the leaders of the different local communities have begun to
think of themselves as members of a wider community and to
recognize and fulfil the responsibilities which membership involves, can a state be formed. When Green says that the state
'only exists as sustaining, securing and completing' the rights
which arise out of other forms of community, his point is that
the leaders of the different local communities will have found
that they can maintain the rights which they and their fellows
already enjoy within these communities, only by forming a
wider community and by accepting the necessary adjustments
and modifications which this involves. It is the logic of the
enterprise of maintaining rights which leads them into the sphere
of citizenship and into the formation of a political community.
They are making explicit the moral implications of the idea of
rights.

But the doctrine that the state exists for the sake of maintaining rights does not mean that it should be regarded merely
as a means to an end. It is an institution of the sphere of citizenship and citizenship is a sphere of rational activity, a way of
living and acting, a context within which questions of ends
and means arise, but itself neither the means to an end nor
an end towards which other actions are the means. Moreover,
citizenship is a sphere of rational activity which sums up and
includes within itself the subordinate spheres of personal relations, work and leisure. It follows that, while the rights which
arise out of the social relations of these lesser spheres are maintained within the state, they will not be maintained in precisely
the same form. The new context will make some difference and

will give rise also to new rights which may properly be called political and new duties. The creation of a political community is thus, on Green's view, a moral and social achievement which is possible only where there has already been a development of rationality beyond the minimum level of morality and some expansion in the range and complexity of the activities of local communities.

2.   Green's objection to the theories which he criticizes is not, however, confined to their inadequate notion of rights. It will be recalled that he also thinks that: 'The power which regulates our conduct in political society is conceived in too abstract a way.' For his own view of the nature and significance of coercive power in the state, we must turn to his critique of John Austin's analytical jurisprudence and especially to his comments on the latter's doctrine of sovereignty. He quotes Austin's own definition. 'The notions of sovereignty and independent political society may be expressed concisely thus: if a determinate human superior, not in the habit of obedience to a like superior, receives habitual obedience from the bulk of a given society, that determinate superior is sovereign in that society and the society, including the superior, is a society political and independent.'[1]

In the course of his comments on this definition Green remarks: 'When the power by which rights are guaranteed is sovereign, as it is desirable that it should be in the special sense of being maintained by a person or persons wielding coercive force and not liable to control by any other human force, it is not this coercive force that is the important thing about it or that determines the habitual obedience essential to the maintenance of rights. That which determines this habitual obedience is a power residing in the common will and reason of men, i.e. in the will and reason of men as determined by social relations, as interested in each other, as acting together for common ends. It is a power which this universal rational will exercises over the inclinations of the individual and which only needs exceptionally to be backed by coercive force.'[2] In another passage, Green says that what he calls 'the real determinant of habitual obedience' must be looked for 'in that impalpable congeries of the hopes and fears of a people bound together by common interests and sympathy which we call the general will'[3]

Green's point is that the state is a moral and social achievement. The basis of habitual obedience is the recognition by the citizens that they have a moral duty as citizens to obey the law. The government has to use coercion only in a small minority of cases where certain individuals for one reason or another fall below the level of morality and would not otherwise obey. But it cannot use coercion regularly, coercion, that is to say, cannot be the basis of the habitual obedience of the great majority because in such a situation the greater coercive force rests with the majority. When Green says that 'the real determinant of habitual obedience' is what we call 'the general will', he is asserting that the basis of any political regime is acceptance of its authority on the part of its subjects. This acceptance may sometimes be grudging or reluctant. A particular government may be supported because, although it arouses little enthusiasm, no available alternative is in sight and any government which can maintain order is better than none. In many cases, habitual obedience will reflect the minimum morality of rule and custom. The 'impalpable congeries of the hopes and fears of a people' may embrace any one or all of these attitudes.

But what about a dictatorial or totalitarian regime? How can they be fitted into this account of the basis of political authority? Green admits that there is a prima facie difficulty. 'It may be objected,' he writes, 'that this view of the general will, as that on which habitual obedience to the will of the sovereign really depends, is at best only applicable to self-governing communities not to those under a despotic sovereign.'[4] In answering this objection, he re-affirms his view that: 'In all organized communities, the power which practically commands the habitual obedience of the people in respect of those acts or forbearances which are enjoined by law or authoritative custom is one dependent on the general will of the community.'[5] But he then goes on: 'It may very well be that there is at the same time another power merely coercive, a power really operating on the people simply through their fears, to which obedience is rendered and which is not in turn representative of a general will.'[6]

Green, that is to say, does not deny that within a political community there may be despotic or tyrannical power, power which commands obedience solely through fear. But in his view, 'Where this is the case, we shall find that such power is only in contact with the people, so to speak, at one or two points, that their actions and forbearances as determined by law and custom are in the main independent of it, that it cannot in any proper sense be said to be a sovereign power over them, at any rate not in the sense in which we speak of king, lords and commons as sovereign in England.'[7] He then proceeds to commit himself to the assertion that: 'If a despotic government comes into anything like habitual conflict with the unwritten law, which represents the general will, its dissolution is beginning.'[8]

A good example of a despotic power in Green's sense, although it is not one which could have occurred to him, is the secret police of a totalitarian state. The secret police operates on the fears of the people and by this means obtains their obedience. But, at the same time, the secret police may fairly be said to be 'only in contact with the people at one or two points', namely those concerned directly with politics. Apart from these, the actions of the people 'as determined by law and custom' are in the main independent of the activity of the secret police. It is not fear of the secret police which makes them observe traffic regulations, refrain from doing violence to the person and property of their neighbours, keep contracts, pay taxes and so forth. It is rather the recognition that these things must be done if there is to be any ordered social life at all. All the same, it may be thought that Green is too optimistic when he asserts that a despotic government which comes into habitual conflict with the general will is paving the way for its own dissolution. He seems to be suggesting that a despotic regime is something superficial, that it cannot seriously affect the way of life of a society against the wishes of the people. Twentieth Century experience of totalitarianism may seem to suggest a different view.

But we must remember that, according to Green, it is 'in all organized communities that the power which practically commands the habitual obedience of the people' is dependent on the general will, and that the general will is 'that impalpable congeries of the hopes and fears of a people bound together by common interests and sympathy.' It is therefore only in an organized community, in which there is some degree of social cohesion, that a despotism will be in contact with the people at only one or two points and will be unable seriously to affect their way of life against their wishes. What he has in mind is an autocracy like Czarist Russia. It was not coercive force which maintained the Czarist regime for so long but the acquiescence, albeit for the most part passive and uncritical, of the Russian people. But when social cohesion breaks down, as eventually happened in Czarist Russia, when, for whatever reason, the bonds of common interest and sympathy are snapped, there is no longer any organized community and no longer any general will. In such a situation, a ruthless well-organized minority may be able for a time to impose itself on a fragmented disorganized majority by coercive force, and obedience which begins through fear may eventually become habitual as a new routine of life develops so that coercion once more recedes into the background.

It may be granted, however, that Green underestimated the capacity of a ruthless, dedicated and well-organized minority to subjugate by force a disunited and disorganized majority. No doubt also he failed to reckon properly with the puppet regime maintained against the wishes of the majority through fear of armed intervention from outside. But, notwithstanding these defects, the core of his doctrine remains significant. A state represents no moral and social achievement, there is no political community except in name, unless the great majority of its members are united by bonds of common interests and sympathy and obey the government not out of fear but as a duty. Where these conditions are not present, where what purports to be a state is kept in being only by force, there is no moral and social achievement. The relations between government and governed are at a level of rationality below that of morality. They are not social relations at all in any real sense. Green was perhaps too optimistic in thinking that such conditions could not last for long but there is nothing in his theory, although he did not realize it, to justify this optimism.

3.   According to Green's original plan, the reason for criticiz-

ing other political theories was in order to develop a truer doctrine of political obligation. We have still to see what that doctrine is. In his view there is a genuine problem of political obligation, but its nature is misconceived if it is stated in a way which implies a conflict between the rights of the individual and the authority of society. 'A right then,' he says, 'to act unsocially, to act otherwise than as belonging to a society of which each member keeps the exercise of his powers within the limits necessary to the like exercise by the other members, is a contradiction.'[1] He then goes on to say that: 'No one can say that unless he has consented to such a limitation of his powers, he has a right to resist it. The fact of his not consenting would be an extinction of all right on his part.'[2] Green's point is that, as a social being, a man has a moral duty to limit the exercise of his powers. He is never entitled to do merely what he likes without reference to his social responsibilities. The condition of his having rights is that he should recognize and fulfil this moral duty.

This principle applies in the case of the citizen and the state. 'Nor can the citizen have any rights against the state,' Green writes, 'in the sense of a right to act otherwise than as a member of some society; the state being for its members the society of societies, the society in which all their claims upon each other are mutually adjusted.'[3] It is not, that is to say, as an isolated individual but as a socially responsible agent that the citizen is morally justified in claiming that the government should secure to him certain powers in respect of his dealings with other men. In describing the state as 'the society of societies', what Green has in mind is that the sphere of citizenship incorporates within itself the various subordinate spheres which embody lower levels of rationality. The various claims to be secured in the possession of certain powers which arise out of the social relations of work and leisure, of family and neighbourhood life, become morally justified only after they have been interpreted and, where necessary, modified and adjusted in the light of the responsibilities involved in membership of the political community. It is the implications of these claims for all the members of that community which must be considered, not merely their effect on the lives of those immediately concerned. No citizen can have a right to act in a way which is incompatible with the responsibilities of citizenship.

This however is not the end of the matter. 'But what exactly is meant,' Green asks, 'by the citizen's acting as a member of his state? What does the assertion that he can have no right to act otherwise than as a member of his state amount to? Does it mean that he has no right to disobey the law of the state to which he belongs whatever that law may be? that he is not entitled to exercise his powers in any way that the law forbids and to refuse to exercise them in any way that it commands?'[4] Green's way of putting his question, namely asking whether the citizen can ever have a right to disobey the law of his state, is somewhat paradoxical. According to him, a right is a morally justified claim to have certain powers secured by law. A morally justified claim to have the power to disobey the law secured by the law itself even under very special circumstances is surely inconceivable. It is a claim that the law should be used in a way which is destructive of law, a claim to have legally secured what is inconsistent with the whole idea of law, and no such claim can be morally justified. But the point behind his question is not paradoxical. He is really asking: is the citizen ever morally entitled to disobey the law of his state, has he ever a moral duty to do so?

Green's question, as thus reformulated, indicates the sense in which there may be a real problem of political obligation. It will appear as a moral problem which arises when the conscientious citizen is in genuine doubt about where his duty lies. As such, it will be a practical problem, the doubt will be about what ought to be done. But the question may arise in either of the two senses distinguished by Green in *Prolegomena to Ethics*. The problem, that is to say, may be primarily one of estimating and evaluating the probable consequence of different courses of action, or it may arise from doubt about the proper conduct of the good citizen in a given situation. Thus it will arise in an acute form in the fuller sense when the citizen asks himself whether it is his duty as a citizen to obey a law which he believes to be morally bad. The question in this form is still practical but as in every case of the fuller sense of the question: 'what ought to be done?' it implies a theoretical question, namely that asked by Green as reformulated above: is it ever the citizen's moral duty to disobey the law of his state? The answer to this question implies a general theory of citizenship. It follows that a problem of political obligation can arise only for a citizen in the proper sense, for a rational agent who has achieved morality at the level of spheres of rational activity. At the level of rule and custom, the problem will not arise for obedience to the law as such will normally be accepted without question as a moral rule. But it is possible that, where a new law comes into conflict with established customs, a stimulus will be given which will, as it were, jerk many people up to the higher level of morality at least for a time.

Can it then ever be the moral duty of the citizen to disobey the law of his state? Discussing this question, Green writes: 'The only unqualified answer that can be given to it is one that may seem too general to be of much practical use: namely, that so far as the law anywhere or at any time in force fulfils the idea of the state, there can be no right to disobey it, or that there can be no right to disobey the law of the state except in the interest of the state, i.e. for the purpose of making the state, in respect of its actual laws, more completely correspond to what it is in tendency or idea, namely the reconciler and sustainer of the rights that arise out of the social relations of men.'[5] For the term 'right' in the above passage, where it is used in connection with disobedience, we must substitute 'moral duty' in order to grasp Green's real meaning. In the nature of the case, the unqualified answer 'is too general to be of much practical use' for the question is a theoretical one and is not intended to provide direct solutions to practical problems. Nor indeed is the unqualified answer satisfactory theoretically. Granted that disobedience is only morally justified for the sake of making the state 'more completely correspond to what it is in tendency or idea', the theory of the state must itself be developed further to make clear what this means. Moreover, we should expect that the result of this further development, while not of direct practical use in the sense of providing rules which can be immediately applied to particular cases, may nevertheless be not without indirect practical significance. It should at least help the conscientious citizen to understand more clearly the nature of the situation in which he is placed.

4.   With the theoretical question raised by the problem of political obligation in mind, Green proceeds to the further development of his theory of the state and of citizenship. 'The general principle,' he writes, 'that the citizen must never act otherwise than as a citizen does not carry with it an obligation under all conditions to conform to the laws of his state, since those laws may be inconsistent with the true end of the state as the sustainer and harmonizer of social regulations.'[1] He then goes on to say that: 'The assertion, however, by the citizen of any right which the state does not recognize must be founded on a reference to an acknowledged social good.'[2] In Green's view, disobedience to any law is justified, if at all, only for the sake of asserting or calling attention to some right which at the time the state does not recognize and therefore does not legally enforce.

Explaining what he means by 'reference to an acknowledged social good', Green writes: 'It is not every power, of which the exercise would be desirable in an ideal state of things, that is properly claimable as a right. The condition of its being so claimable is that its exercise should be contributory to some social good which the public conscience is capable of appreciating, not necessarily one which in the existing prevalence of private interests can obtain due acknowledgement, but still one of which men in their actions and language show themselves to be aware.'[3] His point is that it is not the responsibility of the citizen to act as the member of some hypothetical ideal state. He must act as a member of the political community in which he finds himself, and his responsibility is to try to make it more of a political community, to raise the general level of rationality which it embodies. This means taking account of the particular circumstances, including the 'prevalence of private interests', to say nothing of well established prejudices. The fact that there is a real political community at all, that many rights are recognized and secured by law, will be an indication that there is some consciousness of common interests, some bonds of sympathy uniting the citizens. But there may be a number of rights which are not secured owing to vested interests and long-standing prejudices. These must not be pandered to but neither must they be ignored. In pressing for the recognition of a right, contact must be established with the 'consciousness of common interests'. It must be shown that failure to recognize the right involves inconsistency on the part of the government. That it is not likely to be legally secured in the immediate future is not a ground for failing to press an unrecognized right, but there must be good reason for thinking that the nature of the claim can be pretty generally understood and supported.

It is against this background that the question of the moral justification of disobedience must be considered. 'As a general rule,' Green writes, 'no doubt even bad laws, laws representing the interests of classes or individuals as opposed to those of the community, should be obeyed. There can be no right to disobey them even while their repeal is urged, on the ground that they violate rights, because the public interest, on which all rights are founded, is more concerned in the general obedience to law than in the exercise of those powers by individuals or classes which the objectionable laws unfairly withhold.'[4] It can never, that is to say, be the duty of the citizen to contribute to the undermining of the respect for law, for without general respect for law, citizenship becomes impossible. It can therefore never be the duty of the citizen to press for the recognition of a right in a way which contributes to the destruction of all rights including the one whose recognition is being pressed.

But when all this has been allowed for, there may be circumstances in which disobedience is a moral duty. 'On the other hand,' Green writes, 'there may be cases in which the public interest, not merely according to some remote philosopher's view of it, but according to conceptions which the people are able to assimilate, is best served by a violation of some actual law. It is so in regard to slavery when the public conscience has come to recognize a capacity for right, for exercising certain powers under control of a reference to a general well-being in a body of men to whom legal rights have hitherto been refused, but when some powerful class in its own interests resists the alteration of the law.'[5] In Green's view, when public opinion generally has come to recognize that the slaves are moral agents who are capable of fulfilling social responsibilities, the violation of the laws upholding slavery on behalf of the slaves will represent 'the general sense of right on which the general observance of law depends:'[6] and 'there is no danger of its making a breach in the law-abiding habits of the people.'[7]

Green was writing less than 20 years after the abolition of slavery in the United States and the illustration was a natural one for him to take. Today problems of political obligation arise in less clear-cut but more poignant form. The puppet regime maintained against the wishes of the majority of the citizens through fear of armed intervention from outside is a typical case. What is the duty of the conscientious citizen who is forced to live under such a regime? He has a general responsibility to do what he can to contribute to raising the level of rationality of the political life of his state and he may have good reason to think that he and his compatriots, if left to themselves, would be capable of something better than the current level of achievement. But there may seem little possibility of removing the puppet regime and anything like overt resistance will only make matters worse. It does not follow that his duty is merely to submit passively. It may be that the best thing he can do is to take part in clandestine underground activity against the regime which may at least help to keep alive the idea of a better political life. It may even be that under certain circumstances open resistance is worthwhile for this reason, although it is bound in the end to be crushed. Obviously no rules can be laid down and it ill becomes those who have the good fortune to enjoy a more rational political life to preach to those who are condemned to a lower level. Nevertheless Green's basic point remains. Whatever is done, whether open resistance or outward submission combined with clandestine activity, must be done in the name of citizenship.

Green's illustration of slavery however helps to bring out another point. The laws which uphold slavery are morally objectionable: why? Because, by withholding legal rights, they make it difficult if not impossible for a group of men and women to achieve the level of rationality of which they would otherwise be capable. The relevant standard here is not merely that of citizenship but the ultimate moral community. Slavery is a moral evil because it arbitrarily restricts rational human achievement. It is because they are human beings, not because they are members of a particular national group that the servile status of the slaves is morally objectionable. The underlying point is that the sphere of citizenship is itself subordinate to the higher level of self-consistent human achievement. The moral agent who tries to think out his conduct for himself will find that his duty as a citizen is only one aspect, albeit an important one, of his wider responsibility as a man. The state is the society of societies so far as the legal enforcement of rights is concerned, but it is not the ultimate moral community. As we shall see in the next section, Green recognizes this explicitly at a later stage of his discussion. It is, however, implicit in his doctrine of political obligation.

But the same principle of contemporary relevance applies in the case of the level of self-consistent human achievement. Just as it is not the responsibility of the citizen to act as a member of some hypothetical ideal state, so it is not the moral agent's responsibility to act as a member of some hypothetical ideal humanity. He must take humanity as he finds it and do the best that he personally can to contribute to self-consistent human achievement in a situation in which many levels of rationality will be concurrently embodied. He must do the best he can to act rationally in a situation of imperfect rationality, and to make what contribution he can to raising the general level. He must make the most of what self-consistent human achievement is possible in the circumstances. It is against this background that the moral agent must think out his duty as a citizen.

There is a sense in which, as Aristotle seems to have recognized, there may be a divergence between the good man and the good citizen. It can never be the moral agent's duty to be a bad citizen but it may be his duty to neglect active participation in political activity for the sake of fulfilling some responsibility arising out of family or professional life. There may be some contribution which only he can make in these fields while others who are not in this position can devote themselves actively to politics. Thus the citizen who is forced to live under a puppet regime and who has a growing family to look after, while he recognizes a general responsibility to aid movements which oppose the regime, may very well think that his moral duty is to look after his family and therefore not to take an active part in clandestine political activities. Others without family ties can do this: only he can support his family. Bradley intuitively grasped this aspect of morality and citizenship in his discussion of the Ideal Self in *Ethical Studies* but, owing to his imperfect grasp of the theory of rational activity, was unable to give a satisfactory theoretical account of it. Green does not discuss it explicitly in the *Principles of Political Obligation* and only hints at it in *Prolegomena to Ethics*, but it is implicit in his general position.

C: THE SCOPE AND LIMITS OF GOVERNMENT ACTION

1. From the problem of political obligation, Green turns in the last group of lectures to the third stage of his original plan. This was: 'to consider in detail the chief rights and obligations enforced in civilized states, inquiring what is their justification, what is the ground for respecting them.' By 'civilized states', as we can now see, Green means organized communities in which there is habitual obedience to an established authority on the basis of common interests and sympathy and in which the task of harmonizing and securing rights is accomplished with some degree of success. Throughout his lectures Green has been speaking as the member of such a state. In developing his theory of citizenship and the state, he has been trying to lay bare the implicit rationality of the political life which is familiar in practice both to himself and to his hearers. The inquiry into the chief rights and obligations enforced in civilized states is a continuation of the same process. But the emphasis now will be on the scope and limits of government action, on the nature and significance of the task of securing rights. The chief rights and obligations which Green actually considers are those connected with life and liberty, with property and with the family. In what follows I shall try to summarize the essentials of his doctrine in each case concentrating especially on his view of the scope and limits of government action.

According to Green, there is one right to free life, rather than two separate rights, one to life and the other to liberty. 'No distinction can be made,' he writes, 'between the right to life and the right to liberty, and there can be no right to mere life, no right to life on the part of a being that has not also the right to use the right according to the motions of its own will.'[1] To the question: what is the foundation of this right? Green says: 'The answer is capacity on the part of the subject for membership of a society, for determination of the will, and through it of the bodily organization, by the conception of a well-being as common to self with others.'[2] But the society, membership of which is the moral basis of the right to free life, is the society of mankind, the ultimate moral community. It is not the state, the family or any lesser group. Green admits that: 'We are little inclined to the idea of the universal brotherhood of men, of mankind as forming one society with a common good of which the conception may determine the action of its members.'[3] But he then goes on: 'It is the proper correlative of the admission of a right to free life as belonging to man in virtue simply of his human nature.'[4] It is then as a morally responsible human being that a man has a right to free life. But there are two activities of government, those of war and punishment, which seem prima facie to violate it. Green therefore proceeds to discuss them.

He insists that every war is the outcome of human decisions. The death and suffering involved are human responsibilities not the results of natural disasters or accidents. 'But however widely distributed the agency may be,' he writes, 'which causes the destruction of life in war, it is still intentional human agency. The destruction is not the work of accident or of nature. If then it is to be other than a wrong because a violation of the right of mutual protection of life involved in the membership of human society, it can only be because there is exercised in war some right that is paramount.' But according to Green: 'This argument, however, seems to be only available for shifting the quarter in which we might first be disposed to lay the blame for the wrong involved in war, not for changing the character of that wrong. It goes to show that the wrong involved in the death of certain soldiers does not necessarily lie with the government which sends those soldiers into the field because this may be the only means by which the government can prevent a more serious wrong. It does not show that there is no wrong in their death.'[6]

Thus, although he thinks that war involves moral evil, Green is not a pacifist. Under certain circumstances it may be a government's duty to resort to war if this is the only way in which a worse evil can be prevented. It may be that, by means of war, the general level of rationality in political life can be prevented from sinking as low as it would if pacific policies were adopted. By the same token it may sometimes be the citizen's moral duty to give up his right to free life. But all this does not alter the fact that there is evil involved. Some government must be pursuing a morally indefensible policy if war is necessary as a method of trying to salvage something from international political life. Green objects most strongly to the idea that conflict between states is inevitable, that, as long as there are many states, there are bound to be wars between them. 'There is no such thing as an inevitable conflict between states,' he writes, 'there is nothing in the nature of the state that, given a multiplicity of states, should make the gain of the one the loss of the other.'[7] And in another passage he writes: 'It is nothing then in the necessary organization of the state but rather some defect of that organization in relation to its proper function of maintaining and reconciling rights, of giving scope to capacities, that leads to a conflict of apparent interest between one state and another. The wrong therefore which results to human society from conflicts between states cannot be condoned on the ground that it is a necessary incident of the existence of states.'[8]

In Green's view, national self-interest is no justification for a policy which violates the right to free life of the members of other states. National self-interest, no less than the private self-interest of the individual, must be subordinate to morality. 'It is not the state as such,' Green writes, 'but this or that particular state, which by no means fulfils its purpose and might perhaps be swept away and superceded by another with advantage to the true ends for which the state exists, that needs to defend its interests by actions injurious to those outside it. Hence there is no ground for holding that a state is justified in doing whatever its interests seem to require irrespectively of its effects on other men.'[9] The final standard is that of the ultimate moral community. In the last resort no policy the effects of which are to frustrate self-consistent human achievement can be regarded as morally defensible. 'If those effects are bad,' Green writes, 'as involving either a direct violation of personal rights or obstruction to the moral development of society anywhere in the world, then there is no ultimate justification for the political action which gives rise to them.'[10] But, on the other hand, he is prepared to admit that the policy or political action which is the real cause of the wrong may not be the one which immediately occasioned it. A government may be justified in adopting a policy which has harmful effects on other human beings if this is the only way to avoid greater injury. But the fact remains that some morally indefensible policy has been pursued somewhere. The harm done to human beings is still a wrong even if the government which directly caused it is not morally responsible for it. 'The question can only be,' Green writes, 'as we have seen generally in regard to the wrong-doing of war, where in particular the blame lies.'[11]

I have laid stress on Green's moral condemnation of war and of unbridled national self-interest, because the idea has got about in some quarters that Idealist political philosophy in some way justifies if not positively exalts war as an inherent feature of political life and gives carte blanche to national self-interest as the ultimate arbiter of policy. It is true that those who have adopted this view have usually exempted Green from the general charge against Idealist political philosophy. But they have done so on the ground that, as regards his doctrine of war and international relations, Green is not a true philosophical Idealist. This however is an error. Green's doctrine of war and international relations follows from his general Idealist position. It is the result of a consistent development of the theory of rational activity which is the basis of his entire social philosophy. It is just because he is an Idealist that Green holds the doctrine which he does about war and international relations. But, it may be replied, if this is so, then so much the worse for Idealist political philosophy; for Green's doctrine with its exclusive emphasis on morality is largely irrelevant. It has little or nothing to contribute to the understanding of international relations which for the most part exhibit a level of rationality below that of morality.

I feel some sympathy for this objection although I think that it is misconceived. Green's doctrine is not so much irrelevant as incomplete and therefore one-sided. The consistent development of the theory of rational activity needs to be carried a good deal further than Green takes it in his discussion of war and international relations. But in such a development, his main points would remain. War is not a natural event but the outcome of human decisions. No war is therefore inevitable in the sense of lying beyond the power of human beings to prevent it. To the extent that the way of life of a nation can be maintained only at the cost of depriving other human beings of opportunities for rational self-realization which they might otherwise take, that way of life is tarnished and debased as a rational human achievement. What is missing from Green's doctrine is an adequate recognition and discussion of what is implied in an international political community. He does not seem to have appreciated the nature and scale of the obstacles which stand in the way of its realization. The fact that so much of international political life is at a level of rationality below that of morality might have suggested to him that an international common good, an international consciousness of common interests, is a sophisticated and elaborate moral and social achievement. But in failing to understand all this, he is perhaps only reflecting the somewhat superficial international optimism of his generation. It was because he was a Victorian and not because he was a philosophical Idealist, that he was able to rest content with an incomplete and onesided doctrine of war and international relations.

2.   In punishing offences against its laws and regulations, a government is curtailing, at least temporarily, the right to free life of those whom it punishes. What justifies this curtailment? According to Green: 'The idea of punishment implies, on the side of the person punished, at once, a capacity for determination by the conception of a common or public good, or in other words a practical understanding of the nature of rights as founded on relations to such public good, and an actual violation of a right or omission to fulfil an obligation, the right or obligation being one of which the agent might have been aware, and the violation or omission one which he might have prevented.'[1] He then goes on to say that on the side of the government: 'It implies equally a conception of right founded on relation to public good and one which, unlike that on the part of the criminal, is realized in act, a conception of which the punitive act as founded on a consideration of what is necessary for the maintenance of rights, is the logical expression.'[2]

In Green's view: 'A punishment is unjust if either element is absent: if either the act punished is not a violation of known rights or an omission to fulfil known obligations of a kind which the agent might have prevented, or the punishment is one that is not required for the maintenance of rights, or which comes to the same thing, if the ostensible rights to the maintenance of which punishment is required are not real rights, are not liberties of action or acquisition which there is any real public interest in maintaining.'[3] Thus, according to Green, it is as the agent of the state that the government is justified in punishing crime. As the agent of the state, its task is to secure and protect the rights of the citizens and it punishes crime for the sake of protecting these rights. This is, so far at least, a preventive or deterrent theory of punishment. But the punishment must be just, otherwise there is a failure in the work of protecting rights. If the person punished has not committed a crime, his right to free life is being arbitrarily curtailed. Moreover, if he is not in some degree a moral agent who is responsible for his actions and having a practical understanding of his duties as a citizen in relation to the law, he is not a fit subject for punishment. What he needs is treatment and if this is unavailing, then for his own good as well as for the sake of the general protection of rights, he must be kept under restraint. In such a case, there is no curtailment of his right to free life, because, being below the level of morality altogether, he has no rights to be curtailed. In Green's view, however, this does not justify the government in treating him arbitrarily, for, as we shall see later, we ought not to assume that he is permanently below the level of morality, that there is no hope of his ever attaining to at least a minimum level.

The conditions on the other side are equally important. The right violated by the crime must be a genuine right, a morally justified claim to have certain powers. Nor is this all. 'The justice of the punishment,' Green writes, 'depends upon the justice of the general system of rights, not merely on the propriety with reference to social well-being of maintaining this or that particular right which the crime punished violates, but on the question whether the social organization in which a criminal has lived and acted is one that has given him a fair chance of not being a criminal.'[4] Punishment, that is to say, is not the only method of protecting the rights of citizens. The government must do what it can to prevent the growth of social conditions which breed criminal tendencies. The best contribution which it can make in this direction is to see that the rights which it actually secures are genuine, and that to the best of its knowledge there are no genuine rights which are not enforced by law.

According to Green, the way in which punishment actually operates in the prevention of crime is 'by associating in the mind of every possible doer of them a certain terror with the contemplation of the acts, such terror as is necessary on the whole to protect the rights threatened'.[5] But how much terror is necessary in a given case? How severe must the penalty be to act as an effective deterrent while at the same time remaining just to the criminal who has to bear it? How much allowance should be made for the criminal who in some way seems to have been unfairly treated by society? Green doubts whether any precise rule can be followed. 'For a positive and detailed criterion of just punishment,' he writes, 'we must wait until a system of rights has been established in which the claims of all men as founded on their capacities for contributing to social well-being are perfectly harmonized, and until experience has shown the degree and kind of terror with which men must be affected in order to the suppression* of the anti-social tendencies which might lead to the violation of such a system of rights. And this is perhaps equivalent to saying that no complete criterion of just punishment can be arrived at until punishment is no longer necessary; for the state of things supposed could scarcely be realized without bringing with it an extinction of the tendencies which state punishment is needed to suppress.'[6]

His point is that, although the government must do the best it can only to punish justly, it will never be able to do more than approximate to the standard of perfect justice. There is an inevitable arbitrary element involved in the fixing of the penalty. Apart from the lack of certainty about the severity needed to make it effective as a deterrent, there is no way of computing how much should be allowed for extenuating circumstances, especially for the fact that the criminal may

---

* Sic. Green here uses 'in order to' where modern usage requires 'to secure'.

himself be the victim of unfair social treatment. Green seems
to think that every criminal who is a proper subject for punishment, who is in some degree a moral agent and not a patho-
logical case, has been made what he is at least in part through
his social environment. The injustice of that environment has
fostered the growth of criminal habits. Here he is entering the
territory of empirical psychology and his view may well be
open to criticism in the light of recent work in that field. But
his main point remains unaffected. So far as the severity of the
penalty is concerned, there is an arbitrary element in punishment. In view of this, justice itself seems to require that the
penalty should err on the side of leniency rather than severity.

3. In stressing the preventive function of punishment, Green
does not overlook the sense in which it may be regarded as
retributive. Nor does he fail to take account of its possible reformatory function. In insisting that the government must
punish justly, or as justly as the inevitable arbitrary element in
the penalty will allow, Green is in effect acknowledging the
retributive aspect of punishment. The criminal who is subjected
to a just punishment cannot complain. Because of what he has
done, he deserves to have his right to free life temporarily
suspended. As Green puts it: 'The criminal, being susceptible
to the idea of public good and, through it, to the idea of rights,
though this idea has not been strong enough to regulate his
action, sees in the punishment its natural expression. He sees
that the punishment is his own act returning on himself in the
sense that it is the necessary outcome of his act in a society
governed by the conception of rights, a conception which he
appreciates and to which he does involuntary reverence.'[1] The
criminal, that is to say, has acted in a way inconsistent with his
social responsibilities and therefore has for the time being
forfeited his claim to be treated as a full member of his society.
He must make some amends for what he has done before he
is entitled to be restored to full membership.

But while he admits that there is a retributive element in
every just punishment, Green thinks that it does not concern
the government. The already difficult task of assessing the
penalty must not be further complicated by adding to it the
aim of trying to make the severity of the penalty proportional

to the moral evil of the criminal. No such proportion can be established and in any case it is no part of the government's duty to try to punish immorality as such. 'The notion,' Green writes, 'that the state should, if it could, adjust the amount of punishment which it inflicts on a criminal to the moral wickedness of the crime rests on a false view of the relation of the state to morality. It implies that it is the business of the state to punish wickedness as such but it' has no such business. It cannot undertake to punish wickedness as such without vitiating the disinterestedness of the effort to escape wickedness and thus checking the growth of a true goodness of the heart in the attempt to promote a goodness which is merely on the surface.'[2]

Here Green is simply restating the fundamental point behind his distinction between moral duties and legal obligations. The government can enforce the latter by means of punishment. It cannot enforce the former. But, indirectly, the just punishment of crime contributes to maintaining the general level of morality. Green continues: 'This however is not to be understood as meaning that the punishment of crime serves no moral purpose. It does serve such a purpose and has its value in doing so, but only in the sense that the protection of rights and the association of terror with their violation is the condition antecedent of any general advance in moral well-being.'[3] Punishment contributes indirectly to morality, that is to say, by virtue of its role in the task of securing and protecting rights.

Green thinks that while punishment has a reformatory aspect, this is subordinate to its main function of preventing crime. 'When the reformatory office of punishment is insisted on,' he writes, 'the reference may be and from the judicial point of view must be, not to the moral good of the criminal as an ultimate end, but to his recovery from criminal habits as a means to that which is the proper and direct object of state punishment, namely the general protection of rights.'[4] It is only then as a method of protecting rights that the government should do anything to reform the criminal. But why go to this trouble, it may be asked? Why not simply liquidate him and have done with it? 'Now when it is asked,' Green continues, 'why he should not be put out of the way, it must not be forgotten that among the rights that the state has to maintain are included rights of the criminal himself. These indeed are for the time suspended by his action in violation of rights, but, founded as they are on the capacity for contributing to social good, they could only be held to be finally forfeited on the ground that this capacity was absolutely extinct.'[5] He there- fore concludes that: 'If punishment then is to be just, in the sense that in its infliction due account is taken of all rights including the suspended rights of the criminal himself, it must be, so far as public safety will allow, reformatory. It must tend to qualify the criminal for the resumption of rights.'[6]

Thus, while so far as the government is concerned, punish- ment, including the reformation of the criminal, is justified solely for the sake of protecting rights, in Green's view: 'It is also for the moral good of the criminal himself unless, and this is an assumption that we ought not to make, he is beyond the reach of moral influences. It is morally the best thing that can happen to him.'[7] This is because, in order to fit him for the resumption of his rights, an effort must be made to rehabilitate him morally. Moreover there is a sense in which the reforma- tive function of punishment includes an element of retribution. The criminal, in so far as he is morally rehabilitated and fit to resume his rights, will have come to understand the nature of his offence and to recognize that he deserved punishment. But Green then goes on to make what may seem a surprising state- ment. The just punishment of crime is for the moral good of the criminal, 'even if a true social necessity requires that he be punished with death. The fact that society is obliged so to deal with him affords the best chance of bringing home to him the anti-social nature of his action.'[8]

To some there may be an element of paradox, not to say cynicism, in the suggestion that the morally best thing that can happen to a man is that he should be deliberately killed. Moreover it may seem that Green is guilty of inconsistency for he has just said that the assumption that a man is beyond the reach of moral influences is one that we ought not to make. To kill a man, it may be said, is the one sure way to put him beyond the reach of all human influences, moral or otherwise. But, on behalf of Green, we must remember that he speaks of 'a true social necessity' which requires that the criminal should be pun- ished with death, and of 'the fact that society is obliged so to deal with him'. He is thinking of something like treason in war-time, where there might be some grounds for arguing that the only effective deterrent to those who are likely to commit it is fear of execution. Again the doctrine that we ought not to assume that anyone is beyond the reach of all moral influences does not imply that anyone has an absolutely unconditional right to free life. On the contrary, it may be a man's moral duty to give up his life under certain circumstances.

In the light of these considerations, what Green has in mind may perhaps be stated as follows. Granted that there may be cases such as treason in war-time when the death penalty is justified, admittedly a controversial assumption, then there is a sense in which it is for the moral good of the criminal who is condemned to suffer it. It provides him with the opportunity to atone for his crime by giving up his life to deter other would-be perpetrators. It is his moral duty to do what he can to make amends for what he has done and this can best be discharged by co-operating with the government in preventing further crimes of the same kind. The co-operation required from him involves the loss of his life, but since this is for the sake of fulfilling his moral duty there is no real violation of his rights. Of course he will be executed in any case, whether or not he sees it in this light. But all that can be done for him morally is to help him to see it in this light. The only moral influences which are relevant in his case are those which will lead him to see that it is his duty to accept his execution. But all this of course depends on the initial assumption that the death penalty is justified as the only effective deterrent. The assumption may well be questioned in view of the inevitable element of arbitrariness in the fixing of any penalty. Green himself has misgivings on the point and is inclined to think that it is justified, if at all, only in the case of war-time treason. In war-time every citizen has a duty to give up his life in the interests of public safety.

4.   Green objects to the doctrine that the government should try to punish wickedness as such on the ground that it rests on a false view of the relation of the state to morality. He sums up what he takes to be the true view of this relation in the following pasage: 'The effectual action of the state,' he writes, 'i.e. the community as acting through laws for the promotion of

habits of true citizenship, seems necessarily to be confined to the removal of obstacles.'[1] This is what we should expect in view of his theory of morality, of citizenship and the state, and of rights. But the task of removing obstacles must not be interpreted too narrowly. 'Under this head,' Green continues, 'there may and should be included much that most states have hitherto neglected and much that at first sight may have the appearance of the enforcement of moral duties.'[2]

This statement is in keeping with some remarks in an earlier passage where having laid down the basis of the right to free life, he goes on: 'And though this right can only be grounded on the capacity which belongs to the human nature for freely fulfilling some function in the social organism, we do very little to give reality to the capacity or to enable it to realize itself. We content ourselves with enacting that no man shall be used by other men as a means against his will, but we leave it pretty much to be a matter of chance whether or no he shall be qualified to fulfil any social function, to contribute anything to the common good, and to do so freely, i.e. under the conception of a common good.'[3] This suggests that Green does not subscribe to the doctrine of laissez faire in economic and social policy. The suggestion is borne out by the following passage where he writes: 'The freedom to do as they like on the part of one set of men may involve the ultimate disqualification of many others or of a succeeding generation for the exercise of rights. This applies most obviously to such kinds of contract or traffic as affect the health and housing of the people, the growth of population relatively to the means of subsistence and the accumulation or the distribution of landed property.'[4] It thus appears that the task of removing obstacles by securing and protecting rights may involve considerable intervention by the government in economic and social life. It is against this background that Green discusses the right to private property.

According to Green the basis of the right to private property is: 'that everybody should be secured by society in the power of getting and keeping the means of realizing a will which in possibility is a will directed to social good.'[5] By 'getting and keeping' he means owning what has been acquired by work. On the subject of 'a will directed towards social good', Green says: 'Whether anyone's will is actually and positively so directed does not affect his claim to the power. This power should be secured to the individual irrespective of the use which he actually makes of it, so long as he does not use it in a way that interferes with the exercise of a like power by another, on the ground that its uncontrolled exercise is the condition of the attainment by man of that free morality which is his highest good.'[6] This accords with Green's general theory of rights. They provide conditions under which the moral agent can achieve the highest level of rationality of which he is capable but they do not guarantee that this achievement will be forthcoming. Nor do they depend upon full advantage being taken of the opportunity. A man's right to acquire and own property is not affected by the fact that he makes an improvident or wasteful use of it.

But the right to property, like every other right, is not unconditional. There is an obligation, namely not to use the property in a way which prevents others from becoming property-owners at all. According to Green, 'When the possession of property by one man interferes with the possession of property by another, when one set of men are secured in the power of getting and keeping the means of realizing their will in such a way that others are practically denied the power; in that case it may truly be said that property is theft.'[7] He then proceeds to sum up: 'The rationale of property in short requires that everyone who will conform to the positive condition of possessing it, namely labour, and the negative condition, namely respect for it as possessed by others, should, so far as social arrangements can make him so, be a possessor of property himself, and of such property as will at least enable him to develop a sense of social responsibility as distinct from mere property in the immediate necessaries of life.'[8] The key phrase here is: 'so far as social arrangements can make him so'. The government has a duty to intervene and, where necessary, regulate the use made of private property but only in the name of private property. Green is no apostle of laissez faire but neither is he a socialist. There is nothing wrong with private property as such. On the contrary it is a right, a morally justified claim so long as the correlative responsibility is fulfilled. It is a power which a man must have if he is to be a moral agent and make a rational life for himself.

Inequality in the distribution of private property does not constitute an injustice in Green's view so long as there is no violation of anyone's right to own property. Indeed he thinks that inequality is inevitable. 'Considered as representing the conquest of nature by the effort of free and variously gifted individuals,' he writes, 'property must be unequal. No less must it be so, if considered as a means by which individuals fulfil social functions.'[9] He points out that different kinds of property are needed for different trades and occupations. 'The artist and man of letters require different equipment and apparatus from the tiller of land and the smith.'[10] How is the property necessary for the performance of the various trades and occupations to be supplied and distributed? In Green's view, there are only two alternatives and he is quite emphatic about which is the better. 'Either then,' he writes, 'the various apparatus needed for various functions must be provided for individuals by society, which would imply a complete regulation of life incompatible with that highest object of human attainment, a free morality, or we must trust for its provision to individual effort which will imply inequality between the property of different persons.'[11]

The latter alternative, a system of private enterprise in economic life, implies inequality in the distribution of property because it opens the way to 'the conquest of nature by the effort of free and variously gifted individuals'. The abuses to which such a system might otherwise give rise can be prevented in Green's view if the obligation correlative to the right of private property is legally enforced. The first alternative, according to which the production and distribution of the means of life are planned and directed by the government, is incompatible with a free morality because, in Green's view, the individual would have no real responsibility for looking after himself. Within the sphere of work he would not be a rational agent able to make decisions and plans on his own account, but merely a cog in a machine in the design and operation of which he would have no effective voice. If the sphere of work is to be a genuine sphere of rational activity, one aspect of a rational way of living and acting, the individual must be able to engage in it as a rational agent able to make decisions and plans. Moreover, if work is not a genuine sphere of rational activity, the achievement of a rational way of living and acting is likely to be seriously impaired. A man who is not responsible for looking after himself is unlikely to achieve much as a citizen or husband and father.

But it may be objected that Green is posing extreme alternatives and that we do not have to choose between them. Granted that a society in which the whole of economic life was planned and directed by the government would allow little or no scope for the achievement of higher levels of rationality to its members, it does not follow that the only alternative is complete private enterprise. Indeed in the name of private enterprise itself, for the sake of securing and protecting the right of property, it may be necessary to take certain economic activities out of private hands altogether and entrust them to a public authority. Again, if it is not 'to be pretty much a matter of chance' whether individuals are 'to be qualified to fulfil any social function, to contribute anything to the common good', if the activities of one set of men are not to 'involve the ultimate disqualification of many others or of a succeeding generation for the exercise of rights', if 'the health and housing of the people, the growth of population relative to the means of subsistence and the accumulation or distribution of landed property' are not to be adversely affected by certain kinds of industrial and commercial activity, then the government may well have to undertake considerable supervision and perhaps even direction in certain instances over the general conduct of economic life. The right to acquire and own private property may include the right to make a foolish use of it, but it cannot consistently include the right to use it in a way which can be shown to be injurious not merely to the right to property but to other rights as well.

In view of all this, it may be thought that Green's doctrine on the subject of property and economic life is largely irrelevant. But in fact, like his doctrine of war and international relations, it is not so much irrelevant as incomplete. It needs to be developed a good deal further than he has taken it. No doubt he underestimated the complexity of modern economic life. In posing the alternatives of complete socialism or complete private enterprise he is presenting an unreal choice. But, as in the case of his doctrine of war and international relations, a more complete view would incorporate his main points. If a man is to be a rational agent, capable of looking after himself and capable of taking responsibility for the conduct of his life, he must be able to own and use property. There is nothing unjust about the unequal distribution of property so long as the correlative obligation is fulfilled. Intervention by the government in economic life will be necessary, but it must be intervention on behalf of rights including the right to property.

5.   From property and the economic sphere, Green finally turns to marriage and the family. According to him, the development of family life presupposes that: 'In the conception of the good to which a man seeks to give reality, there is included a conception of the well-being of others connected with him by sexual relations or by relations which arise out of those. He must conceive of the well-being of these others as a permanent object bound up with his own and the interest in it as thus conceived must be a motive to him over and above any succession of passing desires that claim pleasure from or give pleasure to the other.'[1] Without this capacity for social activity, there could be no family life at all. It implies at least some achievement of rationality at the level of morality. Green continues: 'Otherwise there would be nothing to lead to the establishment of the household in which the wants of the wife or wives are permanently provided for, in the management of which a more or less definite share is given to them, more definite indeed as approach is made to a monogamistic system but not wholly absent anywhere when the wife is distinguished from the female, and upon which the children have a recognized claim for shelter and sustenance.'[2]

The reference to a 'monogamistic system' in the last passage suggests that Green regards monogamy as morally superior to polygamy. This is so, and Green gives reasons for his view. In the first place, polygamy arbitrarily excludes some men from the opportunity of marrying at all. 'Under a system of polygamy just so far as it is carried out,' Green writes, 'there must be men who are debarred from marrying. It can only exist indeed under a system of slavery which excludes masses of men from the right of forming a family.'[3] In the second place, polygamy is defective in the treatment given to the wife. 'Nor does the wife under a polygamous system,' Green goes on, 'although she ostensibly marries, form a household or become the co-ordinate head of a family at all."⁴ Moreover she is placed in a position of inferiority vis a vis her husband. 'And further,' Green writes, 'as the polygamous husband requires a strict restraint from his wife which he does not put on himself, he is treating her unequally. He demands a continence from her which, unless she is kept within the confines of slavery, can only rest on the attachment of a person to a person and on a personal sense of duty, and at the same time is practically ignoring the demand which this personal attachment on her part carries with it, that he should keep himself for her as she does herself for him.'⁵

In the third place, polygamy is morally inferior to monogamy because under polygamy the proper claims of children cannot be adequately satisfied. 'For these claims can only be duly satisfied,' Green writes, 'the responsibilities of father and mother towards their children, potentially persons, whom they have brought into the world, can only be fulfilled if father and mother jointly take part in the education of the children, if the children learn to love and obey father and mother as one authority. But if there is no permanent consortium vitae of one husband with one wife, this joint authority over the children becomes impossible.'⁶ Thus, in Green's view, the moral basis of the family as a social institution is to be found in the responsibilities which arise out of the personal attachment and sexual relations between a man and a woman, responsibilities both to each other and to their children. Monogamy is morally superior to polygamy because it is only under monogamy that these responsibilities can be adequately fulfilled.

Green then turns to the question of the proper function of the government in relation to marriage and the family. 'Thus that marriage should only be lawful with one wife,' he writes, 'that it should be for life, that it should be terminable at the infidelity of either husband or wife, are rules of right, not of morality as such but of right. Without these rules, the rights of the married persons are not maintained. Those outward conditions of family life would not be secured to them which are necessary on the whole for the development of a free morality.'⁷ The business of the government is to enforce these rules of right. They are justified because, in Green's view, only if they are observed can marriage become a genuine moral achievement and the responsibilities of the partners to themselves and to their children be fulfilled. It does not follow of course that the mere observation of the rules will make a marriage into a genuine moral achievement. But without them the minimum conditions will not be present.

In another passage, Green sums up his view. 'The ground for securing to individuals,' he writes, 'in respect of their marriage tie certain powers as rights, is that in a general way they are necessary to the possibility of a morally good life either directly to the persons exercising them or to their children. The more completely marriage is a consortium omnis vitae, in the sense of a unity of all interests and for the whole of a life-time, the more likely are the external conditions of a moral life to be fulfilled in regard both to married persons and their children. Therefore the general rule of the state in dealing with marriage should be to secure such powers as are favourable and to withhold such as are unfavourable to the consortium omnis vitae.'[8] Adultery, in Green's view, is the only ground for which the consortium omnis vitae should be legally broken. 'That the wife should be bound indissolubly by a marriage tie to an unfaithful husband or vice versa is a violation of the right of husband or wife as the case may be.'[9] he writes. Broadly his view is that after adultery the injured party is put in approximately the same position as a wife under polygamy, while the adulterer is roughly the moral equivalent of the polygamous husband. The position of the children in a marriage where there has been regular adultery also approximates to that of children under polygamy. The injured party therefore should have the right to end the marriage tie since otherwise he or she and the children are condemned to a morally inferior position.

But in Green's view, although adultery is a violation of the rights of marriage, it should not be made a crime. The rights which arise out of marriage are of such a nature that punishment is not a suitable method of protecting them. 'If a husband,' Green writes, 'who would otherwise be false to the marriage bond, is kept outwardly faithful to it by fear of the punishment which might attend its breach, the right of the wife and children is indeed so far protected. But is anything

F

gained for those moral ends for the sake of which alone the maintenance of rights is of value? The man in whom disloyal passion is neutralized by fear of punishment will contribute little in his family life to the moral development of himself, his wife or his children.'[10] The point is too obvious to need comment. But it follows that strictly speaking there is no right to fidelity in marriage in the sense of a morally justified claim which can be enforced by law. There can only be a right to have a marriage dissolved when there is infidelity, a right which must be left to the injured party to assert. Since adultery is not a crime, that is to say, the initiative in seeking divorce must rest with the injured party and not with the government. All this does not of course alter the fact that there is a moral duty to be faithful in marriage but, like all moral duties, it cannot be enforced by law.

Green discusses at some length the question whether the government should recognize any other ground besides adultery for divorce. He considers both cruelty and incompatibility as possible grounds but is inclined to doubt the wisdom of giving them legal recognition. His conclusion is tentative and any short quotation would scarcely do justice to the spirit of his discussion which is at once candid and realistic. The upshot is, however, that he is inclined to think that if cruelty and incompatibility are made legal grounds for divorce, encouragement will be given to resort to cruelty and to exaggerate differences between husband and wife, as a means of escape from a marriage tie which is felt by one of the parties to be irksome. Many readers today may well find this unconvincing. They may well think that on Green's own doctrine if and when conditions arise which make the continuation of a decent marriage impossible, it should be ended subject to adequate provision being made for the children, who admittedly will be worse off than if their parents had been able to make a success of their marriage, but better off than continuing to live in a home which, except in name, has ceased to be a home at all. But to pursue this question would be to pass beyond the field of political philosophy into that of law. As with his discussion of the rights connected with other spheres, Green's account of the family and marriage is incomplete. It reflects to some extent the tone and temper of the Victorian age. But, as with his discussion of other topics, his main points stand. Marriage is a moral enterprise, the aim of which should be a consortium omnis vitae. It must, if it is to be a moral achievement, be monogamous and the government cannot aid that achievement by making marital offences a crime. It can only secure and protect the right of the injured party to have a marriage dissolved when it is impossible to continue it without moral degradation.

6.   In this chapter I have tried to expound the essentials of the political philosophy developed by Green in the *Principles of Political Obligation* and especially to bring out its relation to his theory of morality. The value of his work lies in the extent to which he has been able to pierce through the immediate circumstances of his time to the nature and significance of citizenship and the state as rational human achievements. Inevitably he is only partly successful. Every philosophy is the product of its time and bears upon it some of the distinguishing marks of the contemporary intellectual and cultural atmosphere. Green's philosophy is no exception. It is pervaded throughout by an air of moral earnestness and, despite the candour and realism of his discussion, there is an underlying note of optimism and confidence in the future destiny of humanity. In our disillusioned mood in the middle of the twentieth Century, these traits are uncongenial. But we must not allow the Victorian flavour of Green's work to put us off.

Green's work is valuable for us not as a conclusion but as a starting point. This was how he regarded the work of his predecessors. It was by criticizing them that he developed his social philosophy. He was able to penetrate further than they into the roots of morality and politics in human experience and to go further in eliciting and exhibiting the implicit rationality of morality and politics because he had a deeper grasp of the theory of rational activity. We can and should apply the same treatment to him. I have indicated in the course of this chapter certain points where his doctrine appears defective. In any case, our emphasis would be different in view of changes in the pattern of political and social life. Green has little or nothing to say about democracy and representative government and touches on nationalism only by implication. His view of the scope and limits of government action as covered by the

work of securing and protecting rights may well seem inadequate against the background of political life today. I do
not suggest that he has said the last word on any topic. But I
am suggesting that, if we are interested in developing a social
philosophy for ourselves, it is by carrying further the work he
has already begun that we shall make most progress.

CHAPTER V

THE THEORY OF THE ABSOLUTE

A : F. H. BRADLEY

1. In our discussion of Idealist social philosophy we have had to take account of certain metaphysical questions which the Idealist philosophers themselves found it necessary to raise. Although in *Ethical Studies* Bradley tried to exclude such questions, he was obliged to consider them in connection with his doctrine of the ideal self. Green found it necessary to raise them at the beginning of *Prolegomena to Ethics* in order to show that a philosophical as distinct from a scientific theory of morality was necessary. But in both these cases, the discussion of metaphysical issues was subordinate to the main problem of the theory of morality. Green died without having done more than indicate the direction which his metaphysical thought was taking but Bradley, whose philosophical career was just beginning when he published *Ethical Studies*, eventually worked out and expounded a systematic metaphysical theory. This was the theory of the Absolute and it has come to be regarded as the official metaphysical doctrine of English Idealism.

Bradley's theory of the Absolute was the outcome of what he described as 'the attempt to comprehend the universe not simply piecemeal or by fragments but somehow as a whole.'[1] It might be thought that in social philosophy* we need not concern ourselves with the universe as a whole but some influential critics of Idealist social philosophy have seen fit to connect it with the theory of the Absolute and to attribute some of its defects to that theory. According to them, the theory of the Absolute has been used by Idealist social philosophers as

---

* In any case, the programme of this book requires some consideration of Idealist metaphysics.

the foundation of an attitude of complacent acquiescence in the social status quo and of resistance to social reform. The existing social order is all right and the evil and suffering which is part of it must be accepted as a necessary price. This reactionary attitude, it was alleged, was given metaphysical support by the theory of the Absolute. L. T. Hobhouse in *The Metaphysical Theory of the State* makes this point in the course of a general indictment of Idealist political philosophy and in particular that of Bernard Bosanquet. Bosanquet had expounded a version of the theory of the Absolute which followed the main lines of Bradley's. 'Dr Bosanquet tells us that he personally believes in a nobler future:' Hobhouse writes 'but since the Absolute is perfection and since evil exists, evil is necessary to perfection and its evanescence seems altogether contradictory.'[2] In another passage, discussing the reactionary social outlook which he believes the theory of the Absolute engenders and supports, he writes: 'There are those again for whom the world, as it is, is the incarnation of the ideal, for whom change is secondary and of no vital significance. For them evil must be justified as essential to good, though a more self-contradictory conception than that of evil maintained by good for its own purposes, cannot well be devised.'[3]

But does the theory of the Absolute really give support to a reactionary social outlook? Even if it does, is it a theory to which Idealist social philosophy is really committed? Does the theory of rational activity, which I have tried to show is the foundation of Idealist social philosophy, somehow imply the theory of the Absolute? To answer these questions, the theory of the Absolute must itself be examined. What is the essence of the theory and what reasons are there, if any, for accepting it? In this chapter I shall attempt a critical examination of the theory of the Absolute. I shall be concerned chiefly with Bradley's version of the theory since he was the metaphysical pioneer among the English Idealists, but I shall also pay some attention to the version later expounded by Bosanquet, partly in order to throw light on certain aspects of the theory, partly because it is Bosanquet's social and political philosophy which has especially been linked with the theory of the Absolute. This programme will necessarily involve reference to Bradley's and Bosanquet's metaphysical writings, but I shall not attempt anything like an exhaustive presentation of their work in that field. I shall confine myself to what is essential for understanding the theory of the Absolute and the reader must not expect a full and detailed statement of all the ground covered by the works to which I shall refer.

2. Bradley's next book after *Ethical Studies* was *The Principles of Logic* published in 1883. His conception of the nature and scope of logic, however, was somewhat different from that which prevails today. For him, logic was the theory of thought, or more strictly of cognitive thought. Its subject-matter was the typical forms of cognitive thought, namely judgement and inference. On this view, logic could be regarded as complementary to ethics. The latter was the theory of morality or practical thought, the former of cognitive thought. Both subjects were quite distinct from psychology, being concerned with the rationality of thought respectively in the context of practice and cognition. It followed that, for Bradley, logic embraced much which many philosophers today would regard as falling within the scope of the theory of knowledge but outside that of logic proper. It followed also for Bradley that logic must include at least some consideration of what cognitive thought was about, of the nature of truth and falsity and of the presuppositions of cognitive thought. One way of expressing the difference between this view of logic and that current today might be to say that for Bradley logic was essentially a philosophical subject which could not be wholly separated from the rest of philosophy, while twentieth-century logicians tend to regard their subject as an independent science which can be studied in its own right without raising any philosophical questions. But while he did not think that logic any more than ethics could be isolated from the rest of philosophy, Bradley thought it desirable that, in the study of cognitive thought, metaphysical questions should as far as possible be set on one side. Some account would have to be taken of them but they should not be pursued more than was absolutely necessary.

So far as the theory of the Absolute is concerned, two things in Bradley's *Principles of Logic* are relevant. One is the bearing of his account of judgement on the nature and scope of empirical knowledge, a point to which we shall return later. The other is a passage in which certain issues are raised which point to metaphysical questions. The passage has to do with the distinction between abstract and concrete in relation to the notions of universal, particular and individual and we may usefully take it as a point of departure. 'The abstract universal and the abstract particular are what does not exist.' Bradley writes: 'The concrete particular and the concrete universal both have reality and they are different names for the individual. What is real is the individual and this individual although one and the same, has internal differences. You may hence regard it in two opposite ways. So far as it is one against other individuals, it is particular. So far as it is the same throughout its diversity, it is universal. They are two distinctions we make within it. It has two characters or aspects or sides or moments, and you may consider it from whichever side you please, or from the side which, for the purpose of the context, happens to be the emphatic or essential side. Thus a man is particular by virtue of his limiting and exclusive relations to other phenomena. He is universal because he is one throughout all his different attributes. You may call him particular or again universal because being individual, he actually is both and you wish to emphasize one side or aspect of his individuality. The individual is both a concrete particular and a concrete universal and as names of the whole from different points of view, these both are names of real existents.'[1]

I shall try to elucidate this passage in the light of the account given of the notion of the concrete universal in Chapter I of this book. We may take first the statement that: 'the abstract universal and the abstract particular are what does not exist.' In saying that the abstract universal does not exist, Bradley seems to mean that attributes like redness, sweetness, loudness and straightness do not exist in their own right. They are not independent realities but abstractions from the things whose attributes they are. By 'abstract particular' I take him to mean the particular instances of general attributes: this red, this instance of sweetness, etc. In saying that the abstract particular does not exist, his point is that what is real is not the particular red, the particular instance of sweetness but the thing which is coloured red and which has a sweet flavour. In other words, in denying that either the abstract universal or the abstract particular has existence, I take him in his own way to be stating the doctrine of the relation between abstract universal and particular which I sketched in Chapter I, section A, in connection with the notion of a class. This interpretation is borne out when Bradley goes on to say: 'What is real is the individual which, although one and the same, has internal diversity.' This is the same as my doctrine that the concrete realities which form the members of a class are individuals. They are what exhibit the attributes upon the basis of which we classify them.

But Bradley then says that the individual is both a concrete universal and a concrete particular. It is particular, 'so far as it is one against other individuals'. This is perhaps not fundamentally different from my account. One individual may be differentiated from others on the ground that it exhibits a particular instance of some attribute which they do not exhibit. But he then says that the individual is universal 'so far as it is the same throughout its diversity'. This is his notion of the concrete universal; the sameness of an individual throughout its diversity. Now, the notion of the concrete universal is the notion of what is real in the context of rational activity. This is always an individual achievement of rationality. The universal in rational activity is rationality, a universal which has a different logical structure from that of the universal in classification and natural science. The reality in rational activity is always an individualized or concrete universal. This is not so in classification or natural science. In these contexts, the individual is opposed to the universal. The former is concrete and real, the latter is not as such real, being an abstraction from the former. But in the context of rational activity this opposition cannot be maintained. The individual cannot be contrasted with the universal as the real with the unreal. Here individual and universal together form one reality.

At first sight it might seem from Bradley's example of an individual, namely a man, that his notion of the concrete universal is not fundamentally different from mine. In support of this interpretation, there is his doctrine of self-realization in *Ethical Studies*, according to which the self is an individual achievement of rationality and, therefore, an individualized or concrete universal. But in the present passage, he says that a man 'is universal because he is one throughout all his different attributes' and is particular 'by virtue of his limiting and exclusive relations to other phenomena'. This suggests that Bradley is regarding a man not as a rational agent but simply as an individual member of a class. It suggests that what he has in mind in his notion of the concrete universal is not an individual achievement of rationality but rather the unity which belongs to a whole such as an organism. Significantly he does not say that a man is universal because he is one throughout his actions but only because he is the same throughout his attributes. A man is said to be particular not by virtue of his limiting and exclusive relations to other men but only to other phenomena, which suggests that other things besides a man could have been given as an example of a concrete universal. It seems, in other words, that for Bradley the notion of the concrete universal is not confined to the context of rational activity; it is not something which arises out of the logical structure of rationality, but is relevant also in other contexts.

That what Bradley has in mind in his notion of the concrete universal is something like the unity of a whole such as an organism is borne out by what he says about an individual in the passage quoted above: 'this individual, although one and the same, has internal differences'. But it is not likely that he has forgotten the doctrine of *Ethical Studies*, according to which the self or rational agent is an individual achievement of rationality. The truth of the matter seems to be that for him the notion of the concrete universal, the principle of sameness in diversity, embraces both the unity of a whole such as an organism and the reality in rational activity, namely individual achievements of rationality. Here he is in direct opposition to the doctrine sketched in Chapter I of this book, according to which only some form of rationality can be an individualized or concrete universal. The unity or structure of an organism is not a form of rationality. It is not something which the organism consciously tries to achieve. It is an empirical unity, something which the organism simply has and which it cannot do anything about one way or the other.

There is, however, a sense in which the unity of an organism is comparable to the unity of the self of the rational agent. The organism has its being in the system of functions of its several organs. The self of the rational agent has its being in a system of activities. This superficial resemblance may have impressed Bradley and led him to overlook the fundamental difference between the two kinds of unity. The difference lies in the fact that the unity of the self of the rational agent is a self- conscious unity while the unity of an organism is not. The rational agent has some idea of what he is doing in each of his various activities and of the bearing of each of them upon the rest. His unity as a self is wrought out in the perpetual attempt to harmonize them. But the organs of an organism carry out their functions blindly and automatically without consciousness of themselves or the system to which they contribute. The point, however, about Bradley's notion of the concrete universal is not so much that in it the self-conscious unity of the self of the rational agent is reduced to the automatic natural unity of an organism as that the difference between the two is glossed over. The principle of sameness in diversity or, as Bradley sometimes calls it, 'identity in difference', blurs what should be kept distinct.

In fairness to Bradley, however, it must be said that he is not himself satisfied with the doctrine set forth in the passage which I have quoted. He readily admits that more development and discussion is needed and claims only to have gone as far as is necessary for the purpose of logic. 'There is here, I confess,' he writes, 'a doubtful point I am forced to leave doubtful. It might be urged that if you press the inquiry, you will be left alone with but a single individual. An individual which is finite or relative turns out in the end to be no individual. Individual and infinite are inseparable characters. Or again, it might be said : the individual is finite and there cannot be an absolute individual. Metaphysics, it is clear, would have to take up these questions and in any case to revise the account which is given in this chapter. But that revision must be left to metaphysics and for the purposes of logic we may keep to the distinctions already laid down.'[2] Whether, however, in his metaphysics, Bradley will revise his notion of the concrete universal so as to bring out the distinction which the present account glosses over, we shall have to see.

3. It was in his third book, *Appearance and Reality*, published

in 1892, that Bradley addressed himself without reservation to metaphysics. 'We may agree perhaps to understand by metaphysics,' he writes in the introduction, 'an attempt to know reality as against appearances, or the study of first principles, or ultimate truth, or again the effort to comprehend the universe not simply piece-meal or by fragments but somehow as a whole.'[1] Passing over the first part of the book, which is devoted to a critical discussion of other metaphysical theories all of which are found to be unsatisfactory, let us try to see what his own positive doctrine is. He thinks that reflection upon human thought indicates a positive criterion of reality. 'For if you think at all,' he writes, 'so as to discriminate between truth and falsehood, you will find that you cannot accept open self-contradiction. Hence to think is to judge; and to judge is to criticize; and to criticize is to use a criterion of reality; and surely to doubt this would be mere blindness or confused self-deception. But if so, it is clear that, in rejecting the inconsistent as appearance, we are applying a positive knowledge of the ultimate nature of things. Ultimate reality is such that it does not contradict itself. Here is an absolute criterion. And it is proved absolute by the fact that either in endeavouring to deny it or even in attempting to doubt it, we tacitly assume its validity.'[2]

According to Bradley's own account, this criterion of ultimate reality, consistency or coherence, is derived from reflection on human thought. Why should it apply to ultimate reality unless ultimate reality is in some way a system of thought or thinking activity? Only thought can contradict itself and only thought can be coherent or consistent. But Bradley goes on to say that, by consistency, he does not mean the bare exclusion of discord. The formal standard of consistency must be combined with the notion of all-inclusiveness. 'We must say,' he writes, 'that everything which appears is somehow real in such a way as to be self-consistent. The character of the real is to possess everything phenomenal in a harmonious form.'[3] He then sums up by saying: 'The universe is one in this sense; its differences exist harmoniously within one whole beyond which there is nothing.'[4] And he adds: 'Hence the Absolute is so far an individual and a system.'[5]

By the 'Absolute', Bradley means ultimate reality or the

universe as a whole. The title is intended to bring out its un-conditional, self-subsistent character. It is all-inclusive and self-maintaining, being neither relative to nor independent on any-thing else, for there is nothing else. In saying that the Absolute 'is so far an individual' Bradley is adopting the doctrine of his *Principles of Logic*. Ultimate reality is 'a sameness in diversity' 'identity in difference'. It is a concrete universal according to Bradley's notion, but not a concrete particular for there are no other individuals with which it can be contrasted. But in Bradley's notion of the concrete universal, as we have seen, the difference between the unity of an organism and an individual achievement of rationality is glossed over. When he says that 'the universe is one in this sense, that its differences exist harmoniously together within one whole', it is not clear whether we should think of this whole as analogous to an organism or to an individual achievement of rationality. All that we can gather so far is that experiences of discord and conflict are for us. They are appearances rather than reality, since reality is a harmonious whole. But just how they are reconciled in the Absolute, just how the differences exist to-gether, remains uncertain.

But Bradley has more to say about the general character of ultimate reality. So far we have been given only a formal out-line of its structure. The Absolute is a system but it must be a system of something. 'When we ask,' Bradley writes, 'as to the matter which fills up the empty outline, we can reply in one word that this is experience.'[6] He goes on to say that: 'Sentient experience in short is reality and what is not this, is not real. We may say, in other words, that there is no being or fact out-side that which is commonly called psychical existence.'[7] In support of this contention, he writes: 'Find any piece of exist-ence, take up anything that anyone could possibly call a fact or could in any sense assert to have being, and then judge if it does not consist in sentient experience? Try to discover any sense in which you could still continue to speak of it when all perception and feeling have been removed or point out any fragment of its matter, any aspect of its being, which is not derived from and which is not relative to this source? When the experiment is made strictly, I can myself conceive of noth-ing else than the experienced.'[8]

Developing this thesis, he writes in another passage : 'I mean that to be real is to be indissolubly one thing with sentience. It is to be something which comes as a feature and aspect within one whole of feeling, something which, except as an integral element of such sentience, has no meaning at all. And what I repudiate is the separation of feeling from the felt, or of the desired from desire, or of what is thought from thinking, or the division I might add, of anything from anything else. Nothing is ever so presented as real by itself or can be argued so to exist without demonstrable fallacy. And in asserting that the reality is experience, I rest throughout on this foundation : You cannot find fact unless in unity with sentience, and one cannot in the end be divided from the other either actually or in idea.'[9] Thus, according to Bradley, matter, in the sense of the inanimate or non-psychical, is not real in its own right. What we call inanimate matter is an abstraction made by us from our sentient experience. The characteristics of matter, its extension, impenetrability and so forth, are really characteristics of our experience. The idea of a material thing is the idea of certain feelings of hardness, extendedness, texture and the like, which form part of some sentient experience.

But it may be objected that in this argument Bradley is guilty of a confusion. Granted that our knowledge of material things is derived from our experience, that it is only because we can see, touch, taste, hear, etc. that we are able to frame ideas of them, it does not follow that material things do not exist in their own right as independent realities. Bradley is confusing what we know with how we come to know it. He fails to see that what we know is one thing and the conditions which make possible our knowledge of it are something else. It does not follow from the fact that we become acquainted with material things through our senses, that material things have no independent existence apart from sentient experience. But in reply to this objection it may be said that the division between what we know and how we come to know it not only presupposes that there is something already there prior to and independent of our cognitive activity, but that in coming to know we do not modify or alter what is already there. The division, that is to say, presupposes that we know things as they are in themselves, as they would be apart from and independently of our cognitive activity. Only if this is so, is how we know irrelevant to what we know. Now Bradley certainly thinks that there is something already there, prior to and independent of our cognitive activity, namely ultimate reality or the Absolute. But he is not committed to holding that, in our empirical knowledge, our knowledge of what can be seen, touched, tasted, etc., we are knowing things as they are in themselves. He might reasonably argue that the nature and status of what we know both empirically and in any other way, is not to be settled by fiat before metaphysical thought begins. It can be settled, if at all, only after a critical examination of our knowledge in all its forms, an examination which must include how we come to know what we claim to know. Now our knowledge of inanimate material things is derived from our experience. It is empirical knowledge. But as we shall see, according to Bradley, a critical examination of empirical knowledge shows that it does not give us knowledge of reality as such but only of appearance. What we know empirically is always altered and modified by the way in which we come to know it.

But it may still be objected that even if inanimate material things are not independent realities in their own right but only abstractions made by us from our sentient experience, it does not follow from this that ultimate reality is sentient experience. Now Bradley does not maintain that the psychical life, which is the stuff of the Absolute is confined to human sentient experience. It is an integral part of his theory that the Absolute is more than human experience. But he insists that it is still experience. 'And if it is more than any feeling or thought which we can know,' he writes, 'it must remain more of the same nature. It cannot pass away into another region beyond what falls under the general head of sentience.'[10] This, however, is the point at issue. Must ultimate reality 'be more of the same'? Why should it not 'pass away into another region'? Bradley has defined ultimate reality in such a way as to exclude the possibility but has he any right to do so? We shall have to return to this point after examining Bradley's critique of empirical knowledge on the basis of which he argues that what we know empirically is always appearance and never ultimate reality. But first let us see how Bradley sums up his argument so far. His conclusion is, he tells us 'that the Absolute is one system and that its contents are nothing but sentient experience. It will hence be a single and all-inclusive experience and hence no feeling or thought of any kind can fall outside its limits.'[11] The Absolute, that is to say, is an absolute individual or concrete universal according to his notion of the individual and the concrete universal. But whether we are to think of it as analogous to an organism or to an individual achievement of rationality is unclear. Our human experience is somehow included within it but just how it figures in the all-inclusive harmonious system has not yet been explained.

4.   The essentials of Bradley's critique of empirical knowledge are to be found in the account of judgement which he gives in his *Principles of Logic*. 'Judgement proper,' he writes, 'is the act which refers an ideal content recognized as such to a reality beyond the act.'[1] In another passage he says: 'In the simplest judgement, an idea is referred to what is given in perception and it is identified therewith as one of its adjectives. There is no need for an idea to appear as the subject and even when it so appears, we must distinguish the fact from grammatical show. It is present reality which is the actual subject and genuine substantive of the ideal content.'[2] When he speaks of reality, he is not referring to the Absolute. That idea has still to be worked out. His point is that every judgement claims to be true and that it must be a judgement about something. This something is not the ostensible subject, not the grammatical subject of the sentence in which the judgement may be articulated. It is reality. Reality for the purpose of logic may be taken to be that which is given in what Bradley calls 'sensuous presentation' or elsewhere 'sentient experience'. 'We have seen already,' he writes, 'and have further to see that all judgements predicate their ideal contents as an attribute of the real which appears in presentation.'[3]

But what appears in presentation is only an aspect of reality. 'It is impossible perhaps,' Bradley writes, 'to get directly at reality except in the content of one presentation. We may never see it, so to speak, but through a hole. But what we see of it may make us certain that beyond this hole it extends indefinitely.'[4] But this aspect of reality which appears in presentation is modified by judgement. 'As soon as we judge,' Bradley writes, 'we are forced to analyse and forced to distinguish. We must separate some elements of the given from others. We sunder and divide what appears to us as a sensible whole.'[5] He calls the judgement of perception 'the analytic judgement of sense' because it involves breaking up and analysing what is given in sentient experience. This inevitable procedure of abstraction vitiates the claim of the perceptual judgement to be true of reality. 'We have separated, divided, abridged, dissected,' Bradley goes on, 'we have mutilated the given and we have done so arbitrarily. We have selected what we chose. But if this is so, if every analytic judgement must inevitably so alter the facts, how can it any longer lay claim to truth?'[6] This inherent defect of the perceptual judgement where we are in direct touch with an aspect of reality, infects all our empirical knowledge. What we know is never reality as such, but the appearances which we have abstracted from it.

In *Appearance and Reality*, Bradley expounds the same doctrine in terms of what he calls 'the dualism of the "that" and the "what"'.[7] He insists that to judge that something exists is, at the same time, to judge what it is, but that the judgement of what it is inevitably falls short of its full reality. The 'what' is never adequate to the 'that'. 'But taking judgement to be completed thought,' he writes, 'in no judgement are subject and predicate the same. In every judgement the genuine subject is reality which goes beyond the predicated, of which the predicate is an adjective.'[8] By the 'predicated' he means the ostensible or grammatical subject. It is of this subject that the ostensible or grammatical predicate is an adjective. The genuine subject is reality and this is always more than the grammatical subject which is an abstraction from some aspect of it given in sentient experience.

There is a parallel between Bradley's doctrine that the judgement that something exists involves the judgement of what it is, and Green's doctrine that there is nothing in human experience which is given ready-made prior to and independent of the work of thought. Both in effect maintain that all attention is also identification. We never merely attend without forming some idea, however rough and provisional, of what it is that we are attending to. We never find ourselves confronted with a mere 'that' which has not in some way been categorized and defined as a 'what'. For Bradley, there is something merely given in human experience but it lies below the level of thought. There is, that is to say, a purely psychical level of human experience which consists simply of feeling as yet undifferentiated and unanalysed by thought. At this level, we are in direct touch with reality but it is a level below that of thought. When we begin to think and so to judge, we abstract from this psychical level and so 'mutilate' what is directly given in sensuous presentation. We are conscious of the given, that is to say, only as a felt background, never as a direct object of thought. For Green, the purely psychical level is a pre-human level of experience, since for him, human experience proper begins only at the level of thought. Both levels are somehow included within the scope of the eternal consciousness but that is a doctrine which we have yet to explore and which must be reserved for a later chapter.

But although in Bradley's view, our empirical knowledge is confined to appearances and cannot reach ultimate reality, we can still, he thinks, know something of the general character of the Absolute. He has already said that the Absolute experience is more than any thought or feeling which we can know. He goes on to say that: 'What is impossible is to construct the Absolute life in its details, to have the specific experience in which it consists.'[9] But knowledge of the main features of the Absolute is possible. 'For these main features,' he writes, 'to some extent are within our own experience and again the idea of their combination is in the abstract quite intelligible. And surely no more than this is wanted for a knowledge of the Absolute? It is knowledge of course which differs enormously from the facts. But it is true for all that while it respects its own limits, and it seems fully attainable by the finite intellect[10] Such knowledge is not empirical but metaphysical. It is to be got through a self-conscious and critical examination of human experience. But it is not human experience at the merely psychical level which must be studied but at all levels. The subject-matter for metaphysical thought is the experience of thinking, rational agents. In metaphysics, that is to say, human thought is reflecting upon itself in all its various forms and it is this self-conscious character which distinguishes metaphysical from empirical knowledge where the subject-matter is human experience at the merely psychical level.

But can metaphysics as thus conceived really lead to knowledge of the main features of ultimate reality and of how in principle they are combined? According to Bradley, we are in direct touch with ultimate reality only at the purely psychical level of experience, a level below that of thought. Once we move from the purely psychical level to a level at which thought is operative, we are no longer in direct touch with ultimate reality. As soon as we begin to think, and so to become conscious of empirical objects, we mutilate the reality given in merely sentient, unthinking experience. It follows that, in reflecting upon our own thinking experience, we are reflecting upon our knowledge not of ultimate reality but only of appearance. On Bradley's own argument, there is no ground for his statement that the main features of the Absolute to some extent are within our own experience since, even if they are, we could not possibly know it. Ultimate reality, the Absolute if we are entitled to give it this title, remains out of reach of our knowledge whether empirical or metaphysical. The self-conscious critical examination of human experience, an examination which is always of thinking experience, may be expected to give knowledge of the main features of human experience. The idea of their combination is no doubt intelligible in the shape of a theory of the general character and structure of human experience. But unless we assume that the main features of ultimate reality are the same as those of human experience, an assumption which is ruled out by Bradley's account of empirical knowledge, we are not able to go further. All that we can say is that ultimate reality is of such a nature as to permit or at least tolerate an experience having the general character and structure of ours. On the logic of his own argument, therefore, Bradley is faced with a dilemma. If he is to preserve his doctrine that empirical knowledge is of appearance and not reality, then the hope of knowledge of ultimate reality must be given up as in principle lying beyond our scope. If, on the other hand, he abandons his doctrine of empirical knowledge and holds, on the contrary, that it affords direct knowledge of ultimate reality, then he has no basis for arguing that ultimate reality is an Absolute system of sentient experience. The ground for the distinction between appearance and reality is cut away. However, at this stage, let us not press these objections but instead see how Bradley sets about the task of showing how in principle what he takes to be the main features of ultimate reality are combined. This will bring us back to his notion of the concrete universal and to the fundamental ambiguity which, as we have already seen, it involves.

5. According to Bradley, the Absolute is an all-inclusive, harmonious system of sentient experience. It is more than merely human experience but, because it is all-inclusive, human experience must fall within it and somehow be a part of it. But how does human experience figure in the Absolute? The Absolute does not think, will or feel after our fashion. Being all-inclusive and harmonious, it has no need to inquire, to formulate and execute purposes, to articulate and express its emotions in finite creations. But thought, will and feeling are somehow preserved in the Absolute, although not as we experience them. According to Bradley, we must envisage the condition of the Absolute as one of permanent and complete satisfaction. 'Such a whole state,' he writes, 'would possess in superior form that immediacy which we find more or less in feeling, and in this whole, all divisions would be healed up and would be experienced entire containing all elements in harmony. Thought would be present as a higher intuition: will would be there where the ideal had reality: and beauty and pleasure and feeling would live on in this total fulfilment.[1]

The reference in this passage to the presence of will in the Absolute, 'will would be there where the ideal had reality', recalls the doctrine of the real ideal self of religion in *Ethical Studies*. But is the idea of how all these aspects of human experience are combined in the Absolute intelligible even in principle? Speaking of the processes of human thought, Bradley says: 'Such processes must be dissolved in something not poorer but richer than themselves, and feeling and will must also be transmuted in this whole into which thought has entered.'[2] But what is the nature of this transmutation? There is a sense in which the transition from a lower to a higher level of rationality may be said to involve a transmutation or trans-

formation of thought, will and feeling. The idea of the transmutation of thought, will and feeling, that is to say, has a basis
in human experience. The movement from a lower to a higher
level of rationality involves a change of perspective with a
modification of our plans and purposes and our feelings about
them. What at the level of merely private self-satisfaction
appears both rational and desirable, appears in a different light
when considered from the standpoint of morality. A course of
conduct which is rational within the sphere of personal relations may have to be revised and modified at the higher level
of citizenship.

It may be thought that when Bradley speaks of the transmutation of thought, feeling and will in the Absolute, he has
in mind something like the change in perspective involved in
the transition from a lower to a higher level of rationality. On
this view, the Absolute would be a level of rationality higher
than any which we can reach but incorporating within itself
the whole scale of human levels. Our highest level of rationality, that of self-consistent human achievement, would be a
subordinate element within the sphere of the Absolute which
would include forms of experience unknown to us as well as
all that we know. But there are fundamental difficulties in the
way of this interpretation. Rational activity at every level is
the activity of rational human agents. But if the Absolute is
the supreme level of rationality, it is not ex hypothesi a level
which is open to human agents. The relation between it and
the highest level in the human scale, therefore, cannot be of the
same kind as the relation between a lower and a higher level
within the human scale. In the latter case, the relation is
between two levels of human activity, in the former it is between a human level and a super-human one. The transition
from the level of self-consistent human achievement to the
Absolute cannot be thought of as the same in kind as the transition from the sphere of personal relations to that of citizenship,
or from the sphere of citizenship to self-consistent human
achievement. The transmutation of thought, feeling and will
which is supposed to take place in the Absolute cannot be
comparable to the change of perspective which takes place
between personal relations and citizenship or between citizenship and self-consistent human achievement, since the Absolute

is not simply one more level in the human scale of rationality.

What then is the nature of the transmutation which thought, feeling and will undergo in the Absolute? The Absolute is a concrete universal according to Bradley's notion. It is a complete all-embracing individual, an identity in difference or sameness in diversity. Is it then something analogous to an organism, human experience being merely one of the organs? On this view, human experience would be contributing to the Absolute as an organ contributes through its special function to the life of the parent organism. But this interpretation is equally difficult to maintain. It must follow either that defects or failures within human experience lead to defects in the Absolute experience, and this conflicts with the doctrine that the Absolute is a perfect experience free from all blemish or discord; or that everything in human experience, all the suffering and misery, cruelty and folly, contributes to the Absolute, is necessary for its life, that whatever is, is ipso facto good. It was this latter interpretation which gave rise to Hobhouse's attack. But the analogy with an organism is difficult to maintain when we recall that, according to Bradley, the Absolute is somehow the complete fulfilment of what is imperfectly achieved in human experience. 'Thought would be present as a higher intuition: will would be there where the ideal had reality: and beauty and pleasure and feeling would live on in this total fulfilment.'

The organic analogy breaks down because an organism cannot be regarded as the complete fulfilment of what is imperfectly achieved by its organs. On the contrary, the life of the organism is maintained through the functions of the organs and imperfections in these functions constitute defects in the life of the organism. We are thus no nearer to understanding the nature of the transmutation undergone by thought, will and feeling in the Absolute. It may be thought that the notion of the complete fulfilment of our imperfect human achievements affords a clue. Perhaps what Bradley had in mind was an ideal system of experience in which everything would be fully achieved, in which there would be no inconsistency, no evil, no folly, no blemish of any kind. But this will not do, for while undoubtedly Bradley does regard the Absolute as the perfect experience, it is no mere ideal but ultimate reality. It is all-inclusive and somehow, although it is perfection, manages to include all the manifold forms of imperfection. But just how this inclusion comes about is not made clear.

According to Bradley the main features of ultimate reality are present in some way in our experience and the principle of their combination is in principle intelligible to us. It is in this connection that his doctrine of the transmutation of thought, will and feeling in the Absolute is important. Thought, will and feeling, which are features of human experience, are also features of ultimate reality, but are transmuted in that setting. If the principle of their combination is to be intelligible, the nature of this transmutation must be made clear. But it is not. Bradley fails to make good his claim. But he does not realize that he has failed. For him, the key to the nature of the transmutation undergone by thought, will and feeling, and to the principle of their combination in the Absolute, is provided by his account of the general character of the Absolute which he has already set forth. He has argued that the Absolute is an all-embracing individual, an absolute concrete universal. But he does not realize that his notion of the concrete universal is itself unclear, blurring, as it does, the difference between the unity of a whole such as an organism and an individual achievement of rationality. Thus, quite apart from the difficulties noticed at the end of the last subsection which have to do with the possibility of our knowledge of ultimate reality, the theory of the Absolute turns out, on examination, not to be a tenable theory. It purports to be a theory of the nature and character of ultimate reality but, owing to the ambiguity in Bradley's notion of the concrete universal, the notion which is the foundation of the account given of the nature and character of ultimate reality, it is not what it purports to be. It contains no intelligible account of the nature and character of ultimate reality.

B : BERNARD BOSANQUET

1.   According to L. T. Hobhouse, Bernard Bosanquet's political philosophy clearly exhibited the reactionary social and political influence of the theory of the Absolute. I shall now briefly examine Bosanquet's version of that theory and in a later chapter will turn to his political philosophy. Bosanquet was

two years younger than Bradley and throughout their respective careers, they were philosophical allies. But, in this relationship, Bradley was the pioneer while Bosanquet was the follower
who undertook the task of consolidating and cultivating the
ground first explored by his more original colleague. His *Logic*
was published in 1885, two years after Bradley's *Principles* and
the latter was enthusiastic in his praise of it. The ground
covered and position expounded are fundamentally the same in
both works. Bosanquet, however, explicitly commits himself
to the view, which is latent in Bradley, that logic and the
theory of knowledge are one and the same. 'The work of intellectually constituting that totality which we call the real
world,' he writes, 'is the work of knowledge. The work of
analysing this constitution or determination is the work of logic
which might be described as the self-consciousness of knowledge or the reflection of knowledge upon itself.'[1] He agrees
with Bradley that the ultimate subject of every judgement is
reality, that we are in direct touch with reality in sentient
experience but that in judgement we inevitably abstract from,
alter and modify what is given at the merely sentient level. Like
Bradley, he tries as far as possible to avoid raising metaphysical
questions while engaged in logic.

   It was not until he was appointed Gifford lecturer for
1911-12 that Bosanquet undertook the task of expounding a
systematic metaphysical theory. By that time Bradley's *Appearance and Reality* had been before the world for 20 years and
Bosanquet took the opportunity afforded by the Gifford Lectures to reformulate and restate the theory of the Absolute in
a way which might meet the criticisms which had been made
against Bradley's work. He also endeavoured to work out more
fully than Bradley had done the implications of the theory for
human life. The first series of lectures was published in a
volume called *The Principle of Individuality and Value*. The
second lecture in this volume has the title: *The Concrete
Universal*. It opens with a passage which will repay examination. Bosanquet writes: 'Thus the true embodiment of the
logical universal takes the shape of a world whose members
are worlds. Whose members are worlds: for the same reason
which made it inevitable for the mere generality to be defective
by the omission of the contents which differentiate the class

members from one another, the universal in the form of a world refers to diversity of content within each member as the universal in the form of a class neglects it. Such diversity recognized as a unity, a macrocosm constituted by microcosms, is the type of the concrete universal.'[2]

The opening statement in this passage, that: 'The true embodiment of the logical universal takes the shape of a world whose members are worlds,' seems at first sight more or less to harmonize with my notion of the concrete universal. Thus it might be thought that what Bosanquet has in mind is the logical structure of the universal, rationality. A given level of rationality sums up and incorporates within itself the levels below it. It may be regarded as a world whose members are worlds. An individual achievement of rationality, e.g. citizenship, includes within itself individual achievements of rationality at lower levels. It will involve various activities each of which will involve series of actions at the level of ends and means. But Bosanquet goes on to say that: 'for the same reason which made it inevitable for the mere generality to be defective by the omission of contents which differentiate the class members from one another, the universal in the form of a world refers to diversity of content within each member as the universal in the form of a class neglects it.' His point here seems to be that the universal in the form of a class is the abstract universal. It fails to bring out the concrete reality of the class members as individuals and merely draws attention to the respect in which they are alike, namely in all exhibiting a particular instance of a general attribute. But the universal in the form of a world 'refers to diversity of content within each member'. This seems to be Bradley's notion of the concrete universal over again. Each class member is an individual, a sameness in diversity or identity in difference. It is a world in the sense of being a whole such as an organism.

Bosanquet concludes by saying: 'Such a diversity recognized as a unity, a macrocosm constituted by microcosms, is the type of the concrete universal.' We have here the same fundamental ambiguity as in Bradley's notion of the concrete universal. Two different things, the unity of a whole such as an organism, and an individual achievement of rationality, are brought together under the principle of sameness in diversity or identity in difference. The distinction between them, the presence in the one case of rationality and in the other of an empirical unity without rationality, is blurred. The fact that Bosanquet speaks in the opening statement of 'the logical universal' which he distinguishes from the 'mere generality' indicates that he thinks that the principle which unites the parts of a whole such as an organism is fundamentally the same as the principle underlying an individual achievement of rationality. The term 'logical' may not unreasonably be applied to the universal in rational activity since rational activity is thinking activity. It cannot properly be applied to the unity of a whole such as an organism. The unity of such a whole is empirical, not logical.

2.   Bosanquet is of course unaware that, in his notion of the concrete universal, the distinction between two different things is obscured. He thinks that it provides a key to the understanding not only of human experience but also of ultimate reality. 'We are regarding it in general,' he writes, 'as the type of complete experience and from this point of view its characteristics are the same, whether we think of it as the object of knowledge, of will or of enjoyment.'[1] On the subject of ultimate reality, he writes: 'It is all one whether we make non-contradiction, wholeness or individuality, the criterion of the ultimately real. We mean by it in each case the same. We mean that which must stand, that which has nothing without to set against it and is pure self-maintenance within.'[2] Bosanquet is here maintaining that non-contradiction, wholeness, and individuality are in the last analysis the same thing. But he is also saying that non-contradiction, wholeness, and individuality are equally criteria of the ultimately real and that the ultimately real is all inclusive and self-maintaining. The ultimately real, that is to say, is free from contradiction, is a whole and an individual, and since it is also all-inclusive and self-maintaining, it must be a single, infinite individual. This brings us to the theory of the Absolute. The ultimately real is an Absolute concrete universal, an all-embracing macrocosm of microcosms. In other words, Bosanquet is saying that if it is agreed that ultimate reality must be all-inclusive and self-maintaining, then we have in the notion of the concrete universal a key to its character. Only a single infinite individual, an Absolute con-

crctc univcrsal, can be all-inclusive and sclf-maintaining.

But this argument gives rise to the same difficulties as Bradley's. It is not clear what an individual or concrete universal is. Under the principle of sameness through diversity two different things are brought together : the unity of a whole such as an organism, and an individual achievement of rationality. Like Bradley, Bosanquet attaches great importance to the principle of non-contradiction or coherence. 'This then is the fundamental nature of the inference to the Absolute;' he writes : 'the passage from the contradictory and unstable in all experience alike to the stable and satisfactory.'[3] This is in essence Bradley's argument that we can take coherence as a positive criterion of reality because it is a fundamental principle in all our thought and in our rational, that is to say, thinking activity. Bosanquet comes to it by way of the coherence theory of truth. 'A true proposition,' he writes, 'is so in the last resort because its contradictory is not conceivable in harmony with the whole of experience, in other words, is not merely a contradiction of facts but a self-contradiction.'[4]

There is a sense in which this view of truth is intelligible when it is taken in conjunction with the doctrine enunciated by Bosanquet at the beginning of his *Logic* to which I referred in the last sub-section. 'The work of intellectually constituting that totality which we call the real world is the work of knowledge.' Taking the real world to be the empirical world and knowledge to be empirical knowledge, the coherence theory of truth as he understands it may be summarized along the following lines. An empirical proposition is not a natural event. It is propounded in answer to a logically prior question which arises within the context of some inquiry. To say that it is true is to say that at the present stage of the inquiry to deny it would be self-contradictory. You cannot deny it without being logically obliged to deny certain other propositions which you have already decided to call true and so contradicting yourself. The decision as to the truth or falsity of a given empirical proposition always involves reference to other empirical propositions upon whose truth you have already decided.

It follows that the decision as to what is empirically true is always provisional, never final. The decision that a proposition is true, made at a certain stage in an inquiry, may have to be revised at a later stage. But when this happens, there will always be other propositions whose truth has already been decided and with reference to which the revision is made. There is an irreducible hypothetical element in all empirical knowledge. What we call empirical truth or fact is never more than an interim report on the progress made so far 'in the work of intellectually constituting that totality which we call the real world', a statement of the provisional results of the current stage of an inquiry. Non-contradiction or coherence is an important principle in empirical knowledge. But its importance is as a principle of procedure rather than of truth. The systematic pursuit of empirical knowledge is a rational activity. Like all rational activity, it is subject to the standard of coherence or self-consistency. We are rational only so far as we aim at being self-consistent and try to avoid contradicting ourselves in what we do and say.

Bosanquet seems to have thought that, from the fact that we try to be self-consistent in our human rational activity, we can infer that ultimate reality is completely self-consistent. Like Bradley, he does not seem to have realized that we cannot infer anything about ultimate reality from our own experience of rational activity except that ultimate reality must be of such a nature at least to tolerate our experience. Like Bradley, he thinks that ultimate reality is not only all-inclusive and self-maintaining but also somehow the consummation and fulfilment of all our imperfect human achievements. The theory of the Absolute is the theory of the nature and character of this all-inclusive self-maintaining perfection. Bosanquet thinks that it provides us with a standard by which we can make a rational critique of human achievement: hence the title of the first series of his Gifford Lectures: *The Principle of Individuality and Value*. Speaking of the theory of the Absolute, he says: 'It is misapprehended if we call on it to put us in possession of an ultimate experience which is ex hypothesi impossible for our limited being. What it will do for us is much more relevant to the transformation of our lives. It exhibits to us in their relative stability and reciprocal suggestions of completeness, the provinces of experience which comprise the various values of life. It interprets the correlation of their worth with their reality and of both with their satisfactoriness to the soul.'[5] But if the theory of the Absolute is to serve as the basis for a critique of human achievement, it must be an intelligible theory, a theory which is free from ambiguity. From what we have seen of it so far, Bosanquet's version has all the defects of Bradley's, being found on the same ambiguous notion of the concrete universal. Let us glance briefly at his subsequent development of the theory to see whether in principle these defects are overcome.

3. Bosanquet's second series of Gifford Lectures was published in a volume entitled: *The Value and Destiny of the Individual.* In it, he attempts further to elucidate his theory of the Absolute and to make good his claim that the theory is of value for the understanding of human life. He argues that the Absolute, being perfection, cannot be adequately conceived in terms of any of our merely human values. 'Now in the first place,' he writes, 'the Absolute cannot be fully characterized by any one of these subordinate excellencies. As the perfect experience, it is more than beautiful, more than pleasant, more than true and more than good.'[1] But the Absolute is an all-inclusive perfection and must in some way be the consummation or fulfilment of these subordinate excellencies. They are present in the Absolute but are transmuted or, as Bosanquet prefers to say, 'transformed'. After the above passage he continues: 'It is plain that the perfection which reconciles all these characteristics must be more than each of them. It cannot be a conjunction, it must, as we have argued throughout, be a transformation.'[2] Bradley, however, was unable to give any intelligible account of his doctrine of transmutation. Whether Bosanquet is able to do any better with 'transformation' remains to be seen.

But the notion of an all-inclusive perfection gives rise to a further problem. What becomes of human failures, of error and evil? Are they somehow transformed in the Absolute? On the subject of error and its relation to the Absolute, Bosanquet writes: 'The Absolute certainly contains error as it contains everything but we cannot say that it is characterized by error, i.e. that when we think of it as the perfection which transcends and completes the nature of truth, we can think of it in this completeness as having error as a constituent member.'[3] Now according to Bosanquet, no human truth is absolutely true and no error is sheer absolute and unmitigated error. Error is partial, misplaced truth and truth is superceded error. But from the standpoint of the Absolute, all human truth in the last resort is error. It is always defective, being one-sided and abstract. 'If then we consider the Absolute, the perfect experience, from the standpoint of truth and error,' he writes, 'we must say: though it contains error, this is a subordinate aspect of its character as truth and can only belong to the ultimate experience so far as imperfect truth belongs to it. But that can only be as an element absorbed in it so that all varieties of relative points of view and one-sided emphasis come together in the one experience of reality and value.'[4] Truth and error, in other words, are for us and not as such for the Absolute. The Absolute does not think and know in the way in which we think and know. But it is somehow the fulfilment and complete achievement of our fallible efforts to think and know. It knows the reality of which we can only know the appearances. Yet, at the same time, our fallible efforts are somehow part of the ultimate experience of reality and value, since that experience is all-inclusive. The nature of this inclusion and of the transformation which it involves remains a mystery.

4.   Bosanquet also discusses good and evil in relation to the Absolute. But before examining his doctrine on this subject, let us see what he has to say about good and evil within human experience. 'Good is primarily the conflict with evil and the triumph over it.' he writes: 'Evil is primarily the rebellion against good.'[1] He goes on to say that: 'There is no simple general choice between worlds of objects antecedently labelled good and bad. The whole positive material of life is in principle before or within the finite self and out of this it has to build itself a symbol or relative world of perfection involving the repudiation of what conflicts with it.'[2] This suggests a doctrine of rational self-realization along the lines of that developed by Bradley and Green, a suggestion which is borne out by the following passage. 'No doubt within every self-conscious finite creature,' he writes, 'there is something of a formed system which constitutes or indicates its attitude to perfection and by

contrast with which what opposes it is evil. But there is no standard or rationale for the identification and estimate of its structure unless we take it in connection with the spiritual organism in which the finite being finds to some extent completion and satisfaction.'[3]

By the 'spiritual organism' he tells us: 'I mean the whole world of achievements, habits, institutions, in which the apparent individual finds some clue to the reality which is the truth of himself. This then, imperfectly as it is realized in connection with himself, stands to him so far for the satisfaction and foundation which his nature demands and his attitude so far as good, is to harmonize his being with it while eliciting from the material of life further harmony for both.'[4] This world of achievements, habits and institutions is presumably a world whose members are worlds, a concrete universal in Bosanquet's sense. It suggests that what he has in mind is something like Green's idea of the sphere or world of self-consistent human achievement. So far as this part of his work is concerned, it seems not unreasonable to interpret Bosanquet's notion of the concrete universal as in essence the notion of an individual achievement of rationality. But the fact that he speaks of the world of achievements, habits and institutions as a 'spiritual organism' betrays the underlying ambiguity in his notion of the concrete universal. For him, an individual whole such as an organism and an individual achievement of rationality are fundamentally the same in character.

According to Bosanquet, evil is not merely the external opposition to good, not merely what obstructs self-consistent human achievement. It is this but also something more. Speaking of the evil attitude, he says: 'It is not merely interested to realize the self against a contradictory element as also is good, but it is interested to realize it in and as a contradiction.'[5] In another passage he writes: 'The essence of the evil attitude is the self-maintenance of some factor in a self both as good and also as against the good system.'[6] Human evil, that is to say, is not merely error in the attempt to achieve rational self-realization. It is not merely what baulks a sincere effort on a given occasion. It is the conscious repudiation of the effort not through weakness or because of overwhelming difficulty, but in the perverse attempt to achieve what the agent knows will conflict with his main purpose. The essence of human evil, in other words, is perversity. The wilful persistence in a self-contradictory course of action knowing it to be self-contradictory yet stubbornly trying to have it both ways. The evil man is the moral agent who knowingly neglects acknowledged duties and responsibilities and who therefore sinks to the level of merely private self-satisfaction in his conduct although capable of the higher level of morality. From the point of view of morality, it is a deliberately anarchic attitude.

But what is the position of human good and evil in the Absolute? According to Bosanquet, the rational agent is inspired by the idea of the Absolute in his efforts to achieve rational self-realization. He is forever striving to reach perfection although, owing to the limits of his finite human nature, he must inevitably fail. 'He is always a fragmentary being,' Bosanquet writes, 'inspired by an infinite whole which he is forever striving to express in terms of his limited range of externality. In this, ex hypothesi, he can never succeed.'[7] But, although this striving must always end in failure, from the standpoint of the Absolute it is not in vain. 'But this effort of his is not wasted or futile.' Bosanquet writes: 'It is a factor of the self-maintenance of the universe and so far is a real achievement. And it constitutes, as we have seen, an element in the Absolute, an element through which the detailed struggle of good and evil is sustained and the relative triumph of good within this conflict is made possible.'[8]

So far as human good and the Absolute are concerned, Bosanquet seems to be repeating his doctrine about human truth. The rational agent can contribute to some valuable human achievement but this will never be an achievement of perfection. No human achievement is ever perfect. Improvement in principle is always possible. The Absolute in some way, how is not clear, is the consummation and fulfilment of imperfect human achievements. In the Absolute, the rational agent's limitations are overcome and his relative achievements are included. But in the case of human evil, matters are different. Evil is not merely error in rational self-realization but the deliberate repudiation of the attempt. How is this conscious perversity to be embraced in all-inclusive perfection? Bosanquet seems to think that, while the evil attitude may dominate some human beings, it cannot gain a permanent hold on them all. Its triumphs are only temporary and, in human life as a whole, it will always be overcome. This must be so if the effort to achieve rational self-realization is, as Bosanquet says it is, 'a factor of the self-maintenance of the universe' and 'an element in the Absolute'. If evil were to gain a permanent triumph, human life would degenerate into the anarchy of utter selfishness. There would be nothing but the separate efforts of finite rational agents to achieve private self-satisfaction with a consequent destruction of all social co-operation. Rational self-realization would be unable to play its part as a factor in the self-maintenance of the universe and human achievements would cease to be an element in the Absolute. But if this was to happen, the Absolute would be affected. It would no longer be perfection and, strictly speaking, no longer Absolute. Thus the triumph of good over evil within human life is guaranteed by the Absolute. Evil can never score more than a temporary success. This is fundamentally Bradley's doctrine of the real-ideal self of religion in *Ethical Studies* over again.

In fairness to Bosanquet however, his point, although he does not make it very clearly, is that, in human life, the struggle with evil itself makes possible human achievements which would not otherwise be realized. Courage, fortitude and self-denial are all called for and in some way these contribute to the Absolute. Thus evil contributes to perfection but only by being overcome. Its contribution, in other words, is purely negative. If it is objected that this means that while evil can never triumph equally it can never be wholly eliminated since, if it were, something would be lost in the Absolute, the answer is that, although evil cannot be eliminated, it may be greatly reduced in scale and extent. The need for courage, fortitude and self-denial will never disappear but their effective exercise can curtail the ravages of evil. But Bosanquet's doctrine does weaken individual responsibility in the struggle with evil. Since the triumph of good is assured, it does not matter whether you or I exert ourselves greatly in opposing evil. There will infallibly be others to take up the good fight, so why should we bother? Why, indeed, should we not ourselves take advantage of what evil may bring to us in the way of private satisfaction? We shall lose the honour of contributing positively to the self-

G

maintenance of the universe, but we shall still be making a negative contribution and we need not worry about destroying the possibility of human life. But these considerations have led us away from the theoretical issues involved in Bosanquet's doctrine to its hypothetical practical consequences. In this section, our purpose has been to see whether Bosanquet, in his version of the theory of the Absolute, is able to get over the difficulties which beset Bradley. From what we have seen of his argument, our conclusion can only be that he has not succeeded where Bradley failed.

C : IDEALISM WITHOUT THE ABSOLUTE

1.   I have said that some critics of Idealist social philosophy, notably L. T. Hobhouse, had seen in the theory of the Absolute a doctrine which engendered a reactionary social and political outlook. I asked whether this was really so and also whether the theory of rational activity which, I have maintained in this book, is the foundation of Idealist social philosophy, somehow carries with it a commitment to the theory of the Absolute. It was in order to answer these questions that I undertook a critical examination of the theory of the Absolute as it was developed by Bradley and Bosanquet. We can now see that the charge of engendering a reactionary social and political outlook is not without plausibility. We saw, in the last section, that, according to Bosanquet, evil is somehow necessary to the perfection of the Absolute albeit in a negative way. The doctrine that the Absolute guarantees the triumph of good over evil, that in human life evil can never score more than a temporary success, tends, as I pointed out, to weaken the responsibility of the individual for combating it. More generally, the distinction between appearance and reality, with the implication that nothing in human life can be of permanent value, that perfection lies beyond our reach, may engender an attitude of indifference to human affairs. Everything is transient and nothing ultimately matters very much. Such an attitude would be an emotional not a logical consequence of accepting the theory of the Absolute, and there is no reason to suppose that either Bradley or Bosanquet would have commended it. We need not, however, deny that accepting the theory of the Absolute might

have such an effect. But more important is my second question: does Idealist social philosophy really carry with it a commitment to the theory of the Absolute? From the criticisms which I have made of the theory in the two preceding sections, the reader will be in no doubt as to my answer. It is: no. I will now briefly summarize these criticisms.

There have been three main lines of criticism. The first was directed against the notion of the concrete universal as Bradley and Bosanquet developed it. For them, the notion is summed up in the principle of sameness through diversity or identity in difference. But in their hands, this principle is ambiguous. It is applied indifferently to an individual whole such as an organism and to an individual achievement of rationality. They fail to recognize the important difference between these two things, that the unity of a whole such as an organism is an empirical unity while that of an individual achievement of rationality is constituted by its rationality. This failure suggests that their understanding of the theory of rational activity is imperfect, a suggestion which, in the case of Bradley, is borne out by the difficulties which arise in the later stages of his argument in *Ethical Studies*.

My second main line of criticism was of certain steps in the argument through which the theory of the Absolute was developed. Both Bradley and Bosanquet argue that, from the fact that in our human rational activity, we try to be self-consistent and avoid contradicting ourselves, we can infer that ultimate reality is coherent and non-contradictory. They assume, that is to say, that, from a characteristic feature of our human experience, we can infer something about the positive nature of ultimate reality. But they also argue that, while at the purely psychical level of experience we are in direct touch with ultimate reality, as soon as we begin to think, we abstract from and mutilate what is given at the purely psychical level. In our rational, i.e. thinking activity, what we experience is appearance, never ultimate reality. It follows that we cannot infer anything about the positive nature of ultimate reality from the characteristic features of human rational activity, because we can never get at ultimate reality as it is in itself to see whether in fact it has any of these features. Ultimate reality is simply what is given at the psychical level of ex-

perience before thought begins to operate and all we can infer
about it is the negative characteristic that, whatever else it
may be, it is of such a nature as to tolerate our human rational
activity. On the logic of Bradley's and Bosanquet's argument,
no knowledge of the positive nature of ultimate reality is possible and the theory that it is an absolute concrete universal, a
self-consistent system of sentient experience is without any
foundation whatever. The upshot of this criticism is that
Bradley and Bosanquet are impaled on the horns of a dilemma.
Either they must maintain their distinction between appearance and reality, in which case there can be no positive knowledge of the nature of ultimate reality and no theory of the
Absolute; or if they renounce the distinction and hold that in
our thinking rational activity we directly experience ultimate
reality they are committed to something like naive realism or
at least dualism in which both thought and matter are ultimate
realities, and once more the theory of the Absolute is without
foundation.

My third main line of criticism was what Bradley called the
'transmutation' and Bosanquet the 'transformation' of human
values and achievements in the Absolute. Setting aside difficulties connected with the possibility of knowledge of ultimate
reality, I asked whether the theory of the Absolute is an intelligible conception. Here the doctrine of transmutation is of
crucial importance. Bradley and Bosanquet tell us that the
Absolute is perfection. It is an all-inclusive harmonious system of
experience in which all our imperfect human values and
achievements are consummated and fulfilled. For this to be
intelligible, we need to know at least in principle how the transmutation comes about. How are human values, to say nothing
of human sins and failures, transmuted in the all-inclusive perfection? But, although we are repeatedly told that it happens,
we are never told how, or upon what principle. The nature,
character and method of the transmutation remains a mystery.
But Bradley and Bosanquet seem to think that in principle the
transmutation has been made intelligible and that the key to it
lies in their notion of the concrete universal. We are thus
brought back to the first main line of criticism. The ambiguity
in their notion of the concrete universal, of which they were of
course unaware, concealed from Bradley and Bosanquet the

fundamental obscurity in their conception of the Absolute. They thought that their notion of the concrete universal was intelligible in the form of the principle of sameness through diversity, identity in difference or a macrocosm of microcosms, and that, in presenting ultimate reality as an Absolute concrete universal, they were putting forward an intelligible conception.

It will now be apparent why my answer to the second question is: no. The theory of rational activity, which is the foundation of Idealist social philosophy, does not carry with it any sort of commitment to the theory of the Absolute. Although both theories involve the notion of the concrete universal, the version employed in the theory of the Absolute is fundamentally confused and the theory of the Absolute reflects this confusion. The version employed in the theory of rational activity has been purged of the confusion and with it of any connection with the theory of the Absolute. It may be objected, however, that even if Idealist social philosophy is logically free from contamination by the theory of the Absolute, nevertheless that theory has in fact been associated with it and may have engendered a reactionary social and political outlook. In others words, the answer to my first question may be: yes, even if the answer to the second is: no. I admit that there may be something in the objection and can only say that one of the aims of this book is to try to dispel the belief that Idealist social philosophy has any necessary connection with the theory of the Absolute. The reader may perhaps agree that, from what he has seen of Idealist social philosophy in this book, there is nothing inherently reactionary about it and that there is something to be said for it on its own merits. In order that these should be appreciated, it is important to lay the ghost of the Absolute.

2. The theory of the Absolute was the outcome of an attempt to know reality as a whole or ultimate reality, such an attempt being in the opinion of Bradley and Bosanquet the proper task of metaphysics. But, according to my second line of criticism, on their own arguments such knowledge is impossible. Why did they fail to see this? What prevented them from recognizing that, on the basis of their critique of empirical knowledge, positive knowledge of reality lies beyond the reach of human

thought, since thought always abstracts from and mutilates the reality given in purely psychical experience? A clue may be found in the notion of reality which plays so prominent a part in their thought. For them it is indubitable not only that there is an ultimate reality but that this reality is knowable. To deny that it is knowable is self-contradictory. Thus, in the introduction to *Appearance and Reality*, Bradley writes: 'To say that reality is such that our knowledge cannot reach it, is to claim to know reality. To urge that our knowledge is of a kind which must fail to transcend appearance itself implies that transcendence: for if we had no idea of a beyond, we should assuredly not know how to talk about failure and success and the test by which we distinguish them must obviously be some acquaintance with the nature of the goal.'[1]

In this passage, Bradley is not arguing that ultimate reality is knowable. He is merely contending that there is no ground, at least before metaphysical inquiry begins, for maintaining that it is not. This at least is all that he is entitled to maintain. But it is difficult to avoid the conclusion that in fact he thinks he has done more. In the body of *Appearance and Reality*, he writes as if the question of whether ultimate reality is knowable has already in principle been settled. Such knowledge is only of its general character and not of its details but it is positive knowledge. Thus the fact that on examination empirical knowledge turns out to be confined to appearance is not allowed to unsettle an issue which has already been settled. Whatever the limits of empirical knowledge may be, the scope of metaphysics is not affected. It never occurred to Bradley and Bosanquet, that is to say, that in the light of their critique of empirical knowledge they ought to revise their assumption that reality is knowable and that it is the task of metaphysics to seek this knowledge. On the contrary, for them the doctrine that empirical knowledge is confined to appearance presupposes another form of knowledge which is not so confined. Their fundamental error is their failure to see that in assuming that reality is knowable and in defining the task of metaphysics as they do, they are from the outset begging important metaphysical questions. What we are to understand by 'reality', whether or in what sense it is an object of knowledge, are questions which properly fall within the body of metaphysics.

They can be answered, if at all, only after metaphysical inquiry has been carried some way. The programme of metaphysics must not be drawn up in such a way that they are settled in advance before real metaphysical work begins.

In the passage quoted above, Bradley fails to come to grips with the real case which he ought to face. It is one which we have already encountered in connection with Green's theory of human experience and it is the basis of my second line of criticism. Briefly summarized it is this. Critical reflection upon human experience and upon the part played in it by thought, leads to the conclusion that there is nothing given ready-made in human experience prior to and independent of the work of thought. There is something given but it is always something categorized and interpreted by thought, never a mere 'this'. There is something already there over and beyond our experience but what it is in itself, as distinct from what it is for us, we do not and cannot know. The nature and character of our experience indicates that there is a 'beyond', but of its positive nature we can have no knowledge. If we choose to call this 'beyond' ultimate reality, then we must say that we can have no positive knowledge of ultimate reality.

Bradley fails to do justice to this case in his opening statement. It is not a matter of asserting that reality is of such a kind that we cannot know it but rather that the nature and character of our experience is such that what we can know is of a certain kind. Nor does the doctrine that our knowledge cannot transcend appearance state the case properly. The case is that what we can know is always something categorized and interpreted by thought. To say this, is not to assert anything positive about the nature of what is already there apart from our experience but only to say something about our experience in general and its cognitive aspect in particular. But what is more important is that the case is not one which could be made at the outset of a metaphysical inquiry. It is itself the outcome of metaphysical inquiry. The proper objection to Bradley's programme of attempting to know ultimate reality is not that reality is unknowable but that the programme has been drawn up in a way which begs important metaphysical questions. If there is to be a metaphysical programme in advance of metaphysical inquiry at all, it must be drawn up in the most general and non-committal terms. We must start in metaphysics, not with a clear-cut problem, but with the aim of reflecting on our experience in all its wealth and variety to see what, if anything, we can learn about ourselves and our situation. By the time we are able to formulate even relatively clear-cut problems, a good deal of fundamental metaphysical thinking will already have been done. Bradley and Bosanquet start with a more or less clear-cut problem, and never give a satisfactory explanation of how and why they came to formulate it as they did.

3.   The doctrine that there is nothing given ready-made in human experience prior to and independent of the work of thought is, as we saw in Chapter 3, the foundation of Green's theory of the character and structure of human experience. It is significant not only as the basis of a case against Bradley's and Bosanquet's metaphysical programme, but also because of its implications for the general position of Idealism as a philosophy. In the next chapter I shall be concerned with this: here it may be useful to recall Green's conviction that knowing makes no difference to what is known. It was this conviction which led him to introduce the notion of the eternal consciousness into his theory of experience. I argued that there are two separate points involved in the idea that knowing makes no difference to what is known. The first is that, if there is to be knowledge, there must be something already there to be known. The second is that, whenever we have knowledge, what we know is unaffected by being known. In knowing it, we are knowing it as it is in itself when it is not being known. I argued that, while the first of these two points is inescapable, the second it not, and in the course of the present chapter I have elaborated this argument. There is however another point, consideration of which I have so far postponed, a point which indicates that there is, after all, something in the conviction that knowing makes no difference to what is known.

The argument which I put forward suggests that I am maintaining both that knowing does make a difference to what is known, and that this is compatible with the necessary condition of knowledge, that there should be something there to be known. But am I maintaining that all knowing makes a difference to what is known, or only that this is so in the case of some knowing? The former view involves a difficulty. If it is a fact that all knowing makes a difference to what is known, could this fact itself be known? To say that knowing does make a difference to what is known is to claim to know something about the character and structure of human experience, namely that it is of such a nature as to involve this consequence for knowledge. Now the character and structure of human experience is something which it has, as it were, in its own right. To know the character and structure of human experience is to have knowledge of something as it is in itself. It is to know something which, ex hypothesi, is unaffected by being known. It follows that, while there may be grounds for holding that some knowing makes a difference to what is known, there are none for holding that this is so in the case of all knowing. The latter view cannot be asserted without implicit self-contradiction, for to advocate it is to claim to have knowledge of the character and structure of human experience, and to claim at the same time that, in the case of such knowledge, what is known is unaffected by being known.

Now the doctrine that there is nothing given ready-made in human experience prior to and independent of the work of thought, does not involve maintaining that all knowing makes a difference to what is known. Nor does it violate the necessary condition of all knowledge, that there should be something already there to be known. Nor again does it deny that human experience points beyond itself, that there is something already there prior to and apart from all human experience. It asserts only that, so far as this independent reality is concerned, we cannot know it as it is in itself. This, however, is not to deny that there is something which is independent of our thought and our human thinking experience. As regards our human experience itself, our experience as rational agents, we can reflect on this and know it as it is in itself, both in its general character and structure and in its individual details, because it is not something which is independent of thought but is itself the work of thought. According to my doctrine, that is to say, knowing makes no difference to what is known, where what is known is our own experience as rational agents. But since we can only know that there is a sense in which some knowing makes a difference to what is known, if we already have knowledge where knowing makes no difference to what is known, it follows that the latter kind is fundamental. It is knowledge in the proper sense, while the former kind is only knowledge in a secondary derivative sense. From this it follows, according to the foregoing doctrine, that knowledge in the proper sense is self-knowledge, knowledge of human experience as regards both its general character and structure and its individual detail. This follows because only in the case of such knowledge does knowing make no difference to what is known. Now this conclusion is of some significance for the general position of Idealism as a philosophy and not least as regards its claims as a social philosophy. I therefore propose in the next chapter to elaborate it and to relate it to the general argument of this book.

CHAPTER VI

HUMANISTIC IDEALISM

A : KNOWLEDGE AS AN INTEGRAL PART
OF RATIONAL ACTIVITY

1. At the end of Chapter I of this book, I gave a provisional statement of the nature, aim and scope of philosophy. It was based on the account which I had previously given of the theory of rational activity and the notion of the concrete universal. I maintained that it is the business of philosophy to know and give an account of the rationality implicit in the various values and standards operative in human life. What gives the work a special character is that, owing to the logical structure of rational activity, the methods of classification and natural science are inappropriate. The philosopher must give his account not in terms of genera and species, or laws of nature, but in terms of the levels in a scale. But I pointed out that this was a provisional definition of philosophy and that it would have to be modified and reformulated as the argument of the book proceeded. In particular, I emphasized that it did not include the theory of the general character and structure of human experience, that such a theory was traditionally a part of philosophy and that it was demanded by the earlier argument of the chapter.

In Chapter III, the question of the nature and scope of philosophy arose in connection with Green's theory of morality. According to Green, if man is to know himself as a rational agent who is capable of knowledge and morality, it must be through philosophy and not through natural science. It was to support this contention that he devoted the first part of *Prolegomena to Ethics* to the exposition of a theory of the general character and structure of human experience, a theory the foundation of which was the doctrine that there is nothing given ready-made in human experience prior to and independent of the work of thought. He argued that human experience is thinking experience, and that it is only in so far as he thinks, that man is a rational agent who is capable of knowledge and morality. I pointed out that this implies that, in so far as human experience is the experience of rational agents, it must have the logical structure of rational activity. Each level of rationality is a level of human experience. On this view, my provisional definition of philosophy could be brought into line with traditional ideas of its nature and scope. The work of formulating a theory of the general character and structure of human experience leads on to the task of giving an account of the various levels of rationality which make up the experience of rational agents. Conversely, the latter task leads back to an inquiry into the general character and structure of human experience which makes possible the various levels of rationality implicit in the values and standards operative in human life, an inquiry which would take account of whatever form or forms of experience are presupposed by and are the foundation of the various levels of rationality.

At the end of the last chapter, I returned to a topic which had arisen in Chapter III, in connection with Green's theory of human experience. This was his conviction that there is knowledge only where knowing makes no difference to what is known. I pointed out that this conviction must be right, at least in the case of some knowledge, and that it does not conflict with the doctrine that there is nothing given ready-made in human experience prior to and independent of the work of thought. According to that doctrine, what is independent of human experience cannot be known as it is in itself, but only as it is for us. In this case, knowing does make a difference to what is known. But in the case of self-knowledge, where what is known is not something independent of human experience but human experience itself, this is not so. Here knowing makes no difference to what is known.

Now if, as I have suggested, it is the task of philosophy to know human experience as regards both its general character and structure and the various levels of rationality which it includes, then philosophy is a form of knowledge in which knowing makes no diffcrence to what is known. Further, if there is a sense in which knowledge in this form is more fundamental than any in which knowing does make a difference to what is known, and if philosophy is the only form of knowledge which explicitly sets out to know human experience in a way which does justice both to its general character and structure and to its range and variety, it follows that there is a sense in which philosophy is the most fundamental form of knowledge. In the present chapter, I shall try to elucidate and develop this conception of philosophy. It is a conception to which all the Idealists adhered, but which they failed wholly to disentangle from other ideas. Prominent among the latter, as we saw in the last chapter, is the view that it is the task of philosophy in the form of metaphysics to know ultimate reality, or reality as a whole. What I shall be attempting, in other words, is to expound the conception of philosophy at which the Idealists should have arrived if they had been wholly self-consistent in their work. On the whole, it was in their social philosophy that they came nearest to putting it into practice and it is a conception which must be made explicit if the significance of their work in that aspect of philosophy is to be understood.

To many contemporary English philosophers, the notion that philosophy is a form of knowledge will be unacceptable. According to the current doctrine, philosophy is an activity of analysis and clarification. It is not concerned with the acquisition of knowledge. I do not question the intellectual significance of much of the work of analysis and clarification which has been done in the name of philosophy in recent years. I question only the propriety of identifying this work with philosophy and of denying that there is anything else deserving of the name. In the rest of this section and the next, I shall mainly be concerned with certain features of knowledge in its non-philosophical forms. In the third, I shall try to elucidate the conception of philosophy as a form of knowledge. This procedure is necessitated by the nature of the conception of philosophy which I am trying to develop. It may also serve to indicate the respects in which my position, and, I should add, the position implicit in Idealism, differs from the current doctrine.

2.   All rational activity is cognitive: at every level of rationality, knowledge is indispensable. But the systematic pursuit of
knowledge, as e.g. in natural science or history, is itself a
rational activity. On the one hand, knowledge is an integral
part of rational activity: on the other, its acquisition may be
made the purpose of rational activity. But knowledge which is
acquired through rational activity cannot be identical with
knowledge which is an integral part of rational activity. There
must be a difference, and discussion of it will occupy us in one
way or another throughout the remainder of this section. I will
begin with the knowledge which is an integral part of rational
activity. This topic has been touched on in earlier chapters. It
arose implicitly in Chapter I, and explicitly in Chapter III in
connection with Green's distinction between the two senses of
the question: 'what ought to be done?'. But so far what has been
said about it has mainly concerned the higher levels of rationality, those of self-consistent human achievement and spheres
of rational activity. I want now to consider it in connection
with the lower levels and will return to the higher levels later.

At the level of ends and means, the rational agent must have
knowledge of the ways in which his various ends may be
brought about. At the level of private self-satisfaction, he must
know enough to enable him to develop a satisfying way of
living in the circumstances in which he finds himself. At the
level of morality, he must have the knowledge necessary for
observing the rules and customs of his society. This suggests
that the knowledge which is an integral part of rational
activity at these levels is practical rather than theoretical. In
terms of the distinction drawn by Gilbert Ryle in *The Concept
of Mind*, it is a matter of 'knowing how . . .' rather than of
'knowing that . . .'. But, while there is truth in this, it is important to realize that no knowledge can be purely practical
without being in part theoretical as well. Every case of 'knowing how . . .' involves some 'knowing that . . .'.

The rational agent who knows how to bring about his ends,
knows that he is an agent who has these particular ends. He
knows that he is in a world in which there are things which can
be handled, manipulated and exploited as means for the bring-

ing about of ends.* He knows what some of these things are and something of their specific properties. If he knows enough to develop a satisfying way of living, he knows something more about himself and his circumstances. He knows that he is an agent with certain capacities and limitations. He knows something of the various pursuits and activities which are possible for one having these capacities and limitations and something also of the different kinds of experience which they afford. If he knows how to observe the rules and customs of his society, he knows what these rules and customs are, that there is a society of which they are the rules and customs and that he is a member of that society. All this is theoretical rather than practical knowledge. It is a matter of 'knowing that . . .' rather than of 'knowing how . . .'. But the point is not that the rational agent must have the theoretical knowledge before he can have the practical. It is that, in acquiring the practical, he at the same time acquires the theoretical. In coming to 'know how . . .' he simultaneously comes to 'know that . . .'. The knowledge which is an integral part of rational activity at these levels is at once practical and theoretical. These are two aspects of it which can be distinguished but not separated. Although the practical aspect is prominent while the theoretical is more or less latent, they are both always present.

It is necessary, however, to take into account two important aspects of rational activity. It is the activity of self-realization and it is always social activity. So far as self-realization is concerned, the point to notice is that the acquiring of the knowledge which is an integral part of rational activity is itself part of the process of becoming a rational agent. Becoming a rational agent involves learning how to act rationally and learning how to act rationally involves acquiring the necessary knowledge. But becoming a rational agent is a process which can never be completed. Self-realization is achieved through a way of living and a way of living is something which is always in the making. One never finishes learning how to act rationally and there is

* Strictly speaking, according to the argument of Chapter I, section B, subsection 3 of this book, it is activities of exploitation, not the things which are exploited, which are the means for bringing about of ends. The rational agent, however, at the level of ends and means will not normally draw this distinction, and for this reason, as well as for the sake of brevity and smoothness of exposition, ordinary language is preferable in the present context.

always more knowledge to be acquired. The social aspect of rational activity introduces rather more complex considerations. At every level of rationality, the rational agent is to some extent conscious of himself as a social being. Why this is so has at least in part already been indicated in Chapter I. A further consideration of the point will however be instructive in the present discussion.

3. The rational agent becomes conscious of himself as a rational agent through his rational activity. The development of rational self-consciousness is part of his process of becoming a rational agent. Each level of rationality constitutes a distinct level of rational self-consciousness. There is a scale of rational self-consciousness corresponding to the scale of rationality. But rational self-consciousness, even at the lowest level, is not developed out of nothing. It presupposes and is a development of lower levels of self-consciousness. Only a subject who already has some consciousness of himself as a distinct person can become conscious of himself as an agent having purposes and plans of his own. Personal self-consciousness is possible only for a subject who is already conscious of the distinction between self and what is other than self. Rational self-consciousness presupposes personal self-consciousness and personal self-consciousness presupposes primary self-consciousness, the bare consciousness of a distinction between self and other. There is a scale of self-consciousness which includes the various levels of rational self-consciousness but also contains lower levels which are pre-rational.

The various levels in the scale of self-consciousness are related to each other in the same way as the various levels in the scale of rationality. Each level in the scale sums up and includes those below it. At the level of personal self-consciousness the subject is conscious of himself as a distinct person. He is also conscious of other persons whom he can identify and distinguish from each other and from himself. Personal self-consciousness is always social consciousness. It is the consciousness of onself as one person among other persons. But the lower level of primary self-consciousness survives within the higher level of personal self-consciousness although in modified form. The bare consciousness of the distinction between self and other has now become the consciousness of the distinction between oneself as a person and other persons. But, in addition, there is also the consciousness of the distinction between the world of persons and what is other than personal. This consciousness of what is impersonal is the consciousness of what comes between oneself and other persons. It is the awareness of the environment within which the world of persons is.

But it is only at the level of morality that the social side of the rational agent's self-consciousness is directly relevant to his rationality. At the level of ends and means, to be rational is to be efficient. At the level of private self-satisfaction it is to make the development of a personally satisfying way of living the guiding principle of all one's conduct. It may be possible for a person to be efficient and to develop a satisfying way of living without being moral. Such a person would observe the rules and customs of his society only when it was in his self-interest to do so. His achievement of rationality would be confined to the level of private self-satisfaction. He would be realizing himself as a rational but not as a social agent. His rational self-consciousness would not include any awareness of personal responsibilities as a member of a society. But his rational self-consciousness would still have a social side. It would include the pre-rational awareness of himself as a person in a world of persons. But the rationality which he achieves does not include any development of this awareness. His rational self-consciousness, being confined to the level of private self-satisfaction, does not add to his social consciousness.

Whether in fact anyone can develop a personally satisfying way of living without also developing at least some loyalty to some human group or association and there achieving some degree of morality, is a question which need not be pursued here. What we have now to notice is the connection between self-consciousness and knowledge. Each level of rationality, I have said, is a level of rational self-consciousness. But there is a sense in which each level of rationality is a level of knowledge, for at each level there is involved the knowledge which is an integral part of rational activity at that level. At the level of ends and means, the rational agent knows that he is an agent who wants to bring about certain ends; at the level of private self-satisfaction, he knows that he is an agent with certain capacities and limitations; at the level of morality, he knows that he is a member of a certain society. At each level, this 'knowledge that . . .' is his consciousness of himself as a rational agent.

But this account leaves out levels below rational self-consciousness. At these pre-rational levels, there is always consciousness of what is other than self as well as of self. Each level in the scale of self-consciousness sums up and incorporates those below it. Thus at the levels of rational self-consciousness there is consciousness of what is other than self, since these levels include the pre-rational levels of primary and personal self-consciousness. At the level of ends and means, the rational agent knows that he is in a world of things which can be handled and exploited as means. At the level of private self-satisfaction, he knows that there are certain activities which are possible and which yield certain kinds of satisfaction. At the level of morality, he knows that there is a certain society with a certain body of rules and customs. At each level, this 'knowledge that . . .' is his consciousness of what is other than self.

Thus my statement that, at a given level of rationality, the rational agent's self-consciousness is an aspect of the theoretical side of the knowledge which is an integral part of rational activity at that level, is not strictly correct. Since self-consciousness is always consciousness of what is other than self as well as of self, rational self-consciousness at a given level of rationality is strictly speaking equivalent to the whole of the theoretical side of the knowledge which is integral to that level. But, since in speaking of rational self-consciousness the intention is normally to place the emphasis on self rather than what is other than self, it is not unreasonable to equate rational self-consciousness with an aspect of the theoretical side of the rational agent's knowledge, namely his knowledge of himself as a rational agent. There is no harm so long as it is realized that what is other than self is not excluded from rational self-consciousness but that the emphasis is placed on self. In fact, the rational agent's self-consciousness at a given level of rationality and the theoretical side of the knowledge which is an integral part of rational activity at that level are one and the same thing, but in the first case the emphasis is upon self and in the second upon what is other than self. We can speak in terms of one or the other according to which side we wish to emphasize.

4. It follows from this argument that the various levels of rational self-consciousness constitute a scale of levels of knowledge. It consists of the theoretical side of the knowledge which is an integral part of rational activity at each level of rationality. At each level, the lower levels of this knowledge are incorporated but in a form appropriate to that level. But rational self-consciousness, we have seen, presupposes pre-rational levels of self-consciousness. If we regard the various levels of rational self-consciousness as a scale of knowledge, then we must regard the pre-rational levels of self-consciousness as pre-rational levels of knowledge. Although this may sound rather paradoxical, it amounts only to saying that the knowledge which is an integral part of rational activity at least on its theoretical side is not developed out of nothing. It pre-supposes and is developed out of knowledge which is prior to all rational activity.

It might seem, however, as if we had overlooked the point that the theoretical side of the knowledge which is an integral part of rational activity is subordinate to its practical side. The rational agent comes to 'know that . . .' through coming to 'know how . . .'. But this relation is a feature of the pre-rational levels of self-consciousness. Regarded as levels of knowledge, they are at once practical and theoretical and in each case the practical side is primary, the theoretical secondary or subordinate. Thus the practical side of primary self-consciousness, the bare consciousness of the distinction between self and what is other than self, is the activity of attention. It is through the practical activity of attention that the subject becomes conscious of the distinction between self and other. Without it, the distinction would not be drawn and there would not even be primary self-consciousness. At the level of personal self-consciousness, the practical work of attention is supplemented by the activity of identification* and, as the subject's capacity develops, communication. It is as he becomes able to recognize

---

* Embryonic identification is already at work at the level of primary self-consciousness but it is negative only, being the mere identification of what is other than self as 'something which is not self'.

other persons, to distinguish them from himself and from each other, and in a embryonic way to communicate with them, that the subject becomes conscious of himself as a person in a world of persons. He is not yet capable of rational activity but he already has a rudimentary form of knowledge which is at once practical and theoretical and without such knowledge he could not go on to determine himself as a rational agent.

The important point to notice is that at no level of self-consciousness, either pre-rational or rational, and therefore at no level of knowledge, is there anything given ready-made prior to and independent of the work of thought. Bradley's doctrine of the 'what' and the 'that' may be conveniently adapted to express the point. At every level of self-consciousness, we never merely 'know that . . .', we always also 'know what . . .'. We always, that is to say, have some idea, however provisional and indefinite, of what it is that we are conscious of. At the primary level of self-consciousness this 'knowing what . . .' is so rudimentary as to be almost non-existent. It is merely the bare awareness of what is different from self and apart from this lacks all determinateness. But even this bare consciousness of difference involves thought in its most primitive form. The 'other' which the subject is conscious of at this primary level is not some independent reality as it is in itself apart from the work of thought. It is something as it is for thought. It is what the subject's thought is able to make out and present to him at this level. What is true at the primary level of self-consciousness is true of every higher level. What we know is never something as it is in itself apart from human experience but always something as it is for human experience and therefore for consciousness and for thought. This is not to deny that there is always a 'given' character about our consciousness at each level. It is only to insist that we are always conscious of what is given as mediated through our thought. In this connection, the activity of communication which first begins at the level of personal self-consciousness is of special significance. In learning how to communicate, the subject learns how to think in terms of systems of ideas and thus to expand the range of his consciousness. Each level above personal self-consciousness involves a development of the systems of ideas already at work at lower levels.

It is in connection with the theoretical side of the knowledge which is an integral part of rational activity at the level of ends and means, that the doctrine of the last paragraph is at variance with every-day common sense ideas. At this level, the rational agent knows that he is an agent who wants to bring about certain ends. He also knows that he is in a world of things which can be handled, manipulated and exploited as means. We normally regard this world as an independent reality, something which is already there prior to and independently of rational activity and indeed of human experience altogether. So far as the individual rational agent is concerned, this common sense conviction is quite correct. So far as he is concerned, the world of things which can be exploited as means is already there and is independent of his private experience. But it is not independent of all rational and all human experience. It is already there so far as the individual rational agent is concerned because it is an aspect of the experience of other rational agents who are already engaged in rational activity before he begins. From the private standpoint of the individual rational agent, rational activity is already there or, more accurately, already going on, independently of his own personal achievement of it.

What the rational agent knows then, when he knows that there is a world of things which can be handled, manipulated and exploited as means, is not something as it is in itself independently of human experience. On the contrary, what he knows is an aspect of human experience, in particular an aspect of the experience of rational agents engaged in rational activity at the level of ends and means. I said in the last chapter that human experience is not self-maintaining or all-inclusive, that it does seem to point beyond itself. My point there and here is that we never know ultimate reality as it is in itself but only as it is for our experience. What we know as a world of things which can be exploited as means, no doubt is part of some larger reality but what it is as belonging to that reality we cannot know.

So far we have been discussing knowledge which is an integral part of rational activity and what this knowledge presupposes. We have seen that it is knowledge which is at once practical and theoretical and that the practical side is prior, the theoretical side is secondary. We come to 'know that . . .' through coming to 'know how . . .'. But we have yet to consider the knowledge which may be made the purpose of rational activity, e.g. natural science and history. Such knowledge is at least predominantly theoretical in character. We aim at coming to 'know that . . .' rather than at coming to 'know how . . .'. We can now see that the roots must lie in the theoretical aspect of rational activity. In the pursuit of it, rational activity turns back upon itself as it were, and attempts to expand and develop what is already an integral part of itself. We can also see that such knowledge, because of its origins in rational activity cannot escape from its characteristic limitations. It can never be knowledge of an independent reality as is in itself apart from human experience. It can only be knowledge of our human experience.

B : KNOWLEDGE AS THE OBJECT OF RATIONAL ACTIVITY

I. As examples of the knowledge which may be made the purpose of rational activity, I have cited natural science and history. They are highly developed forms of such knowledge. In this section I shall propound a thesis about each of them. But these theses are not intended to be complete theories of science and history. What I have to say in each case is strictly relevant to the purpose of this chapter. That purpose, it will be recalled, is to sketch the conception of philosophy which I believe to be implicit in Idealism. We have already seen something of this conception in previous chapters. Its nucleus consists of the notion of the concrete universal and the theory of rational activity expounded in Chapter I, together with the theory of the character and structure of human experience which we first encountered in Chapter III in connection with the work of T. H. Green. At the beginning of the present chapter I tried to sum up the result of preceding discussions and suggested the conclusion is that there is a sense in which philosophy is the most fundamental form of knowledge. My theses about science and history are intended to elucidate this conclusion.

I will begin with natural science. Its roots lie in the theoretical knowledge which is necessary for rational activity at the level of ends and means. At this level, the rational agent knows that he is in a world in which there are things which can be handled, manipulated and exploited as means. It is out of this knowledge that natural science is developed. What for the rational agent at the level of ends and means is a world of things to be exploited, for the scientist becomes a world of things to be classified and analysed and of events to be correlated and systematized, not for the sake of applying knowledge to the realization of ulterior ends but simply for the sake of knowing more about the world. The pursuit of knowledge has become the purpose of his rational activity.

I have tried to characterize the essence of the scientific attitude and to indicate its genesis. Certain amendments and qualifications however are necessary. I have said that the scientist's world is a world of things to be classified and analysed and of events to be correlated and systematized. In a sense, so also is the rational agent's world at the level of ends and means. He too classifies and analyses, correlates and systematizes. But he does so in order to discover how to bring about his various ends. What the scientist does is to develop, for its own sake, a way of knowing, initially developed in the course of rational activity at the level of ends and means. I said also that the scientist aims at clarifying, organizing and expanding what he already knows as an integral part of his rational activity at the level of ends and means. The emphasis perhaps should be on 'expanding'. Not only is the scientist not tied down to what he already knows as means to his ends, he is not restricted to any scheme of classification or types of events. His world is a world of whatever can be classified and analysed, correlated and systematized. Finally, it is important to remember that the scientist qua scientist is not a philosopher. Like the rational agent at the level of ends and means, he regards his world as an independent reality, something which is already there independently of human experience. As a scientist, he takes it for granted that what he knows is something to which no difference is made by being known. The things which he classifies and analyses, the events which he correlates and systematizes, exist and happen whether or not anyone knows about them.

2.   My thesis about natural science is a thesis about what it is the scientist really knows through his work as a scientist. We have seen that the roots of science lie in the theoretical side of rational activity at the level of ends and means. We have seen in the last section that this is not knowledge of anything as it is in itself, apart from human experience. It is knowledge of an aspect of human experience, of an aspect namely of the experience of all rational agents. Apart from the experience of rational agents, there is no such world. The scientist's world is developed out of the rational agent's world of things which can be exploited as means. Since it is developed out of what is an aspect of human experience, it cannot be a reality independent of human experience, scientific opinion to the contrary notwithstanding. If the scientist's world is not what he takes it to be, what does he really know as the result of his work? My thesis is that what he knows is always something of the following kind: that if he performs certain precisely specified operations in precisely specified circumstances, certain precisely specified events will happen, events which he will be able to experience. According to this thesis, the complex body of classificatory schemes, scientific laws and theories which is the result of the work of science, is really a complex of systems of ideas in terms of which scientists can specify sets of operations and predict what will be experienced when they are carried out.

The view of science contained in my thesis has something in common with two doctrines: Phenomenalism and Instrumentalism. As I understand it, according to Phenomenalism, these schemes, laws and theories form systems of ideas in terms of which scientists can specify sets of operations and predict the sensations which will be experienced when they are carried out. But according to my thesis, what is predicted is never merely sensations as such but observations, e.g. pointer-readings. The experience of observing a certain pointer-reading is not merely the experience of having certain sensations, although it certainly involves having sensations. It is an experience which is possible only for rational agents. But Phenomenalism makes no reference to rational activity and seems not to recognize the significance of the work of thought in human experience. As regards Instrumentalism, there is no difference from my account of what it is that scientists know as the result of their scientific work. But there is a difference as regards the essence of the scientific attitude. For Instrumentalism, as I understand it, the scientist is interested in specifying operations and predicting the experiences which follow them only for the sake of applying this knowledge to the bringing about of ends which arise outside science. The scientist, that is to say, is still only the rational agent at the level of ends and means, although he is now a much more efficient and competent one. But, according to my view, the scientist is more than this. What animates him is not merely the desire to increase his efficiency, but the desire to acquire knowledge for its own sake. As a scientist, he does not grasp the real nature and significance of the knowledge which he acquires, since he puts the emphasis on the things and events which he classifies and correlates rather than on the operations and the results which follow them. But this does not alter the fact that his aim is knowledge and not practical skill.

It follows from my thesis that scientific knowledge is knowledge of an aspect of human experience. It is the same aspect as that which is known through rational activity at the level of ends and means but through the work of science, knowledge of it is expanded and enlarged. What the scientist knows is not merely the by-product of the practical work of bringing about particular ends but is the result of deliberate systematic activity. But it may be objected that even if my thesis is compatible with those sciences which are devoted to the discovery of natural laws, e.g. physics and chemistry, it is inapplicable to the quasi-historical natural sciences, e.g. geology, paleontology and certain parts of astronomy. The point about these sciences, it may be said, is that they afford knowledge of what is inherently independent of human experience because prior to the existence of human life. Much of geological knowledge e.g., is knowledge of a state of affairs before man evolved as a distinct species, while parts of astronomy are concerned with past events which were independent not only of human but of all life.

My reply to this objection is to repeat once more that the doctrine that we cannot know anything as it is in itself apart from human experience does not involve denying that there is something beyond our experience. On the contrary, our experience points beyond itself to something which we cannot experience and cannot know as it is in itself. The geological past and the astronomical past are conceptions in terms of which we think about what lies beyond our experience. But in thinking in terms of these conceptions, we do not gain knowledge of something as it is in itself apart from human experience. The accounts of part series of events given by geology and astronomy are not literally true. They do not tell us about past events as they really were but of how they would have been for us had we been able to experience them although, ex hypothesi, we could not have experienced them. The significance of these ways of thinking about what lies beyond our experience is that they enable scientists to enlarge the scope of their work. By thinking in terms of them, scientists can precisely specify many more sets of operations and the predictable experiences which follow them. The essence of the quasi-historical natural sciences is that they extend the theoretical framework within which science is carried on and so increase the range of science.

I have said that scientific knowledge is enlarged and expanded knowledge of the same aspect of human experience which is known through rational activity at the level of ends and means. It follows that, for knowledge of human experience which will do justice to its range and variety and at the same time exhibit its general character and structure, we need something more than science. We shall not get this knowledge by thinking in terms of the categories and theories of natural science, for these categories and theories are relevant only to the purposes of science. The scientist, we have seen, is a rational agent who already has the knowledge which is an integral part of rational activity at the level of ends and means. He cannot however gain knowledge of himself as a rational agent through science. The roots of science lie in the knowledge of the world of things which can be exploited as means. The scientist reflecting upon what he already knows as a rational agent at the level of ends and means, places this world in the focus of his attention. He does not qua scientist take account of his consciousness of himself as a rational agent. He takes account of himself only as one more thing in the world of things which can be exploited as means. The categories and theories in terms of which he classifies and analyses, correlates and systematizes, do not add to his knowledge of himself as a rational agent; nor do they directly afford knowledge of the general character and structure of human experience. What they do is to enable him greatly to increase his knowledge of possible sets of operations and the experiences which follow them. This is certainly an increase of his knowledge of human experience but it is an increase, as it were, on the same plane. It does not deepen and broaden it.

But to say that something more than science is necessary for adequate knowledge of human experience is not to disparage science. For the sake of expository convenience, I have spoken above of 'the scientist'. But, in fact, natural science in its developed modern form is a great co-operative enterprise, a social as well as an intellectual achievement. We have seen in earlier chapters that as a rational activity it belongs to the highest level of rationality, that of self-consistent human achievement. Its work is of general human significance, for the aspect of human experience which it explores is relevant to all rational activity. Regarded as an achievement of critical intelligence embodying disciplined imagination, insight and tenacity, it is one of the great human triumphs. To say that, as knowledge, it is confined to an aspect of human experience is in no way to question its status as an achievement of rationality.

3. From natural science I turn to historical knowledge.* By 'historical knowledge' I mean knowledge of the human past as distinct from the quasi-historical natural sciences. The roots of historical knowledge lie in the rational agent's self-consciousness. At the level of ends and means, he knows not only that he is a rational agent but that he is a rational agent who lives through time. At any given moment, he knows that he is engaged in trying to bring about certain future states of affairs and that he has already taken certain steps and must now take others to realize these ends. At the level of private self-satisfaction, this temporal aspect of his self-consciousness is increased.

* The reader familiar with Collingwood's work in the philosophy of history will recognize my indebtedness in what follows. But my doctrine is not identical with that of *The Idea of History* and in some respects is closer to that outlined in *Speculumentis*.

His knowledge of how to live in a satisfying way includes his knowledge of his own past activities and of the experiences which they afforded. At the level of morality, his knowledge of his own past includes at least some knowledge of the past of those members of his society with whom he is in intimate contact. In Chapter I, section 4, sub-section 1, when elucidating the notion of the concrete universal, I pointed out that all rational activity is activity in a historical situation. It is to act in a situation in which rational activity is already going on, a situation which is what it is as the result of past rational activity. The rationality of any course of action must be assessed with reference to the historical situation in which it was done. The knowledge which is an integral part of rational activity always includes some knowledge of the relevant historical situation. This knowledge forms part of the rational agent's self-consciousness on any given occasion.

The essence of the historical attitude is an interest in past rational activity not merely for the sake of current action but for its own sake. The historian is a rational agent who, reflecting upon what he already knows about past action through his own rational activity, sets out to increase his knowledge of it. He has become aware that the historical situation which he knows as an integral part of his current rational activity is only the latest phase of a past process of rational activity which seems to stretch back indefinitely. He sets himself the task of finding out in detail what some of the earlier phases of that process were. This attitude is possible only for one who already knows how to live as the member of a society. Unless he had already gained, through his current rational activity, some knowledge of the past rational activity of other agents besides himself, the idea of a process of rational activity stretching back into the remote past could not arise. The historian, that is to say, is a rational agent who must have already achieved rationality at the level of morality and gained some social experience.

No doubt the historian will already have become acquainted with traditional ideas about the past in the course of learning to live as a member of his society. But he is interested not in traditional beliefs but in knowledge. He wants to base his ideas about the past not on tradition, hearsay or legend but on evidence. His aim is to make an intellectual reconstruction of the various phases of the past process of rational activity on the basis of the evidence of these phases, which has survived into the present. This evidence takes the form of documents, artifacts, buildings and even customs and rituals, all of which originated in past ages. It is through inference from these relics that he must make his reconstruction. The world of things which can be exploited as means becomes, for the historian, a world in which there are things which have been exploited as means and which have been used as material components of ways of living. For the individual historian, as for the individual rational agent, these things are independent realities. They are already there, prior to and apart from his experience. But they are not prior to and independent of all human experience. They are the products of rational activity and it is only because he is a rational agent already participating in rational activity that they can enter the historian's experience. They belong to a world which has its being within the experience of rational agents and which exists just so long as there is rational activity.

4. From the standpoint of the doctrine that we cannot know anything as it is in itself independently of and apart from human experience, historical knowledge presents no difficulties. The historian sets out to know in detail the past process of rational activity. Historical knowledge, in so far as it is attained is knowledge of human experience. But is it adequate as knowledge of human experience? Can we find in it what we failed to find in natural science, namely a form of knowledge which will do justice to the range and variety of human experience and, at the same time, exhibit its general character and structure? My thesis is that historical knowledge fails to meet these requirements. It is indeed a way of knowing human experience but the knowledge which it affords is partial and incomplete.

To appreciate the grounds for this thesis, we must return again to the argument of Chapter I. In section D, sub-section 1, I maintained that the concrete reality in rational activity is always an individual achievement of rationality. An individual achievement of rationality, it will be recalled, is always an achievement in terms of one of the levels in the scale of rationality. It is an action done as a means to an end, an activity carried out as a phase or moment in the development of a satisfying way of living, the discharge of some recognized obligation, or a contribution to some sphere of rational activity. The subject-matter with which the historian deals is past achievements of rationality. But is his way of knowing adequate for his subject-matter? In this connection we must recall another point from Chapter I. In order to know what an individual achievement of rationality is, it is necessary to evaluate it as an achievement. This means evaluating it as an achievement in the historical situation in which it was done. But it means also not merely evaluating it in terms of the level of rationality at which the agent was consciously acting but in terms of the highest level in the scale. This at least is necessary if the achievement is to be known for what it really is.

Now the historian is concerned with past individual achievements of rationality not as achievements of rationality but as constituting a temporal process. As we have seen, they always do constitute a temporal process. All rational activity is activity in a historical situation. On any given occasion, the rational agent finds himself confronted by rational activity which is already going on. The situation in which he has to act is what it is as the result of what he and other rational agents have been doing. The historian looks back to past situations. He tries to discover what they were and how one changed into another through the actions of the agents concerned. The process which he reconstructs is the process of these actions and the account which he gives of it is in terms of the beliefs, ideas, purposes and plans of the agents. The record of change which results from his work is a record of changing beliefs, ideas, purposes and plans, the changing beliefs, ideas, purposes and plans in terms of which successive generations of rational agents thought and acted. Moreover, the account which he gives is always of some definite activity which formed part of the life of a past society, e.g. its politics, its economy, its art or its science. This is because his concern is with what past agents believed themselves to be doing on given occasions which is always something in particular, however vague and confused their ideas may have been about it.

It is not the historian's task qua historian to evaluate the various actions which make up the past process of rational activity which he reconstructs. The account which he gives takes the following form. 'On a given occasion, an individual agent A, believing himself to be in a certain situation, pursues a certain course of action. This course of action appears to other agents B, C and D in the light of their respective beliefs about the situation, to be of a certain kind and to involve certain consequences. They therefore initiate courses of action which appear to A and to other agents E and F to call for further courses of action . . .' and so on. It is not the historian's business to evaluate these courses of action as individual achievements of rationality. He may personally consider them to have been wise or foolish, well-judged or ill-considered. He may think the beliefs of the various agents to have been prejudiced or erroneous, or again to have been well-informed and clear-sighted. But it is not his business to pass judgement. His concern is with what past agents on given occasions believed themselves to be doing when they acted, and with the process constituted by their actions. He accepts the various agents' own evaluation of their achievements because he is interested not in evaluating them but simply in what happened next as seen through their eyes.

But why should the historian not evaluate the past actions which he narrates? In practice, it may be said, most of them invariably do and are they not specially qualified to do so by virtue of their special knowledge of past situations? Now it may be recalled that, in Chapter I, section D, sub-section 2, in my provisional account of philosophy, I said that the work of evaluating individual achievements of rationality is the work of the critic. Every rational agent must to some extent be a critic. There is no reason why the historian should not turn critic and evaluate the actions he narrates as individual achievements of rationality. But it is essential to realize that, when he does so, he is no longer, strictly speaking, a historian. His evaluations imply a theory of rational activity and this theory is not the product of his historical work. It is something which he gets from elsewhere and when he uses it to evaluate past courses of action he is no longer speaking with the authority of a historian. But it would be a mistake to regard his evaluations as unfortunate lapses from the straight and narrow path of historical scholarship. The historian is himself living and acting in historical situations. He is a member of a particular society during a certain epoch in its life, and his work is addressed to his contemporaries. He must make his narrative intelligible to them and, in order to do this, he will find it necessay to evaluate as well as merely narrate. So long as he does not conceal the fact that he is evaluating and indicates at least the general standpoint from which he is doing it, there is no detraction from his work as an historian. It follows that there is a sense in which the much discussed distinction between fact and interpretation in history is significant. Fact is what the historian qua historian narrates. Interpretation is what he does as a critic, namely evaluate the facts. But it must be remembered that, on this view, interpretation is no longer part of the work of history proper but a necessary literary embellishment.

This distinction between fact and interpretation or between the historian qua historian and the historian qua critic, has a bearing on the question raised earlier: namely whether the historical way of knowing is adequate for its subject-matter. The subject-matter is past individual achievements of rationality. The historian qua historian does not know his subject-matter adequately. He does not know past individual achievements of rationality for what they really were but only as constituting a temporal process. So far as the rationality of the actions which he narrates is concerned, he accepts the verdict of the agents who did them or were affected by them. On the other hand, while the historian qua critic does attempt to know his subject-matter in a way which is in principle adequate, for he does evaluate the actions which he records, it remains an open question whether the theory of rational activity in terms of which he evaluates is an adequate theory. This question takes us out of the province of historical knowledge. We must regard historical knowledge properly so-called as the way of knowing of the historian qua historian, not of the historian qua critic. It follows that the knowledge of rational activity which can be gained through history is imperfect, being partial and incomplete.

From the standpoint of knowledge of human experience, history is equally defective. Its perspective is confined to what rational agents in the past believed about human experience. The historian qua historian does not ask whether they were

right or wrong. It is not his task to inquire into the presuppositions of rational activity or to elicit the character and structure
of human experience implicit in the activities whose history
he narrates. Yet what he knows, so far as it goes, is a form of
knowledge in which knowing makes no difference to what is
known. What he knows, the past process of rational activity in
terms of the beliefs and ideas of the agents concerned, is something which is already there and which, in principle, he can
intellectually reconstruct without in the process altering or
disfiguring it. What the historian knows, in other words, is
what he sets out to know. From this point of view, history is
more adequate as knowledge than science because what the
scientist knows is not what his categories and theories lead him
to suppose that he knows. Moreover, the historian's knowledge of human experience, although limited, is greater than
that of the scientist. His perspective includes that of the scientist
in the sense that, as the historian of science, he can trace the
process of scientific thought down to his own time and can
see it as the scientist qua scientist cannot, as the outcome of
intellectual endeavour. I do not however mean to suggest that
history is a greater intellectual triumph than science. From this
point of view, they both stand on the same level, that of self-
consistent human achievement.

C : PHILOSOPHY

1. According to the conception of philosophy summarized at
the beginning of this chapter, philosophical knowledge is knowledge of human experience. As we saw in the last section, the
same is true of natural science and history but the knowledge
which they afford of human experience is partial and incomplete. Philosophical knowledge is knowledge of human experience as the experience of rational agents and it includes
also knowledge of levels of experience below that of rational
activity. It is a way of knowing which exhibits the general
character and structure of human experience and does justice
to its range and variety. It is the most fundamental form of
knowledge in the sense that, in it, knowing makes no difference
to what is known and what is known, namely human experience, is known more adequately than in any other form of

H

knowledge. But, as the systematic pursuit of knowledge, philosophy no less than science and history, must have roots in the
knowledge which is an integral part of rational activity. To
discover these roots we must go to the higher levels of rationality, those of spheres of rational activity and self-consistent
human achievement.

At these levels, the rational agent directs his conduct in the
light of his judgement of the responsibilities which face him in
his work, his leisure, his personal relations, as a citizen and as
a member of the wider human community. Knowing how to
identify these responsibilities and how to assess their relative
importance on any given occasion is the practical side of the
knowledge which is an integral part of rational activity at these
levels. On its theoretical side, this knowledge involves knowing
something in detail of the current situation immediately confronting him in each of the various spheres of rational activity.
But it also involves knowing something of the value and significance of work, leisure, personal relations and citizenship for
human life. But the theoretical side of this knowledge remains
subordinate to the practical side. Here, as elsewhere, the
rational agent comes to 'know that . . .' through coming to
'know how . . .'. It is through his efforts to think out his
responsibilities for himself instead of relying on the prescriptions of established rules and customs that the rational agent
gradually gains knowledge of the value and significance of
work, leisure, personal relations and citizenship for human life.
It is through these efforts that he gradually comes to see them as
concentric spheres of rational activity within a way of life which
is in principle open to all rational agents. It is through these same
efforts again that he comes to see the value and significance of
activities like art, science, history and philosophy as distinctively
human achievements. But he does not articulate this knowledge
into systematic theory. It remains more or less implicit, being
expressed, if at all, only in the form of working conceptions in
the course of his efforts to think out the demands of the situations which confront him.

The roots of philosophy lie in the theoretical side of the
knowledge which is an integral part of rational activity at the
higher levels of rationality. The essence of the philosophical
attitude is the desire to know human experience as the ex-

perience of rational agents and to know it in a way which will do justice to all its facets and aspects. In coming to know the value and significance for human life of the various spheres of rational activity, the rational agent has implicitly adopted the philosophical attitude. He begins to philosophize when he becomes interested for its own sake in the theoretical side of what he already knows as an integral part of his rational activity and sets out to make it explicit in the form of systematic theory and to pursue its implications. From this point of view, he regards all the standards, values and general ideas in terms of which rational agents think and act as different forms of rationality and his aim is to discover the degree and kind of rationality they represent within the general structure of human experience. On the other side, his aim is to discover the general character and structure of human experience which makes possible the various kinds and degrees of rationality.

I have said there is a sense in which the perspective of historical knowledge includes that of natural science. Science, being a rational activity, has a history, and history includes the history of science down to its latest phase. The perspective of philosophy includes both science and history. Science and history are both distinctive human achievements. It is the proper task of philosophy to discover the nature and significance of each and the structure of human experience which makes them possible. Science, history and philosophy may be regarded as the three distinct levels of knowledge, each of which incorporates but goes beyond the perspective of the level below it. But, while philosophy is theoretical knowledge in its most complete and systematic form, there is a sense in which it too is impartial and inadequate. The knowledge which it affords to human experience is always knowledge of it in terms of some aspect which has been selected as the point of departure. Just as all history is the history of specific activities, e.g. of politics, economics, art and so forth, so all philosophy is the philosophy of some standard, value or idea which has been selected as the point of departure. It is always knowledge of the character and structure of human experience as revealed through morality, art, science, politics or whatever the point of departure may be. These various points of departure are not mutually exclusive. The theory of morality will have implications for the theory of knowledge, the theory of knowledge for the theory of art and so on. The account of the character and structure of human experience derived from one case must be compatible with that derived from another. In one sense, in coming to know a given standard, value or idea in terms of the character and structure of human experience, the philosopher always transcends his point of departure. But he never transcends it completely. His knowledge of human experience always retains something of his original angle of approach of his special point of departure.

Philosophy may also be characterized in terms of the notion of the concrete universal. The universals of science are abstract. Those of philosophy are not. They are the universal side of individual achievements of rationality. The universals of philosophy cannot therefore be analysed into genus and mutually exclusive species. They are forms of rationality and are related as levels in a scale of levels, each level in the scale summing it up to that point. This holds not only of explicit forms of rationality but also with forms of human experience in general. Human experience is the experience of rational agents. Its structure is the structure of the universal rationality, those forms which constitute pre-rational experience, e.g. primary and personal self-consciousness, being levels of experience below the levels of rationality but surviving in them. Failure to grasp the structure of rationality and to realize that its various forms constitute a scale of levels, emasculates the attempt to philosophize. The purely analytic philosophy current in the English-speaking world today is a case in point. As an intellectual activity it is not without interest. From the point of view of the logic of the abstract universal, its procedure is impeccable. But as philosophy proper, according to the conception here being expounded, it fails to qualify.

2.   There is another point which must be taken into account in considering the scope and limits of philosophical knowledge. The philosopher as a rational agent finds himself in a given historical situation. He is a member of a certain society and is already caught up in its life. The standards, values and ideas in terms of which that life is carried on have a history. In the past rational agents have thought and acted in terms of standards,

values and ideas which, if not wholly different from those currently in vogue, at least are not identical with them. In the course of the past process of rational activity, many shifts of emphasis have occurred. Some ideas have become obsolete, others have been expanded and developed. Some values have ceased to be important while others have come into prominence. Old standards have been applied to new contexts and have been reformulated and revised in the process. The current standards, values and ideas which confront the philosopher are part of the given historical situation in which he finds himself. They have come into being as the result of the gradual modification, adjustment and development of earlier standards, values and ideas. Even if, in some cases, they are formulated in the same terms, they are no longer understood in precisely the same way as in the past.

What are the implications of this historical aspect of his subject-matter for the philosopher? He is interested in standards, values and ideas as forms of rationality within the general structure of human experience. It is the permanent significance of moral rules and customs, work and leisure, personal relations and citizenship, art and science, that concerns him. While there is a sense in which the current standards, values and ideas of his society have a special claim upon him, a point to which I will return later, he must not confine his attention to them. He must know their history and the account which he gives of the general character and structure of human experience must be such as to make intelligible the kind and degree of rationality, embodied in the standards, values and ideas of past ages as well. As a political philosopher, he must come to know political life in a way which makes intelligible the standards, values and ideas of the city states of antiquity and of feudalism, in addition to those of the nation-state. As a philosopher of science, he must understand the kind and degree of achievement embodied in Aristotelian as well as modern natural science. The account which he gives of the character and structure of human experience must do justice to both and bring out the significance of the transition from the one to the other.

In this connection, it is important to realize that philosophy itself has a history. The philosopher, no less than the scientist and the historian, must build upon the work of his predecessors.

He must bring together the history of standards, values and ideas and the history of philosophical thought about them. But he must approach the latter not merely from a historical but from a philosophical point of view. He must look on it as a series of attempts to think out and come to know the permanent significance of standards, values and ideas and he must consider each attempt on its merits. He must ask, that is to say, of each past philosophy: how far does the general view of human experience, which it presents, make intelligible the kinds and degrees of rationality embodied in the various standards, values and ideas in terms of which in different ages rational agents have thought and acted? Inevitably, no one philosophy of the past will be adequate when judged from this point of view. Apart from other defects which it may possess, it will be limited by the author's inability to foresee future developments, so that he will not do justice to the standards, values and ideas of ages later than his own. It will be characterized by the perspective of the author's point of departure and will inevitably exhibit the limitations of the idiom of his age. But at the same time, it will also contain something positive which, so far as it goes, is genuine philosophical knowledge. It will make intelligible at least some of the standards, values and ideas in terms of which rational agents have thought and acted.

The philosopher must make a critical study of the history of philosophy in order to elicit the genuine philosophical knowledge which is embedded in the philosophies of the past. He must try to work out for himself a view of human experience which will incorporate this knowledge and, at the same time, go beyond it by making intelligible standards, values and ideas inadequately treated in past philosophies. His aim must be to sum up the history of philosophy in his own philosophy, purging it of its defects while preserving its achievements and at the same time adding to them. But these past achievements will not be preserved in their original form. They will be reformulated and integrated into his own view of human experience. His own philosophy, however, cannot escape the fate of the past philosophies which he has been criticizing. Even in the rather unlikely event of its appearing to his contemporaries to be the last word in philosophical development, it will eventually pass into the history of philosophy and become subject-matter for criticism by philosophers of the future. They must criticize it if they are to understand it. Inevitably they will find in it at least the defects which he found in the best of the past philosophies which he criticized. They must work out their own philosophies for themselves just as he has done. What he may hope is that they will find something of permanent significance in his work which, after being modified and restated, will be integrated into their philosophies.

I said that the philosopher, no less than the scientist and the historian, builds on the work of his predecessors. There is, however, a difference in the two cases. Scientists and historians build on the work of their immediate predecessors. This they must assimilate and criticize. But, in order to criticize it, they need not go further back to the work of previous generations. They can criticize it directly, in the one case through experimental tests and in the other through an examination of the evidence and the inferences based on it. As a result of this critical procedure, some of the work of their immediate predecessors will appear in various ways to have been erroneous. New problems will be posed and new questions suggested. In so far as there is continuity between one generation and the next, it follows that current work in science and history incorporates all the achievements of the past. But this happens automatically without conscious effort on the part of scientists and historians. The case of the philosopher is different. In assimilating and criticizing the work of his immediate predecessors, he cannot use experimental tests or historical evidence. He must assess it on its own merits by deciding how far it makes intelligible all the various standards, values and ideas in terms of which rational agents have thought and acted. If it does this with any degree of success, it will incorporate in itself the genuine knowledge contained in past philosophies. The philosopher must go back to these past philosophies and see how well it incorporates their achievements. Only if he does this, has he any independent check on the account given by his immediate predecessors.

The history of philosophy thus remains alive in current philosophy in a way in which the history of science and historiography does not in current work in these subjects. Scientists and historians have no need to ask whether the work of their immediate predecessors incorporates the achievements of earlier generations. To the extent that it withstands experimental tests and confrontation by evidence, it does so. The nature of the philosopher's task precludes experimental testing and confrontation by evidence. Among other things, he is concerned with a view of experience which must make intelligible the procedure of experimental testing and inference from evidence. But the success with which a given philosophy sums up the history of philosophy in itself is not the only relevant consideration in criticizing it. Equally important are self-consistency and freedom from ambiguity. A philosophy which contains internal inconsistencies may not, on that account alone, be lacking in all merit. It may be possible to reformulate the general view of experience which it presents in a way which will remove them. Again, along with inconsistencies which cannot be removed by reformulation, there may be genuine philosophical knowledge not to be found in any previous philosophy. Hume's philosophy, especially his theory of knowledge, is a case in point. What is then called for is a philosophical reconstruction which will incorporate the new insight without the attendant inconsistencies and, at the same time, preserve the achievements of earlier philosophies.

As regards ambiguity: a given philosophy may seem at first to have reached a view of the character and structure of human experience which incorporates the main philosophical achievements of the past, but, after examination of its positive doctrines, may be found guilty of ambiguity. English Idealism in the hands of Bradley and Bosanquet is a case in point here. The ambiguity lies in their notion of the concrete universal. What is then needed is a reconstruction which will remove the ambiguity and at the same time preserve the positive achievements both of the philosophy in question and of past philosophies. This book is intended to be a contribution to such a reconstruction of English Idealism. Its aim is to exhibit the main achievement of English Idealism, its social philosophy and, by reformulating the notion of the concrete universal in terms of the theory of rational activity, to purge away the ambiguities of the original notion. The conception of philosophy which I am here developing I call 'Humanistic Idealism' to distinguish it from the Absolute Idealism of Bradley and Bosanquet.

For the sake of simplicity, I have spoken in preceding paragraphs of 'the philosopher'. In fact, the work of philosophy is of a complexity and scale which necessitates co-operation and collaboration. By 'a philosophy', I do not necessarily mean the work of one man, although it may sometimes be that, but the work stemming from a distinct view of the character and structure of human experience. By a 'school of philosophy', I understand the collective work of a group of thinkers who share roughly the same general view of human experience and, in consequence, the same general conception of philosophy. But in this connection it is important to remember what was said at the end of the last sub-section. The view of experience presented in a given piece of philosophy, which is expounded on a given occasion, will always bear upon it the marks of its author's point of departure. It will be the view of experience which is revealed from the angle of the theory of morality, of art, of scientific or historical knowledge. What is traditionally called metaphysics is no exception. It represents the view of experience revealed by the consideration of what it is to know and what there is to know, both questions being taken together. Every view of experience is partial and incomplete, since it reflects the perspective of the angle of approach to it. What is important is not that futile efforts should be made to overcome this inevitable limitation but that the different views revealed by different angles of approach should be checked against one another and, where incompatibilities are revealed, efforts should be made to remove them by revising the theories in question.

3. Has philosophy, on the conception of it here being expounded, any practical significance? So far as the actual business of living is concerned, does it make any difference whether the work is done or not? Philosophical knowledge is knowledge of human experience as the experience of rational agents. In what way, if any, does it facilitate rational activity? We have already touched on these questions in Chapter III in connection with Green's theory of morality and its implications for moral practice. But, in the light of the discussion of the present

chapter, it is appropriate to consider them briefly again. In this connection, we must recall what has been said about individual achievements of rationality. Rational activity consists of individual achievements of rationality. To know what an individual achievement of rationality is, you must evaluate it as an achievement. This must be done with reference to the relevant historical situation. But if it is to be done fully and completely, it must be done in terms of the highest level in the scale of rationality. Making such evaluations is the work of criticism. Every rational agent must be a critic. In order to act rationally, you must, to the best of your ability, recognize current individual achievements of rationality for what they are.

One might describe the philosopher as the rational agent who is exploring and trying to know the basis of his own critical procedure. Will such knowledge make him a better critic? In so far as he knows something of the various levels of rationality within the general structure of human experience his evaluations of individual achievements of rationality will be less likely to be marred by irrelevance and one-sidedness. He will know that ultimately it is in terms of the highest level of rationality that a given achievement must be judged. He will therefore not be taken in by appeals to immediate considerations and interests however pressing these may be. His perspective as a critic will be enlarged by his philosophical knowledge. He will have a clearer idea on any given occasion of what sort of things to take into account and how much importance to attach to each of them. But it must not be forgotten that evaluations of individual achievements of rationality must always be with reference to their historical context. Knowledge is necessary of the intimate details of the situation and to this philosophy has nothing to contribute beyond emphasizing that it is necessary. Thus while philosophy can help the rational agent in his work as a critic, something more is necessary if that work is to be well done. In the terminology of this book, individual achievements of rationality are concrete universals. Philosophy is concerned with their universal rather than their concrete side although not denying but, on the contrary, affirming that they are both.

There is a sense in which criticism is the essence of all

rational activity. The rational agent appraises and criticizes his own and other people's conduct in the course of defining the situation in which on any given occasion he stands. He defines the situation so as to identify his responsibilities and decide what in particular he shall do. But this decision itself involves further criticism. The agent evaluates possible courses of action as individual achievements of rationality and decides upon that which embodies the highest achievement. As a rational agent it is his duty always to embark on that course of action which is the highest achievement of rationality open to him. In defining the situation, criticism is retrospective. In deciding what shall be done, it is prospective. But the principle in both cases is the same. Thus philosophy is not without practical significance both as regards defining the situation and deciding what shall be done. It is relevant to prospective criticism in the same way as it is relevant to retrospective criticism, namely in enlarging the critic's perspective. But no more in the case of prospective than in the case of retrospective criticism is philosophy by itself enough. Before the agent can evaluate possible courses of action as individual achievements of rationality, he must know what courses are possible. This involves knowing the consequences of various alternatives and has nothing to do with philosophy. In so far as it is defective, the agent's prospective criticism will be irrelevant.

In so far as it can help to make the rational agent a better critic, philosophy is not without practical significance. More generally, it can help us to understand better what we are trying to do as rational agents and how well we are doing it. But we must remember that philosophy as the systematic pursuit of knowledge has its roots in the knowledge which is an integral part of rational activity. In one sense the rational agent in his work as a critic always does his own philosophizing. When, in the course of identifying his responsibilities and deciding which on a given occasion is the strongest, he thinks out the value and significance for human life of the various spheres of rational activity, he is implicitly philosophizing. So far as the actual business of living is concerned, it is this implicit philosophizing that matters. To be of practical significance, academic philosophy, the systematic pursuit of philosophical knowledge, must influence it. No doubt, this influence can best be secured if academic philosophy is an integral part of higher education. In this connection a point touched on earlier becomes relevant. I said that current standards, values and ideas are of especial importance to the philosopher. They are so in the sense that they are the medium through which he must communicate with his non-academic contemporaries. As we have seen, he must not in his work confine his attention to them. But, if he is to have any practical influence, he must make them intelligible as forms of rationality and, in expounding his work, emphasis must be placed upon them. To do as much is indeed his social responsibility as a philosopher.

CHAPTER VII

BERNARD BOSANQUET'S POLITICAL PHILOSOPHY

A : THE REAL WILL

1. In Chapter V of this book I expounded and criticised the theory of the Absolute developed by Bradley and Bosanquet. I argued that it is not a tenable theory and that the error which gave rise to its lies in an ambiguity in the notion of the concrete universal as formulated by Bradley and Bosanquet and employed in their metaphysical writings. My point was that, when the notion of the concrete universal is properly understood and the distinction between a whole such an an organism and rational activity is grasped, the theory of the Absolute does not arise. The latter theory is not an integral part of Idealist philosophy but, on the contrary, arises from an error in the development of that philosophy. In the last chapter I attempted to sketch the outlines of a conception of philosophy based upon a consistent development of the central ideas in English Idealism, ideas which, in the course of preceding chapters, had already been examined and discussed. I contended that this conception of philosophy, which I called 'Humanistic Idealism', enables the genuine philosophical achievements of traditional Idealism to be preserved and in particular its achievements in social philosophy. In the present chapter, I shall try to substantiate this contention in connection with Bosanquet's political philosophy.

Boscanquet's best known work in political philosophy is his *Philosophical Theory of the State*, a book which was first published in 1899. In the opening chapters, he tries to make clear the nature of the task on which he is embarking and in particular what he means by a philosophical theory. 'It is assumed then for the purpose of a philosophical treatment,' he writes, 'that everything, and more particularly in this case the political life of man, has a nature of its own which is worthy of investigation on its own merits and for its own sake.'[1] Later he goes on to say that for philosophy, 'society is an achievement or utterance of human nature, of course not divorced from nature in general, having a certain degree of solidity so to speak i.e. being able, up to a certain point, to endure the tests and answer the questions which are suggested by the scrutiny of human life from the point of view of value and completeness. Is the social life the best or the only life for a human soul? In what way through society and in what characteristics of society does the soul lay hold upon its truest self or become in short the best that it has in it to be?'[2]

There is nothing in these statements of the nature and scope of philosophy to suggest the theory of the Absolute. Indeed the general position which they indicate is not unlike Humanistic Idealism. No doubt Bosanquet would say that from the standpoint of metaphysics, which for him is the theory of ultimate reality, the conclusions of political philosophy need to be modified. No merely human achievement, on the theory of the Absolute, is more than appearance. But we can take his political philosophy on its own merits and need not concern ourselves with the problem of interpreting it from the standpoint of the theory of the Absolute since, as we have seen, that theory is untenable and no part of a consistent Idealist position. This is not to say, however, that Bosanquet's political philosophy when taken on its own merits is not open to criticism. In fact, as we shall see, the ambiguity in the notion of the concrete universal which gave rise to the theory of the Absolute seems to have exerted a deleterious influence at certain points in Bosanquet's political philosophy. In this chapter I shall expound and criticize the essentials of his political philosophy. I shall be concerned for the most part with the argument of the *Philosophical Theory of the State* which is Bosanquet's most systematic and elaborate work in political philosophy. But I shall also refer to certain other writings at various points in order to bring out more clearly some features of his position.

2.   Bosanquet begins his main argument in the *Philosophical Theory of the State* with a criticism of the atomistic theory of

society which was the basis of the Utilitarian moral and political philosophy. All such doctrines he calls 'theories of the first appearance', and he says that they 'are characterized by accepting, as ultimate, the absolute and natural independent existence of the physical individual, and therefore regard government as an encroachment on the self, and force as an oppression'.[1] He argues that if human society is nothing but an aggregate of separate physical individuals, then morality and self-government are impossible. The view gives rise to what he describes as the paradoxes of ethical and political obligation. 'The paradox of ethical obligation,' he writes, 'starts from what is accepted as a self and asks how it can exercise authority or coercion over itself, how a metaphor, drawn from the relations of some persons to others, can find application within what we take to be the limits of an individual mind.'[2]

His point is simply that if authority and coercion is thought of solely in terms of physical force, as it is in theories of the first appearance, then it is impossible to see how a man can discipline and exercise control over himself. He can only discipline and control others against whom he can bring to bear physical force. Equally, it is impossible to see how there can be such a thing as self-government. 'The paradox of political obligation,' Bosanquet continues, 'starts from what is accepted as authority or social coercion and asks in what way the term "self", derived from the individual mind, can be applicable at once to the agent and patient in such coercion, exercised prima facie by some persons over others.'[3] The point here is that no society can be said to govern itself, if government and self are thought of in purely physical terms. There can only be the exercise of physical control and coercion by one group over another. There can be no such thing as political obligation any more than there can be such a thing as moral obligation. People simply do what they want unless and until they are forcibly restrained by other people. It is all a matter of physical force and nothing else. But this conclusion has been reached by starting with the conception of human society as nothing but an aggregate of separate physical individuals. Bosanquet therefore sets himself the task of developing a conception of society which will do justice to the political and moral life with which we are in practice familiar.

3.   It is in the doctrine of a real or general will that Bosanquet finds the basis of a theory of society which will make morality and self-government intelligible. He acknowledges Rousseau as the original exponent of the doctrine but thinks that the latter's account fails to bring out all its implications. His version is intended to be a clear and consistent statement of an idea only partially understood and imperfectly developed by Rousseau. He introduces it to the reader of the *Philosophical Theory of the State* in the following passage. 'A comparison of our acts of will through a month or a year is enough to show that no one object of action as we conceive it when acting exhausts all that our will demands. Even the life that we wish to live, and which on the average we do live, is never before us as a whole in the motive of any particular volition. In order to obtain a full statement of what we will, what we want at any moment must be at least be corrected and amended by what we want at all other moments and this cannot be done without also correcting and amending it so as to harmonize it with what others want, which involves an application of the same process to them. But when any considerable degree of such correction and amendment has been gone through, our own will will return to us in a shape in which we should not know it again, although every detail would be a necessary inference from the whole of wishes and resolutions which we cherish; and if it were to be supplemented and re-adjusted so as to stand not merely for the life which, on the whole, we manage to live but for a life ideally without contradiction, it would appear to us quite remote from anything which we know. Such a process of harmonizing and re-adjusting a mass of data to bring them into a rational state is what is meant by criticism and criticism, when applied throughout to the will, shows that it is not our real will or, in the plainest language, that what we really want is something more and other than at any given moment we are aware that we will, although the wants that we are aware of lead up to it at every point.'[1]

This passage can best be understood if we interpret it as an attempt by Bosanquet to expound the essentials of the theory of rational activity in terms of 'will'. Taken by themselves, our day to day acts of will, what Bosanquet sometimes calls our 'actual will', embody rationality at the level of ends and means.

When we attempt to amend and correct what we want at any one moment in the light of what we want at all other moments, we have moved to rationality at the level of private self-satisfaction. We are no longer thinking in terms of particular ends and means but of a satisfying way of living. When we go further and take account not only of our own wants but also of those of others, attempting to correct and adjust ours to harmonize with theirs, we have moved to the level of morality. We are now thinking in terms of a social, and not merely a privately satisfying, way of living. When Bosanquet says that : 'In order to obtain a full statement of what we will, what we want at any moment must at least be corrected and amended by what we want at all other moments and this cannot be done without also correcting and amending it so as to harmonize it with what others want . . .', he is emphasizing the social character of human personality. When we reflect on ourselves and our situation, we realize that a rational way of living must be a social way of living.

When Bosanquet says that : 'when any considerable degree of such correction and amendment has been gone through, our own will will return to us in a shape in which we should not know it again . . .' his point is that most of the time we consciously think and will in terms of particular ends and means. It is from this limited perspective that our real will, what we really want as rational and therefore social and moral agents, appears quite remote. But if, for most of the time, we think and act only at the level of ends and means, how is it possible for us to achieve a social way of living? Bosanquet's answer is that the laws, institutions and customs of a given society provide the frame-work of a social way of living for its members and that, by observing the rules and conventions which they embody, the members can live socially without having to go through a process of correction and amendment every time they act. The laws, institutions and customs of a given society, that is to say, provide a working formula for rational conduct. The members can concentrate the bulk of their attention on day to day problems of ends and means making sure only that they observe the rules and conventions of established laws, institutions and customs. In this way, their day to day acts of will are automatically corrected and amended so as to express their real will without explicit thought on their part.

'The laws and institutions of any community,' Bosanquet writes, 'are, so to speak, the standing interpretation of all the private wills which compose it and it is thus possible to assign to the general will an actual concrete meaning as something different at once from any private will and from the vote of any given assembly, and yet as standing on the whole for what the one and the other necessarily aim at sustaining as the framework of their lives.'[2] Bosanquet agrees that the established rules and conventions will themselves be imperfect from the standpoint of the real will. But in his view the important point to realize is that, although imperfect, they provide the individual agent with a much better indication of a social way of living than he could work out for himself on any given occasion of action. 'It is needless to observe,' he goes on, 'that such a representation of the real will is imperfect since every set of institutions is an imperfect embodiment of life and any given system of life is itself incomplete. It is more important to remember that, although always incomplete just as the system of sciences is an incomplete expression of truth, the complex of social institutions is, as we have seen, very much more complete than the explicit ideas which at any particular instant move any individual mind in volition'.[3]

This account of laws and social institutions suggests that what Bosanquet has in mind is something like rationality at the level of moral rules and custom. In saying that a complex of social institutions although an incomplete embodiment of life is 'very much more complete than the explicit ideas which at any particular instance move any particular mind in volition', he seems to be insisting that moral rules and customs embody a higher level of rationality than action at the level of ends and means. But is this all that he has in mind? His account of laws and social institutions is strongly reminiscent of Bradley's doctrine of the social self in *Ethical Studies*, the doctrine of 'My Station and its duties'. That doctrine, as we saw in Chapter II, conceals an uncertainty on Bradley's part about the higher levels of rationality. He fails to develop the theory of rational activity satisfactorily beyond the level of moral rules and customs and in particular fails to grasp the conception of spheres of rational activity. Is Bosanquet simply following

Bradley and repeating his errors? The fact that he shares the latter's notion of the concrete universal together with its ambiguity and repeats the same errors in metaphysics gives substance to the question. But, on the other hand, Bosanquet was a close student of Green's work in ethics and political philosophy and, as we have seen, Green avoids Bradley's errors and develops the theory of rational activity fully and consistently. If Bosanquet really understood Green, then surely he would not simply repeat Bradley's errors. In fact, his understanding of Green was imperfect and he does not seem ever to have realized that Green's theory of morality was essentially a criticism and development of Bradley's. He tends throughout all his social philosophy to oscillate back and forth between the doctrines of *Ethical Studies* and *Prolegomena to Ethics* without realizing the respects in which the two differ. It is here that the chief weakness in his work lies, a weakness which, as I shall suggest later, is ultimately due to the ambiguity in his notion of the concrete universal.

4. Green's influence on Bosanquet's political philosophy can be seen in the following passages from the *Philosophical Theory of the State*. Discussing the value and significance of social life he writes: 'In any case we have seen enough to suggest that society prima facie exists in the correlated dispositions by which a plurality of individual minds meets the need for covering the ground open to human nature by division of labour in the fullest sense.'[1] His point is that social life should be regarded as a co-operative way of living in which human potentialities are realized to the fullest possible extent. He then goes on to insist on the importance of the function of contributing to the realizing of human capacities. 'But we have further pointed out,' he writes, 'that the true particularization of the human universal does not necessarily coincide with the distinction between different persons and that the co-relation of differences and the identity which they constitute remain much the same whether they chance to fall within a single human being or are dispersed over several. The stress seems therefore to lie on the attainment of the true particularization which does justice to the maximum of human capacity rather than the mere relations which arise between the members of a

de facto plurality, not that the claim of human nature in any individual does not constitute a claim that it should be perfected in him but that its perfecting must be judged by a criticism addressed to determining real capacities and not by the accidental standards of a given plurality."[2]

In these passages Bosanquet is expressing in his own way the doctrine that the ultimate moral community is the community of mankind and that the highest standard of rationality is the level of self-consistent human achievement. From a superficial reading of his argument it might appear that he is denying value and significance to individual personality but this is not his intention. He is not maintaining that 'the presence of human nature in any individual does not constitute a claim that it should be perfected in him'. His point is that it is a claim to achieve the rationality of which the individual is capable and that it must be evaluated accordingly. Each individual, that is to say, is a rational agent in the making and is entitled to be treated as such. But individuals are variously and unequally gifted. In the social division of labour through which human capacities are realized the difference between functions does not correspond to the difference between individual persons. Each man should perform those functions which he has the ability to perform. A gifted individual will be able to perform a variety of functions, another will find his personality in the performance of a few simple ones. What matters is that each should be able to make the best contribution of which he is capable to self-consistent human achievement, not that each should be subjected to uniform treatment.

All this suggests that the laws and institutions of a given society should be criticized and evaluated from the standpoint of self-consistent human achievement. How far do they enable the members of the society to realize the capacities which they possess? How far do they thwart or restrict the achievement of rationality by the members of other societies? Bosanquet seems to be committed to this doctrine by what he says about 'covering the ground open to human nature', 'the true particularization of the human universal', 'the attainment of the true particularization which does justice to the maximum of human capacities', and that 'the presence of human nature in any individual' constitutes 'a claim that it shall be perfected in him'. On this view, the real will is the will for self-consistent human achievement. Each level of rationality may be regarded as a level of will and at the highest level, that of the real or general will, the lower levels are summed up and incorporated in modified and revised form. Rational activity is not merely a matter of intellect. It is practical and this may be emphasized by expounding it in terms of volition. But, as we shall see later, Bosanquet does not consistently maintain this doctrine. There is no reason why the theory of rational activity should not be expounded in terms of the doctrine of a real or general will but Bosanquet's version cannot be regarded as a satisfactory rendering of it.

B : THE THEORY OF THE STATE

1. The doctrine of the real will was put forward by Bosanquet to solve the paradoxes of ethical obligation and self-government. These paradoxes arise in theories of 'the first appearance' which identify the self with the physical organism and government with force. For such theories, freedom is nothing but the absence of restraint. The doctrine of the real will however provides the basis for a deeper and more adequate theory of freedom. Bosanquet's theory of the state may be most conveniently approached through an examination of this theory of freedom. 'Liberty no doubt as Rousseau has told us,' he writes in the *Philosophical Theory of the State*, 'so far agreeing with Mill, is the essential quality of human life. It is so, we understand, because it is the condition of our being ourselves. But now that it occurs to us that in order to be ourselves we must always be becoming something which we are not, in other words, we must always recognize we are something more than we have become, liberty as the condition of our being ourselves cannot simply be something which we have, still less something which we have always had, a status quo to be maintained. It must be a condition relevant to our continued struggle to assert the control of something in us which we recognize as imperative or as our real self but which we only obey in a very imperfect degree.'[1]

Bosanquet's point is that to be free or at liberty is to be in a position to act rationally. But the value and significance of freedom depends upon how rational activity is conceived. For theories of 'the first appearance', rational activity is thought of simply in terms of ends and means and freedom is therefore merely the absence of restraint upon the agent's efforts to bring about his ends. But when it is realized that rational activity is something more than merely action at the level of ends and means, that it is the activity of rational self-realization and that there is a scale of levels of rationality, the conception of freedom as simply the absence of restraint upon the agent's attempts to bring about his ends is seen to be inadequate. To be free is to be in a position to realize oneself as a rational agent but everything turns on what being a rational agent is thought to involve. It is not merely a matter of bringing about particular ends which happen to be desired, but of trying to live and act in a certain way. As Bosanquet puts it, it is a 'continued struggle to assert the control of something in us which we recognize as imperative upon us or as our real self'. In terms of the doctrine of the real will, to be free is to be in a position to realize not merely our actual or day to day will, but our real will.

Bosanquet argues that freedom as the condition of being in a position to realize the real will is essentially a condition of mind. It is a matter of having reached a stage of moral and intellectual development at which one is not at the mercy of desires and impulses as they arise but is capable of self-discipline for the sake of acting in a socially responsible way. He proceeds to contrast this view of freedom with the absence of restraint theory. 'In the case of liberty conceived as a condition of the mind,' he writes, 'just as in the case of liberty conceived as the absence of physical menace or coercion on the part of other persons, the root of the matter is the claim to be determined only by ourselves. But in the literal case, what we mean by ourselves is the given self, the group of will and wishes, of feelings and ideas associated from time to time with my particular body; in short the casual, uncriticized mind as we experience it all day and every day.'[2]

In calling the absence of restraint theory 'the literal case', Bosanquet is following Green. The latter's point was that the absence of restraint theory reflects accurately the use of the word 'freedom' in every-day life. Describing his own theory of

freedom as the metaphorical case, Bosanquet continues: 'In
the metaphorical case, we have made so much progress in self-
criticism as to know at least that our self is something of a
problem. We know that the given self, the mind from day to
day, is not satisfactory and we throw the centre of gravity outside it and place the true self in something which we rather
want to be than actually are, although at the same time it is
clear that to some extent we are this something or we should
not want to be it.'[3] Bosanquet is in effect saying that if we take
seriously the notion that freedom is freedom for rational
activity, a notion which is implicit in the theories of 'the first
appearance', we shall be led beyond the conception of absence
of restraint on the attempt to bring about particular ends. To
be in a position to act rationally is to have attained the appropriate stage of moral and intellectual development. It is to be
free from the defects of character and the impediments of
ignorance which prevent the achievement of rational activity
at the level of morality.

In all this, Bosanquet is repeating the essentials of Green's
theory of freedom, the main outlines of which were traced at
the end of Chapter III of this book. According to this theory,
the scale of levels of rationality may be regarded as a scale of
levels of freedom. The man who is capable of rational activity
at the level of morality is more free than the man who is only
capable of achieving the level of private self-satisfaction
because he has a more adequate conception of his self and his
situation and is less subject to the restraints of ignorance and
caprice. To the man who is only capable of rational activity at
the level of private self-satisfaction, the rules and customs of
his society appear as irksome restraints upon his attempt to
achieve a personally satisfying way of living. Equally the man
who is capable of achieving the higher levels of rationality is
more free than the man who is limited to the level of customary morality. He is no longer at the mercy of the arbitrary
element in established rules and customs and is able to criticize
them, obeying them not blindly but because he understands
the reasons for them. There is a sense in which freedom at
every level of rationality is the absence of restraint. The error
of the theories of 'the first appearance' lies in thinking that the
only restraints which can arise are those which impede the

bringing about of particular ends, restraints which directly or indirectly are always of a physical kind.

We can now see how for Bosanquet the paradox of ethical obligation is overcome. The man who disciplines his personal desires and inclinations for the sake of discharging his moral obligations is acting freely. In deciding to do what he ought to do as distinct from what he would like to do merely from the point of view of his immediate impulses, he is acting in accordance with his real will. A paradox arises only if rational activity is identified with action at the level of ends and means, and freedom with the absence of physical restraint. Once it is realized that rational activity is something more than merely action at the level of ends and means and that a man can discipline himself not only from fear but also for the sake of doing what he believes to be right, the paradox disappears. As regards the paradox of self-government: it arises from a view which regards a human society merely as an aggregate of separate self-contained agents. It disappears when a society is seen to be a way of living for rational agents who freely accept and fulfil the obligations which membership of such a group entails. But this is not all. For Bosanquet, organization and explicit regulation is necessary if a society is to succeed in the practical achievement of self-government. A self-governing society must be a political community or state.

2.   Expounding his theory of the state, Bosanquet first remarks that: 'The term "state" accents indeed the political aspect of the whole and is opposed to the notion of an anarchical society.'[1] His point is that social life must become political if it is to avoid becoming anarchical. He goes on to argue that we must think of the state not as a separate community contrasted with other forms of social life but as the frame-work within which rational social life is lived. 'But it (the state) includes the entire hierarchy of institutions by which life is determined,' he writes, 'from the family to the trade and from the trade to the church and the university. It includes all of them not as the mere collection of the growths of the country but as the structure which gives life and meaning to the political whole while receiving from it mutual adjustment and therefore expansion and a more liberal air. The state, it might be said, is thus con-

ceived as the operative criticism of all institutions, the modification and adjustment by which they are capable of playing a rational part in the object of human will, and criticism in this sense is the life of institutions.'[2]

From the standpoint of the theory of rational activity, this notion of the state as the framework of social life is quite intelligible. It is fundamentally the notion of citizenship as a sphere of rational activity, a sphere which includes the lesser spheres of work, leisure and personal relations. That this is what Bosanquet seems to have in mind is suggested by the following passage. 'It follows that the state in this sense is not a number of persons but a working conception of life. It is, as Plato has taught us, a conception by the guidance of which every living member of the commonwealth is enabled to perform his function.'[3] Bosanquet goes on to say that he does not regard it as a criticism of his argument that in it 'state' and 'society' seem to be equated. He writes: 'We have hitherto spoken of the state and society as almost convertible terms and in fact it is part of our argument that the influence of society differs only in degree from the powers of the state and that the explanation of both is ultimately the same. On the other hand, it is also part of our argument that the state as such is a necessary factor in civilized life, that no true ideal lies in the direction of minimizing its individuality or restricting its absolute power. By 'the state' then we mean society as a unit rightfully exercising control over its members through absolute physical power.'[4]

This reference to power brings out an important feature of Bosanquet's theory. 'The state as the operative criticism of all institutions,' he writes, 'is necessarily force and in the last resort it is the only recognized and justified force. It seems important to observe that force is inherent in the state and that no true ideal points in the direction of destroying it.'[5] But by 'force' he means something more than merely physical coercion. 'We make a great mistake,' he writes, 'in thinking of the force exercised by the state as limited to the restraint of disorderly persons by the police and punishment of internal law-breakers. The state is the flywheel of our life. Its system is constantly reminding us of duties from sanitation to the incidence of trusteeship which we have not the least desire to neglect but which we are either too ignorant or too indolent to carry out apart from instruction and authoritative suggestion.'[6] The force which is inherent in the state is the force of routine, organization, tradition and custom as well as physical compulsion. 'Without such power,' Bosanquet writes, 'or where if anywhere it does not exist, there could be no ultimate and effective adjustment of the claims of individuals and the various social groups in which individuals are involved.'[7]

This account of the nature and role of force brings us back to the doctrine of the real will. We saw in the last section that according to Bosanquet, 'The laws and institutions of any community are, so to speak, the standing interpretation of all the private wills that compose it . . .'. The real will, that is to say, is embodied in the complex of laws and institutions of a given society. We are now told that 'The state is the fly-wheel of our life. Its system is constantly reminding us of duties . . .'. These duties, 'which we have not the least desire to neglect', are duties which 'we are either too ignorant or too indolent to carry out apart from instruction and authoritative suggestion.' The complex of laws and institutions which embody the real will, that is to say, act upon us with the force of routine, tradition and custom. Our real will is our will to live and act as citizens and we realize it by conforming to the rules and conventions of the laws and institutions of our society. But what gives system and direction to the complex of laws and institutions is that our society is politically organized. To put it another way: only in so far as we are members of a politically organized society can we effectively realize our real will, our will to live and act as socially responsible persons, because only in a politically organized society can the complex of laws and institutions of social life be given system and direction. Social life which is not politically organized will tend towards anarchy and confusion, and the achievement of a socially responsible life, the effective realization of our real will, will be difficult if not impossible.

The force of routine, organization, tradition and custom does not restrict freedom. The man who acts in accordance with his real will is more free than the man who acts only in accordance with his day to day will. The real will is the will to live and act as a citizen and this means to live and act in conformity with the complex of laws and institutions of one's society, a complex which is given unity and direction through political organization. The force of routine, organization, tradition and custom comes to the citizen as what Bosanquet calls 'instruction and authoritative suggestion'. He does not find it a restraint but rather a necessary guide in assisting him to become what he ought to be. What is restrained is not the citizen's real will but his actual will in so far as taken by itself it conflicts with socially responsible living. The man who responds to the discipline of routine, organization, tradition and custom and controls his immediate impulses and desires is for Bosanquet as for Rousseau 'being forced to be free'. The use of physical compulsion is a final resort in imposing the discipline of social living on recalcitrant individuals who are unable or unwilling to respond to 'instruction and authoritative suggestion'. What is coerced by this compulsion is their anarchic day to day will. In so far as physical compulsion is used against them, they are not being forced to be free, for they are capable only of the lower levels of freedom and not of the freedom of citizenship. Unless and until they become able to respond freely to the discipline of the complex of laws and institutions of the political community they must be subjected to physical compulsion in order to protect other citizens.

The paradox of self-government arose out of a view which equated force with physical compulsion and government with force. For Bosanquet, force is inherent in the state and therefore in government but it is by no means identical with physical compulsion. The members of a politically organized society govern themselves in so far as they respond to the 'instruction and authoritative suggestion' of routine, organization, tradition and custom not from fear of punishment but from a desire to fulfil their social responsibilities. For Bosanquet, that is to say, self-government is to be understood as a necessary feature of rational social living. Now it seems to follow that every politically organized society must be self-governing. This is true in the sense that no politically organized society can exist on the basis of physical compulsion alone: those who supply the physical compulsion at least cannot be physically coerced. But on this view, there is no significant difference between a tyranny and a constitutional state. For Bosanquet, the important thing is that routine, organization, tradition and custom should provide the 'instruction and authoritative suggestion' necessary to enable the citizens to act in accordance with their real will and no doubt this can happen only under a constitutional regime and not a tyranny. But the question now arises as to the adequacy with which the laws and institutions of a given political community embody the real will. According to Bosanquet, the state is 'a working conception of life' and 'the operative criticism of all institutions'. This suggests that the complex of laws and institutions must be criticized in the light of a working conception of life which is among other things a conception of political life or the life of citizenship. But what is this conception and can it itself be criticized? Our next step must be to see how Bosanquet answers these questions.

3. Near the end of the *Philosophical Theory of the State*, Bosanquet takes up the question of the grounds on which states ought to be criticized. 'The state then exists to promote good life', he writes, 'and what it does cannot be morally indifferent. But its actions cannot be identified with the deeds of its agents or morally judged as private volitions are judged.'[1] He then goes on to explain why this is so. Referring to the state, he writes: 'Its acts proper are always public acts and it cannot as a state act within the relations of private life in which organized morality exists. It has no determinate function within a larger community but is itself the supreme community, the guardian of the whole moral world and not a factor within an organized moral world. Moral relations presuppose an organized life but such a life is only within the state not between the state and other communities.'[2]

When Bosanquet says that the actions of the state 'cannot be identified with the deeds of its agents', his point is that the personal failure of an official or politician is something different from the failure or inadequacy by the whole political community. An official may be dishonest, a politician may be politically inept, but this does not provide grounds for condemning the state of which they are members. It is their personal inadequacies and limitations which deserve censure. It is inappropriate to judge a state by the standards of personal conduct. Bosanquet's doctrine on this point does not conflict with the theory of rational activity. Citizenship and personal relations are distinct spheres of rational activity. A man may behave well by the standards of the latter and at the same time badly by the standards of the former as when he allows loyalty to family or friends to lead him into acquiescing in crime. Being a good citizen is not the same thing as being a loyal friend or member of a family. But the two spheres are not mutually exclusive. They are concentric, that of citizenship including that of personal relations. Being a good citizen does not involve repudiating loyalties to family and friends. It means modifying these loyalties to harmonize them with the responsibilities of citizenship. When Bosanquet says that the state 'is the supreme community' he is, at least in part, expressing this relation between the responsibilities of citizenship and private life.

But the statement that 'the state is the supreme community', taken literally, cannot be reconciled with the theory of rational activity. According to the latter theory, the supreme community is the human community. A man's responsibilities as a human being take priority over his responsibilities as a citizen of a particular state. To be moral is not merely to be a good member of a family and friend, nor even a good citizen, although it involves these things. It is to be a good human being. Loyalties to family, friends and to nation must be modified and where necessary revised to harmonize them with loyalty to mankind. Now the passages which I quoted from the *Philosophical Theory of the State* in section A, sub-section 4 of this chapter, where Bosanquet speaks of the social division of labour for 'covering the ground open to human nature', and of 'particularizing the human universal', suggest a position basically like Green's in which the ultimate moral community is the human community. The statement in the first of the two passages quoted above, that 'the state exists to promote good life' also suggests the same position. But the statements in the second passage that 'the state is the guardian of the whole moral world' and that the state 'is not a factor in a larger community', suggest that for Bosanquet the ultimate moral community is the political community, that morality is to be equated with citizenship. When Bosanquet says that 'moral relations presuppose an organized life', he is developing a point made earlier in his theory of the state, that a society will tend towards anarchy unless it becomes politically organized. In an anarchic situation socially responsible conduct and hence morality is difficult if not impossible. But granted that in the absence of settled conditions and social stability, morality can hardly be achieved, the question remains as to what the various moral obligations and loyalties are and how they are related. It does not follow merely from the fact that a society without political organization tends towards anarchy, that the state is the ultimate moral community and citizenship the highest form of morality.

But we have still to see what Bosanquet's positive doctrine of political criticism is. Referring to the state, he writes: 'The means adopted by such a supreme power to discharge its responsibilities as a whole are of course subject to criticism as respects the conception of good which they imply and their appropriateness to the task of realizing it.'[3] He goes on to say that: 'The nearest approach which we can imagine to public immorality would be when the organs which act for the state as such exhibit in their public actions on its behalf a narrow, selfish or brutal conception of the interests of the state as a whole in which, so far as can be judged, public opinion at the time agrees. In such a case the state as such may really be said to be acting immorally, i.e. in contravention of its main duty to sustain the conditions of as much good life as possible.'[4]

Bosanquet here seems to be saying that there are two levels of political criticism. On the one hand, a given state should be criticized on the basis of the general conception of life implied in the complex of laws and institutions which it tries to maintain. On the other, particular policies and measures should be criticized from the standpoint of their efficiency. A given state, that is to say, is an individual achievement of rationality and must be evaluated as such. In addition, the work of its government should be criticized in detail on the grounds of technical and economic efficiency but this latter criticism must be subordinate to the former. To the extent that the conception of life implied in a given complex of laws and institutions is narrow selfish or brutal, the state in question is a poor achievement of rationality. But it does not follow that a state which is a relatively poor achievement of rationality should necessarily be condemned as immoral. It may be the best that the citizens are capable of. A narrow, selfish or brutal conception of life may result from ignorance, stupidity or bigotry. A given state would strictly deserve censure as immoral only if there was good reason to think that its citizens were capable of a better achievement of rationality and that owing to lack of integrity in its public life on the part of at least some citizens, politicians and officials, things were worse than they need be. Immorality must not be equated with ignorance and prejudice although no doubt, where the latter are widespread, the former will also be present. In other words, the reasons why a given state represents a poor achievement of rationality will always be complex. In part it will be due to ignorance and prejudice: in part to immorality in those who could do something to improve the situation but fail to make the necessary effort.

Setting aside the point about immorality, however, it seems that, in his positive doctrine of political criticism, Bosanquet is taking up a position fundamentally the same as that of Green. The good life which the state exists to maintain is something more than merely the life of citizenship. It is the life of self-consistent human achievement and the ultimate moral community is not the state but the community of mankind. But this is inconsistent with the negative side of his doctrine of political criticism summarized in the two passages quoted at the beginning of this sub-section in which he maintains that the state is the ultimate moral community and that morality is equivalent to citizenship. Thus, on the one hand, he speaks of the state as 'the guardian of the whole moral world' and says that it 'is not a factor in an organized moral world'. On the other hand, he speaks of 'the duty of the state' and of its 'responsibilities'. How can it have a duty and responsibilities if it is not in some sense a factor in a larger moral world, if not necessarily an organized one? We can now see that Bosanquet's answer to the questions posed at the end of the last sub-section is ambiguous. Those questions were: what is the working conception of life which the state represents? can this conception itself be criticized? In his positive doctrine of political criticism, he is following Green and maintaining that the state as a working conception of life is only an aspect of a larger moral conception. On this view, the working conception embodied in actual states can be criticized in the light of the larger moral conception. But on the negative side of his doctrine, he seems to want to say that the state is the ultimate moral conception of life, that it is the supreme community and that there is no larger moral community beyond. On this second view, it is not clear how a given state can be morally criticized although it might still be criticized on the grounds of efficiency.

4. Earlier in this chapter, I said that, in his political philosophy, Bosanquet oscillates between Bradley's theory of morality in *Ethical Studies* and Green's in *Prolegomena to Ethics*. The inconsistency in his doctrine of political criticism is the outcome of this oscillation. It also affects his theory of international relations. For Bosanquet, the theory of international relations is part of the theory of the state. There are many states and the question arises: how ought we to regard the relations which grow up between them? Now Bosanquet has said that the term 'state' 'emphasizes the political aspect of the whole and is opposed to the notion of an anarchic society'. If we take literally his statement that the state 'is the supreme community' and 'the guardian of the whole moral world', it follows that relations between states are essentially non-moral. Indeed they must tend towards anarchy since there is no world state. On the other hand, if the supreme community is the human community, if the state is only an aspect of a larger way of life, then international relations have a moral foundation.

Bosanquet turns to the subject of international relations near the end of the *Philosophical Theory of the State*. He begins by rejecting the idea of a cosmopolitan or international political community. 'Putting aside the impossibility arising from succession in time,' he writes, 'we see that no such identical community of experience can be presupposed in all mankind as is necessary for the active membership of a common society and exercise of a general will.'[1] The fact that mankind is too diverse to share a common life means, according to Bosanquet, that a common tradition of habits and institutions cannot be developed. There is then nothing in which a real or general will of mankind can be embodied and there can therefore be no international political community. But Bosanquet also repudiates the idea that the international situation is one of moral anarchy. He continues: 'It does not follow from this that there can be no general recognition of the rights arising from the capability for good life which belongs to man as man. Though insufficient as variously and imperfectly realized to be the basis of an effective community, they may as far as realized be a common element of tissue or connection running through the more concrete experience on which more effective communities rest.'[2]

In the first of these two passages, Bosanquet seems to be adhering to something very like Bradley's doctrine of 'My Station and its duties'. Morality is equated with citizenship but citizenship is not regarded as a sphere of rational activity. It is thought of in terms of conformity to the rules and conventions of the laws and institutions of a given society. Like Bradley, Bosanquet has not grasped the distinction between the level of moral rules and customs and the level of spheres of rational activity. He has not understood the conception of spheres of rational activity as a level of rationality above that of moral rules and customs. He recognizes that laws and institutions with their rules and conventions grow out of a common way of life and since there is not a common life of mankind there can be no one set of laws and institutions for all mankind. Hence there can be no international society for there can be a real society only where there is one set of laws and institutions. All this is the same line of thought which led him to say that the state 'is the supreme community', 'the guardian of the whole moral world' and 'not a factor in an organized moral world'. Given the moral of 'My Station and its duties', these statements follow.

But in the second passage when he speaks of 'the rights which belong to man as man', Bosanquet seems to be reverting to Green's position. For Green these rights are moral rights. They imply the responsibilities which 'belong to man as man'. They imply that the ultimate moral community is the community of mankind. But Bosanquet is unwilling to admit that they are strictly moral rights. He denies that they can 'form the basis of an effective community' although at the same time he agrees that they 'form a common element of tissue or connection'. It is at this point that we can see that he has not fully understood Green's theory of morality. He has not understood, that

I

is to say, the way in which the theory developed by Green in *Prolegomena to Ethics* goes beyond Bradley's theory in *Ethical Studies* and overcomes the defects of the latter. Indeed he does not seem to be aware that Bradley's theory has any defects. But, at the same time, he seems to have been impressed by the notion of mankind or humanity in Green's theory of morality although he cannot grasp the idea of a moral community of mankind. As we have already seen in sub-section 4, section A of this chapter, he seems to have some understanding of the idea of self-consistent human achievement and he reverts to the idea again in his discussion of international relations.

The main point which he seems anxious to make is that while the notion of humanity is what he calls 'an ethical idea', it does not mean accepting as the standard of human worth the common or average attainments of mankind. To him : 'It is plain that humanity as an ethical idea is a type or problem rather than a fact. It means certain qualities at once realized in what we take to be the crown of the race and includes sensibilities to the claims of the race as such.'[3] He then goes on to point out that 'Sensibilities to the claims of the race as such is least of all qualities common to the race as such. The respect of states and individuals for humanity is then after all in its essence the duty to maintain a type of life, not general but the best we know which we call the most human, and in accordance with this to recognize and deal with the rights of alien individuals and communities. This conception is opposed to the treatment of all individual human beings as members of an identical community having identical capacities and rights. It follows our general conviction that not numbers but qualities determine the value of life. But qualities of course become self-contradictory if they fail to meet the demands imposed on them by numbers.'[4]

The thought here seems to be that while it is the duty of the state to bring about and maintain conditions favourable to the development of the best human qualities of its own members, this must not be done at the expense of the rest of mankind. The latter must not be deprived of the opportunity of developing their own capacities in their own way. But this is in essentials the doctrine that the highest standard of rationality and value is self-consistent human achievement. If self-consistent human achievement is to be made the ultimate standard, there must be a moral duty to respect it. Bosanquet, in spite of himself, is tacitly admitting that the ultimate moral community is not the state but mankind. If it is not, what is the reason for respecting and dealing with 'the rights of alien individuals and communities'? It should be noted incidentally that the doctrine that the ultimate moral community is the community of mankind does not involve any idea of identical human beings with identical rights or that the standard of human worth is what is common or average to mankind. Bosanquet's insistence on human qualities is safeguarded in the notion of self-consistent human achievement as the highest level of rationality. Thus it appears that, in spite of his statements to the contrary, Bosanquet's real view is that the world of international relations is fundamentally a moral world, that the state is not the supreme community nor the guardian of the whole moral world.

5. In this section I have tried to expound and elucidate Bosanquet's theory of the state and to bring out the inconsistency in which it is entangled. But why did Bosanquet fail to notice this inconsistency? Why did he fail to see that Green's theory of morality is a development of Bradley's based on a criticism of the latter's? Why did he fail to see that he could not adopt Green's idea of humanity without accepting its moral implications and giving up a doctrine along the lines of 'My Station and its duties'? An answer may be found in the notion of the concrete universal which he shared with Bradley. In Chapter I of this book, I expounded a notion of the concrete universal according to which a concrete universal is an individual achievement of rationality. In Chapter V, I tried to show that Bradley and Bosanquet in their notion fail to make a distinction between an individual achievement of rationality and a whole such as an organism. Their principle of 'identity in difference' applies equally to both. This, as I tried to point out, gives rise to a fundamental ambiguity in their notion. At times when they refer to a concrete universal or individual, they seem to mean an individual achievement of rationality; at times an organic whole; at times something which is supposed to be both. The Absolute is a case of the last kind.

Bosanquet's doctrine of the real will reflects the essential ambiguity in his notion of the concrete universal. The real will is said to be embodied in the laws and institutions of a given society. Bosanquet seems to be thinking of a politically organized society as a kind of moral organism. Its structure is supposed to be in principle the same as the structure of any whole. To be moral, to act in accordance with the real will, is to play one's part as an organ in the moral organism. Bradley uses similar language in his account of 'My Station and its duties' and takes the same view. Unless a society is politically organized, it cannot become an effective whole with a unified system of laws and institutions. Hence the conclusion that the state is the supreme society and the guardian of the moral world. As a working conception of life, it is the structure of the moral organism. But Bosanquet also thinks that the state is an individual achievement of rationality. The real will is the rational will. It is not the mere uncriticized day to day will for particular ends, but the will to live a coherent responsible life. Because he fails to see that there is any fundamental difference between the structure of an organic whole and an individual achievement of rationality, Bosanquet regards the real or rational will as the will to play one's part in the life of what he calls 'an effective community', that is to say in a politically organized society or moral organism.

The view that a human society is a moral organism is not without plausibility and, as a metaphor, the expression 'moral organism' may sometimes be apt. The individual moral agent finds himself in a society which is already there. Its way of life with its institutions, traditions and customs is a going concern and by the time he has become conscious of himself as a moral agent, he is already caught up in it. He finds his personality as a moral agent by learning how to participate in the life of his society and this means learning how to observe its rules and conventions. From this point of view, he may be regarded as a part in the social whole, an organ in the moral organism. Again, among organized societies the nation-state is undoubtedly the most elaborate and developed. From a sociological standpoint, it may fairly be described as the supreme community. But a philosophical theory of the state is not merely a sociological description. What is wanted is a theory which elicits and exhibits the rationality of political activity and its value and significance in human experience.

Now a theory of the rationality of political activity and of its value and significance in human experience must at the same time be a theory of rational activity and of the general character and structure of human experience. Its account of these latter topics will inevitably be one-sided and incomplete, being limited by the special perspective of political activity, but it cannot avoid, at least by implication, putting forward a theory of them. So far as the theory of rational activity is concerned, Bosanquet clearly grasps the distinction between the levels of ends and means and private self-satisfaction and sees that the latter is a higher level of rationality than the former. The relation between the day to day will and the real will, neglecting the social aspect of the latter, is his way of expressing distinction. He also recognizes that morality represents a higher level of rationality than private self-satisfaction and that morality arises from the social context of all rational activity. This is brought out in his doctrine that the real will is a social will. But he fails to understand adequately the nature of morality as a form of rationality. In particular, he fails to grasp the distinction between the level of moral rules and customs and spheres of rational activity and seems to have no real understanding of the latter conception at all.

The reason why Bosanquet fails properly to distinguish between rationality at the level of moral rules and customs, and spheres of rational activity lies in the ambiguity in his notion of the concrete universal. He sees that a whole such as an organism is not simply a class of things which have in common some attribute. A whole, that is to say, is not merely the class of things which are its parts. There is a system which gives structure to the parts and makes them into a whole. A whole is not merely the sum of its parts. In the same way, he sees that a human society is not merely the class of its members. It is not a mere sum of individual agents. Its structure is the systematic rational activity of a number of agents. But there is a fundamental difference between a whole such as an organism and a human society, which Bosanquet does not see and which is the source of the ambiguity in his notion of the concrete universal. A human society is an individual achievement of rationality but it is also made up of individual achievements of rationality, namely the activities of its members as members. To live and act as a member of a society is an individual achievement of rationality by a rational agent and a society of such agents is in its turn an individual achievement of rationality. A human society, made up of selfconscious rational agents, is a genuine macrocosm of microcosms. But this is not true of a whole such as an organism. The parts are not self-conscious: the organism is not an organ of organs. A whole such as an organism is not an individual achievement of rationality. It is not rationality which gives a structure to its parts but a merely empirical or de facto system, a system which is intelligible in terms of events and their relations but not in terms of agents and their actions.

Bosanquet, and the same is true of Bradley, has been deceived by the superficial resemblance between a whole such as an organism and a human society. He has seen that they are alike in that neither is a mere sum or aggregate. He has seen that both have a unity which is not the mere unity of a class. But he has failed to see that they are fundamentally different: that the unity in one case is that of an empirical system, in the other, of rationality. All this is to say that Bosanquet's understanding of rationality, and especially of its logical structure, is inadequate. He has enough understanding of it to realize the defects of utilitarianism and to have some idea of the scale of levels of rationality, but he is unable to get beyond the point reached by Bradley in 'My station and its duties'. Yet like Bradley, he seems to realize that something more is required. Bradley attempted without success to get further through the doctrine of the Ideal self. Bosanquet tries to do the same by making use of Green's idea of humanity. As we have seen, this involves him in inconsistency and indicates that his understanding of Green is imperfect. As regards a theory of the general character and structure of human experience which will exhibit the value and significance of political activity, Bosanquet does his best to follow Green but without accepting the moral implications of the latter's position. That this is inconsistent with his doctrine of the state as a moral organism does not occur to him because he is of course unaware of the ambiguity in his notion of the concrete universal.

C : POINTS OF PERMANENT INTEREST IN BOSANQUET'S POLITICAL PHILOSOPHY

1. So far in this chapter I have dwelt on the defects of Bosanquet's political philosophy rather than on its merits. I must now try to redress the balance. Despite the great fissure of inconsistency which runs through his theory of the state, there is much in Bosanquet's political philosophy of permanent significance. It is to be found in that part of his work where he is following in Green's footsteps rather than Bradley's and may be regarded as an extension of the political philosophy first developed by Green. In certain respects indeed Bosanquet's doctrine is an improvement on Green's, being a fuller and more penetrating statement of what the latter had in mind. In this section I shall try to indicate at least some of the things in Bosanquet's work which I think would have to be incorporated into any political philosophy worthy of the name, notwithstanding the fact that they may be inconsistent with some of his other doctrines.

It may be appropriate to begin with some of Bosanquet's later thoughts on international relations, since this was the last topic discussed in the previous section. In a volume of essays and addresses published in 1917 under the title of *Social and International Ideals*, Bosanquet returns to the subject of international relations. Discussing patriotism, he asserts that: 'No patriotism and no politics are trustworthy unless they are kept sweet and clean by a real and a fundamental love of the things that are not diminished by being shared, such as kindness, beauty and truth.'[1] The thesis which Bosanquet advocates in his discussion is that patriotism and cosmopolitanism rightly understood are not antagonistic but complementary. The patriotic member of what Bosanquet calls 'a civilized nation' must be cosmopolitan in the sense that his loyalty is to humanity at its best not to humanity in its average achievement. The true cosmopolitan standpoint, that is to say, is that of a member of the community of mankind. The rational basis of the community of mankind is loyalty to self-consistent human achievement and this must also be the basis of loyalty to the nation-state. But in order to act on this loyalty and contribute to self-consistent human achievement, we must look not to what is common to all humanity but to what is best.

Thus Bosanquet writes: 'A great proportion of the human race lead lives which give us no guidance as to what is desirable for mankind. We cannot get any common purpose out of them and say: "this is the humanity we have to realize".'[2] He then goes on to assert that: 'The fact is that the quality of humanity, whether cultural or humaneness, is rather to be discovered in the life of the great civilized nations with all their faults than in what is common to the life of man.'[3] His point is that it is in the life of the great civilized nations that we are likely to find those values 'which are not diminished by being shared' and not in the values which as a matter of fact most of mankind actually respect. The patriot must be loyal to his nation not simply because it is his nation but because it stands for human values, values which are open to all mankind to cherish and pursue even though in fact only a minority at a given time recognize them. Such patriotism is, at the same time, cosmopolitanism in the true sense.

But granted that true patriotism must be cosmopolitan, what bearing has this upon the actual conduct of international relations? International relations have to be carried out from day to day in the world as it is, which means in a world in which there is much uncosmopolitan patriotism and widespread respect for values and interests which are as likely to generate conflict as co-operation. No doubt citizenship should be thought of in international rather than national terms and the political community as a community of nations but how can these principles be given practical expression in an imperfect world? Bosanquet is fully alive to these difficulties and in another essay in the same volume he discusses them. 'Once you have a vitally coherent community,' he writes, 'intimately bound together by feeling and type of experience and allegiance to the same values and aspirations, then you possess the constituents of a true general will and how you go to work to realize its aims becomes a purely practical matter. At present the difficulty is to find such a common constituent throughout any area exceeding what is usually called the territories of a nation.'[4]

Bosanquet has in mind here the problem of giving practical expression to the idea of international political co-operation. His point is that an organized political community is built upon the

foundation of shared experience and common values. The problem is to find a basis of shared experience and common values for
an international political community. His use of the term 'general will' in this connection may be taken to express the idea of
socially responsible conduct. It is an application of his original
doctrine of the real will but in a form which is unexception-
able. He thinks that a unity transcending the limits of national
frontiers can be achieved only if there is a practical need for
international co-operation to protect things which each nation
values and which are not competitive. There must be a widespread recognition of this need among the citizens of the several
nations. They must regard international co-operation as a
responsibility of citizenship, a responsibility arising out of the
facts of the current situation.

'If, on the one hand, there were to exist,' Bosanquet writes,
'in one or more communities a prevailing general will, i.e. a
concordant sense of supreme objects which by a plain deriva-
tion demand a certain concerted action in favour of peace, for
example, then there would so far be a solid foundation for
practical steps towards international cosmopolitan unity.'[5] He
goes on to point out that international co-operation cannot be
achieved merely by drawing up paper constitutions and legal
frameworks. 'It cannot be done by setting up machinery,' he
writes, 'though to do it would need a machinery. This would be
the consequence not the cause. It can only be done by making
evident in the inner life of groups a devotion to the great ends
of humanity so as to offer a sure foundation for precautions to
be taken in their relations with each other against the obstruction of those ends which all of them genuinely desire and
mould their lives upon.'[6]

In all this, Bosanquet is inculcating a realistic but in no sense
cynical attitude towards international relations. His fundamental point is that lasting international co-operation in
politics is possible only to the extent that people are prepared
to think and act internationally and this in turn is possible only
to the extent that they desire and cherish genuinely human
values. Lasting international political co-operation giving rise
to real international citizenship, that is to say, is possible only
where there is a genuine recognition that the ultimate moral
community is the community of mankind and at the same time

a genuine desire to act on this recognition. This may not be strictly compatible with Bosanquet's doctrine in the *Philosophical Theory of the State* but it fits in well enough with the theory of rational activity and the general spirit of Green's political philosophy. It follows that we must not expect more international co-operation than the conditions prevailing at a given time make possible. In so far as the responsibilities of the ultimate moral community are imperfectly realized and the meaning of self-consistent human achievement as the highest level of rational activity is not understood, then we must make do with something less than lasting international political co-operation. It does not follow that we must resign ourselves to permanent international conflict but it does follow that we must live amidst disputes and tensions and must adapt ourselves accordingly. Bosanquet's teaching is as much a warning against naive optimism as it is a prophylactic against cynical pessimism. Its permanent significance is that it provides the basis for a critical assessment of the values, principles and general ideas in terms of which international politics are carried on.

2.   From international relations let us now turn to the subject of socialism and private property. Bosanquet has something to say about both these topics. Discussing the issues involved in socialism in a volume called *Aspects of the Social Problem* which was published in 1895 and to which he contributed several essays, Bosanquet writes : 'I believe in the reality of the general will and in the consequent right and duty of civilized society to exercise initiative through the state with a view to the fullest development of the life of its members. But I am also absolutely convinced that the application of this initiative to guarantee without protest the existence of all individuals who are brought into being, instead of leaving the responsibility to the uttermost possible extent to the parents and the individuals themselves, is an abuse fatal to character and ultimately destructive to social life. The abolition of the struggle for existence, in the sense in which alone that term applies to human society, means, so far as I can see, the divorce of existence from human qualities and to further the existence of

human beings without human qualities is the ultimate inferno to which any society can descend.'[1]

When he says that he believes in the reality of the general will, Bosanquet's point is that a society is not merely an aggregate of separate human atoms but a corporate way of living and acting. He is rejecting the Utilitarian view. His reference to the struggle for existence is intended to emphasize the importance of individual responsibility in the life of every society. What he is clearly against is the idea of a paternalistic state providing services for its members who passively receive them without taking any responsibility for their provision. In another essay in the same volume with the title of 'The Principle of Private Property', he develops the same point. After remarking that in the case of a child, 'his relation to things has no correspondence to his moral nature, no nerve of connection runs through his acts and dealings with the external world',[2] he goes on to assert that: 'Private property is not simply an arrangement for meeting successive momentary wants as they arise on such a footing as this. It is wholly different in principle as adult and responsible life differs from child life which is irresponsible.'[3]

The principle of private property, according to Bosanquet, 'rests upon the conception of a common good to be realized in individuals as moral and rational agents.'[4] It is 'the unity of life in its external and material form, the result of past dealing with the material world and the possibility of future dealing with it, the general or universal means of possible action and expression corresponding to the moral self which looks before and after as opposed to the momentary wants of a child or of an animal. A grown man knows that if he does this, he will not be able to do that, and his humanity, his power of organization, his intelligent self-assertion depends on this knowledge.'[5] This does not mean that Bosanquet should be branded as a doctrinaire exponent of economic *laissez faire*. As he says: 'Clearly the principle does not demand an unlimited acquisition of wealth.'[6] In his view, 'The question of the organization of industry is really a separate question.'[7] He continues: 'The London and North-Western Railway cannot be effectively private property in the sense in which a wheel-barrow can be.

Whether it is managed by the state or not makes little practical difference in this impossibility.'[8]

Bosanquet is not opposed to socialism as such. 'If socialism means the improvement of society by society,' he writes, 'we are going on that track more or less today as civilized society has always gone, and the collective organization of certain branches of production is a matter open to discussion with a view to its consequences.'[9] But he is opposed to that conception of socialism according to which private property is regarded as nothing but an instrument for the satisfaction of wants without reference to personal responsibility. 'Is it not enough,' he asks, 'to know that one can have what is necessary and reasonable?'[10] and he replies: 'No; that makes one a child. A man must know what he can count on and judge what to do with it. It is a question of initiation, plans, design, not of a more or less in enjoyment.'[11]

From the standpoint of the theory of rational activity Bosanquet's principle of private property is intelligible in terms of the level of spheres of rational activity. It is a social principle being related to the conception of a common good. Private property must be acquired and used in a way which is compatible with the conditions of social living. But it is also a necessary condition for the achievement of what Bosanquet calls 'personal responsibility'. He does not develop this notion at any length but what he has in mind is essentially the idea of spheres of rational activity. The agent who is to achieve a rational and at the same time moral and social way of living in his work, his leisure, his personal relations and as a citizen, must be able to acquire, own and use property. Unless he is able to do this, he cannot take responsibility for his conduct in these spheres. He cannot look ahead and make plans; he cannot exercise initiative or experiment. He cannot fully appreciate that food and clothing, goods and services, comforts and the material conditions of well-being, do not simply turn up but can be had only through human exertion and human forethought. He remains in the condition of a child who is not personally responsible for his life. A child may be and normally is capable of rationality at the level of moral rules and customs. One way of expressing the difference between this level and that of spheres of rational activity is to say that the one is still that of childhood while the other is essentially the level of adult life. To think of private property simply as a means to ends is to think of it in terms of the levels of ends and means and private self-satisfaction and to miss its real significance. On the contrary, it should be thought of as a constituent of a rational way of living and not merely as a tool. But all this does not mean that all property must be private. It in no way excludes the role of public property but, on the contrary, helps to make clear the distinction between the two.

3.   From a discussion of socialism and private property, the question naturally arises: what should be the scope and limits of government action? For Bosanquet's answer we must go back to the *Philosophical Theory of the State*. 'The state is in its right,' he says, 'when it forcibly hinders a hindrance to the best life or common good.'[1] He is here re-stating Green's doctrine and he agrees with Green that the best life cannot be directly promoted by government action. 'On every problem the question must recur:' he writes, 'is the proposed measure bona fide confined to hindering a hindrance or is it attempting direct promotion of the common good by force? For it is to be borne in mind throughout that wherever acts are enforced they are, so far as the force operates, withdrawn from the higher life. The promotion of morality by force, for instance, is an absolute self-contradiction.'[2] He argues that because of this limitation and in order to prevent misguided or inappropriate government action, 'We ought as a rule when we propose action involving compulsion to be able to show a definite tendency to growth or a definite reserve of capacity which is frustrated by known impediments, the removal of which is a small matter compared to the capacities to be set free.'[3]

In terms of the theory of rational activity, Bosanquet's doctrine may be restated as follows. A government acts by making and enforcing rules. It can therefore affect directly only the three lower levels of rationality: those of ends and means, private self-satisfaction and moral rules and customs. Moreover, so far as the third level is concerned, it cannot make people moral. In so far as it has to compel obedience to its rules, it operates only at the level of ends and means and private self-satisfaction. But where people already recognize that they ought to obey the rules and customs of their society, it can affect what they do by the rules which it makes and facilitate their attempt to act in a socially responsible way. So far as the higher levels of rationality are concerned, government can only 'hinder the hindrances'. The levels of self-consistent human achievement and spheres of rational activity demand something more from the rational agent than merely conscientiously obeying established rules. But established rules and customs may obstruct or facilitate the achievement of the higher levels of rationality in various ways. Government can do something indirectly to help this achievement through the rules which it makes and enforces. What it can do will depend upon the capacity of its citizens for rational achievement. This must already be there and government can do no more than assist in its liberation. But in so far as this liberation depends upon the organization and systematizing of certain aspects of social life, the contribution of government will not be negligible.

Bosanquet goes on to link his account of the scope and limits of government action with his doctrine of the force of routine, organization, tradition and habit, this force being inherent in the state. 'The social system under which we live,' he writes, 'taking it as one which does not demand immediate revolution, represents the general will and the higher self as a whole to the community as a whole and can only stand by virtue of that recognition being recognized. Our loyalty to it makes us men and citizens and is the main spiritualizing force of our lives.'[4] This passage is influenced by his conception of society as a moral organism but the central thought is not affected by that conception. He continues: 'But something in all of us and much in some of us is recalcitrant through rebellion, ignorance, indolence or incompetence, and it is only on these elements that the public power operates as power through compulsion or authoritative suggestion. Thus the general will, when it meets us as force and authority resting on force and not as a social suggestion which we spontaneously rise to accept, comes to us ex hypothesi as something which claims to be ourself but which, for the moment, we more or less fail to recognize.'[5]

In this last passage Bosanquet is in effect restating Rousseau's doctrine that in being forced to obey the general will, 'we are being forced to be free'. His point is that while social discipline may be irksome when we are feeling lazy or preoccupied with our own private affairs, it is something which, in our better moments, we know to be necessary. In obeying the government as the agency which enforces social discipline, we are obeying our better self. Without government to act as the agency of social discipline, most of us would be less scrupulous in conforming to the laws and conventions of our society. This lapse would not be due to wickedness so much as to laziness and selfishness and there is therefore a real sense in which government helps us to be our best self by stimulating us to overcome these human defects. The stimulus of government action, that is to say, may help us to rise from the level of private self-satisfaction to that of morality, assuming that we are already capable of achieving the higher level and have fallen back only temporarily. But all this assumes, as Bosanquet has said, that the social system under which we live 'is one which does not demand immediate revolution'. It must be a social system which is itself on the whole morally defensible. For Bosanquet's view of what this means as well as for further insight into his view of the scope and limits of government action, we must turn to his theory of rights.

4. Bosanquet introduces the subject of rights in the course of his discussion of the scope and limits of government action. 'And if we ask in general,' he writes, 'for a definition and limitation of state action, as such, the answer is in a simple phrase that state action is co-incident with the maintenance of rights.'[1] He then says that: 'All rights are powers instrumental to making the best of human capacities and can only be recognized or exercised upon this ground.'[2] He then turns to the relation between a right and a duty. 'In this sense,' he writes, 'the duty is the purpose with a view to which the right is secured and not merely a corresponding obligation equally derived from a common ground; and a right and duty are not distinguished as something claimed by self and something owed by others but the duty is distinguished as an imperative purpose and the right as a power secured because instrumental to it.'[3]

In all this Bosanquet is following Green. By 'a duty' he means something different from 'an obligation'. A duty is the moral basis of the claim to a right. But an obligation is the correlative of a right. It is what must be done by others in order to secure the right. 'Rights are claimed, obligations are owed,' Bosanquet writes, 'and prima facie rights are claimed by a person and obligations are owed to a person, being his rights as regarded by those against whom they are enforced.'[4] This reference to obligations being enforced recalls Green's distinction between moral duties and legal obligations. Legal obligations may be, and no doubt usually are, moral duties. But moral duties cannot as such be made legally obligatory because they can only be done for their own sake. No one can do his duty unless he recognizes that he has a duty and that he ought to do it irrespective of whether or not it is legally enjoined. Bosanquet continues: 'Thus the distinction between self and others, which we refused to take as the basis of society, makes itself prominent in the region of compulsion. The reason is that compulsion is confined to hindering or producing external acts and is excluded from producing an act in its relation to the moral end, i.e. the exercise of a right in its true sense, though it can enforce an act which in fact favours the possibility of acting towards a moral end, i.e. an obligation.'[5]

What lies behind Bosanquet's account of the relation between duties on the one hand and rights and obligations on the other, may be brought out by restating it in terms of the theory of rational activity. At the level of moral rules and customs, the rational agent's duty is to observe the established rules and customs of his society. At this level therefore, there is no distinction between duties on the one hand and rights and obligations on the other. The agent's duty is to claim the rights and fulfil the obligations prescribed in the established rules and customs. But at the higher levels of rationality the situation is different. The rational agent's duties are his responsibilities, the responsibilities which he has as a human being and which he must identify and meet in his work, his leisure, his personal relations and as a citizen. It is no longer enough merely to claim established rights and discharge established obligations. He must think out his responsibilities for himself and on occasion this may involve claiming new rights and neglecting established obligations. The rational justification for claiming that a certain right should be secured and the corresponding obligation fulfilled is that it is necessary if the responsibilities of the higher levels of rationality are to be met. It is in this sense that a duty is the imperative purpose for which a right is claimed. The relation between duties on the one hand and rights and obligations on the other, reflects the relation between the higher levels of rationality and the level of moral rules and customs. At the latter level, there can be no rational justification for the claim that a new right should be secured. Duty at this level is confined to claiming those rights and fulfilling those obligations which are already established.

So far as government is concerned, its task is to secure rights by enforcing the corresponding obligations. But the rights which it ought to secure are those for which there is a rational justification, not merely those which are part of established rules and customs. Where the latter lack any rational justification and obstruct the meeting of responsibilities, government ought to do what it can to change them by making and enforcing new rules. But before going further, there is another aspect of Bosanquet's doctrine to be considered. 'Rights then are claims recognized by the state,' he writes, 'by society acting as ultimate authority for the maintenance of conditions favourable to the best life.'[6] But he then goes on to say that rights cannot exist and be unrecognized. 'Thus then a right, being a power secured in order to fill a position, is simply a part of the fact that such a position is recognized as instrumental to the common good. It is impossible to argue that the position may exist and be unrecognized for we are speaking of a relation of minds and, in so far as minds are united into a single system by their attitudes towards each other, their positions and the recognition of them are one and the same thing.'[7]

Bosanquet is aware of the objection which this argument is likely to arouse. 'If we deny that there can be unrecognized rights,' he goes on, 'do we not surrender human freedom to despotism or to popular caprice? The sting of the suggestion is taken out when we thoroughly grasp the idea that recognition is a matter of logic working on and through experience and not of choice or fancy.'[8] He then proceeds to explain: 'No person and no society is consistent with itself and the proof and amendment of their inconsistency is always possible. And one inconsistency being amended, the path is open to progress by the emergence of another. If slaves come to be recognized as free but not as citizens, this of itself opens the road by which the new free man may make good his claim that it is an inconsistency not to recognize him as a citizen.'[9]

Bosanquet's point is that a right is a rationally justified claim. The bare fact that a claim is asserted does not mean that a right exists. To be a right, the claim must be made because it is rationally justified. A given right comes into existence when someone recognizes that certain conditions are necessary for the fulfilling of certain responsibilities and on this basis proceeds to claim the conditions. The fact that the government of the day or public opinion fails to acknowledge the claim does not mean that it is not a right. The government and public opinion may well be guilty of inconsistency or of failing to understand what is involved. But someone must have thought out the situation, seen that the conditions are rationally justified and proceeded to claim them for that reason before the right came into existence. It may be objected that the claim to certain conditions may be rationally justified but that no one has yet noticed it. But the point is that the right comes into existence only when someone does notice it and makes the claim on the basis of its rational justification. It might well be that a given right might have come into existence earlier than in fact it did but this does not alter the basic point. It follows that the rights which are embodied in the established rules and customs of a given society are not necessarily genuine rights. They are genuine rights only in so far as there is a rational justification for them and this rational justification is understood.

After repeating that the recognition of rights is a matter of fact and logic, not of fancies or wishes, Bosanquet sums up his argument. 'If I desire to assert an unrecognized right,' he says, 'I must show what position involves it and how that position asserts itself in the system of recognitions which is the social mind and my point can only be established universally with regard to a certain type of position and not merely for myself as a particular A or B.'[10] When Bosanquet says that a right 'must be established universally with regard to a certain type of position', his point is that to be a right, a claim must be rationally justified for any one who has to meet the responsibilities of some aspect of the life of a given society. A man must be able to show that the conditions which he claims are necessary to enable him to do his work as a doctor, a scientist, a merchant, a manufacturer or as a labourer, or again to meet his responsibilities as husband and father of a family. The conditions claimed are claimed universally in that they are necessary for any member of the society in question to meet these responsibilities and not merely for a particular individual in special circumstances. What is claimed as a right, that is to say, must be capable of being brought within the scope of a general rule which will apply without exception to all concerned in the society. The work of government in securing rights by enforcing the corresponding obligations is therefore limited to what can be brought within the scope of general rules. Because 'no society is consistent with itself', this work is never finished. Legal and customary rights must continuously be overhauled to see whether they are rationally justified, and as conditions change, new rights will come into existence and will require to be secured by government action.

In this section, I have tried to indicate certain features of Bosanquet's political philosophy which, notwithstanding the inconsistency in his theory of the state, are of permanent significance. I do not mean that he has said the last word about international co-operation, socialism and private property, the scope and limits of government action or the theory of rights. My point is that these are topics of lasting interest in political philosophy and that what Bosanquet has to say about them, while needing to be supplemented and amended, is of positive value and should be incorporated into any political philosophy worthy of the name. While what he has to say is in essentials the same as Green, this is itself something worth noting. Critics of Idealist political philosophy have been especially severe in their comments on Bosanquet while tending to be more lenient towards Green. While not denying that Bosanquet's general position is more vulnerable than Green's, I think that, in fairness to him, the basic agreement between them on many important points needs to be brought out. In this chapter I have tried to show where the weakness in his political philosophy lies and how it arises, and at the same time to indicate its merits.

CHAPTER VIII

THE MORAL PHILOSOPHY AND
METAPHYSICS OF JOSIAH ROYCE

A : THE THEORY OF LOYALTY

1. In Chapter III of this book, we saw that Green thought it necessary to supplement his theory of the general character and structure of human experience with a doctrine of an eternal consciousness. I argued in that chapter that in fact this doctrine is not needed. Green thought that it was, because of his conviction that there can be knowledge only if knowing makes no difference to what is known, a conviction which he does not seem to have subjected to any analysis or criticism. He seems to have assumed that there must be something already there prior to and independent of knowledge, and that what we know when we acquire knowledge is some aspect or fragment of this independent reality. The doctrine of an eternal consciousness was introduced to bridge the gap between this conviction and his theory of human experience, the central thesis of which was that there is nothing given ready-made in human experience prior to and independent of the work of thought. My point was that, while there must be something already there prior to and independent of knowledge, there is no need to assume that we must be able to know this reality or some aspect or fragment of it as it is in itself apart from all human experience. It is enough if we assume that we know it as it is for us, that we know it as categorized and identified by thought. If we make this more limited assumption, the need for the eternal consciousness disappears.

Neither Green's theory of morality nor his political philosophy is directly connected with the doctrine of the eternal consciousness and I made no further reference to it in my discussion of these topics. In the course of discussing Bradley's and Bosanquet's theory of the Absolute, I returned to the view that knowing makes no difference to what is known, developing and partly modifying what I had said about it in Chapter III. I did not find it necessary however to re-introduce the eternal consciousness. But it may well be thought that I have set aside the doctrine in too cavalier a way. It may fairly be regarded as an alternative to Bradley's and Bosanquet's theory of the Absolute. Indeed it would be more accurate to say that their theory is an alternative version of it, since the doctrine of an eternal consciousness is at any rate much more like Hegel's theory of spirit. Moreover, rightly or wrongly, the doctrine has been held to be an integral part of Idealism, to provide, as it were, an ultimate foundation for Idealist theories of ethics, politics and society, to say nothing of religion. I therefore propose in this chapter to consider the doctrine a little more fully and it is in this connection that Josiah Royce is of special relevance.

Towards the end of the nineteenth century there occurred in the United States a development of Idealist philosophy similar to that which was going on in England. Josiah Royce, who was a few years younger than Bradley and Bosanquet, played a leading part in this movement and was one of its outstanding figures. His first book, *The Religious Aspects of Philosophy*, was published in 1885 and in it he sketched the outlines of a philosophical position which in the next thirty years he restated, developed and expanded but never fundamentally altered. The essence of this position is that it is an attempt to unite ethics, religion and metaphysics into a single intellectual system. In the introduction to *The Religious Aspects of Philosophy*, he writes: 'These three elements then go to constitute any religion. A religion must teach some moral code, must in some way inspire a strong feeling of devotion to that code and, in so doing, must show something in the nature of things that answers to the code or that serves to reinforce the feeling. A religion is therefore practical, emotional and theoretical. It teaches us to do, to feel and to believe and it teaches the belief as a means to its teaching of the action and the feeling.'[1]

For Royce, the theoretical element in religion is philosophy. In so far as it is the reasoned theory of a moral code, it is ethics or moral philosophy. In so far as it is the attempt to show something in the nature of things that answers to the code, it is metaphysics. The two are bound up together. The reasoned theory of a moral code leads eventually to metaphysics. Incidentally his use of the term 'moral code' is somewhat misleading. It suggests a body of moral precepts but what Royce has in mind is rather the general notion of moral conduct. The task of moral philosophy is to work out a theory of what moral conduct is, a theory which will have practical implications but which is not itself a list of practical rules. Moral philosophy, that is to say, is concerned with the theoretical basis of a moral code, not with elaborating its details. Moreover, while he thinks that moral philosophy when fully developed must pass into metaphysics, he agrees that a distinction may be drawn between them and that it is possible to go a good way in moral philosophy without embarking on metaphysics.

That this is his view is borne out by the plan of *The Religious Aspects of Philosophy*. It is divided into two books. Book I is devoted to moral philosophy without metaphysics and Book II to metaphysics. The metaphysics of Book II is intended to be the further development and culmination of the moral philosophy of Book I but it is possible to consider the argument of Book I on its own merits without reference to Book II. The theory developed in Book I has strong affinities with Green's theory of morality and the central thesis of Book II is a doctrine of an eternal consciousness. It is for this reason that Royce is of interest to our present discussion. His general philosophical position is an Idealist one and at its core is a doctrine of an eternal consciousness. But *The Religious Aspects of Philosophy* was Royce's first book. It was the product of his formative years and for a mature statement of his position we must go to his later work. His doctrine of an eternal consciousness was expounded most fully and systematically in his Gifford lectures, which were published under the title of *The World and the Individual*. In sections B and C of this chapter I shall try to summarize the essentials of his argument. But first it may be of interest to examine a later statement of his moral philosophy. This is to be found in his *Philosophy of Loyalty*, a book which was published more than twenty years after *The Religious Aspects of Philosophy*. It is in this book that Royce's general social philosophy and his relation in this connection to English Idealism is most clearly exhibited.

2. Like several of his books, Royce's *Philosophy of Loyalty* is the text of a course of public lectures. Some of his best work took this form. The task of explaining himself to an audience unversed in systematic philosophy seems to have stimulated in him an effort to express himself with simplicity and lucidity. In books written primarily for his professional colleagues he was content with a rather lower standard in this respect. The lectures on loyalty were first given at a summer school in 1906 and were published two years later. In this section I shall first summarize the essentials of his argument and will then attempt some interpretation and comment. In the introductory lecture, he tells his audience that: 'In loyalty, when loyalty is properly defined, is the fulfilment of the whole moral law. You can truthfully centre your entire moral world on a rational conception of loyalty.'[1]

Royce then goes on to give a preliminary account of loyalty which he proposes to expand, criticize and revise in the ensuing lectures. 'Loyalty shall mean,' he says, 'according to this preliminary definition, the willing and practical and thoroughgoing devotion of a person to a cause. A man is loyal when first, he has some cause to which he is loyal, when secondly, he willingly and thoroughly devotes himself to this cause, and when thirdly, he expresses his devotion in some sustained and practical way by acting steadily in the service of his cause.'[2] Royce makes it clear that he does not consider mere uncritical obedience to be loyalty. Nor is it the unimaginative adherence to routine or custom. Loyalty demands initiative and responsibility. 'The loyal man,' Royce says, 'may often have to show his loyalty by some fact which no mere routine predetermines. He may have to be as inventive of his duties as he is faithful to them.'[3] Nor is loyalty opposed to freedom. On the contrary, there is no loyalty unless there is voluntary devotion to a cause. Royce insists that: 'true loyalty, being a willing devotion of the self to its cause, involves some element of autonomous choice.'[4]

As examples of possible causes to which loyalty may be given, Royce suggests friendship, the family and the state. Summing up his illustrations, he writes: 'Our initial illustrations of possible causes were first, a friendship which unites several friends into some unity of friendly life; secondly, a family whose unity binds its members' lives together; and thirdly, the state, in so far as it is no mere collection of separate citizens, but such a unity as that to which the devoted patriot is loyal. As we saw, such illustrations could be vastly extended. All stable social relations may give rise to causes that may call forth loyalty.'[5]

But if loyalty must be freely given and if there are many possible causes to which a man may be loyal, upon what principle is he to choose? Royce remarks that: 'nobody can be equally and directly loyal to all of the countless actual social causes that exist.'[6] He goes on to point out that: 'It is obvious also that many causes which conform to our general definition of a possible cause may appear to any given person to be hateful and evil causes to which he is justly opposed.'[7] So far indeed the conception of loyalty does not seem to be very promising as a key to the understanding of morality. It seems on the contrary to lack positive moral significance, since it has nothing to say about which causes are deserving of loyalty. But as yet, we have been concerned only with the preliminary account of the conception. Will a deeper and more searching examination reveal something of more positive moral significance?

Royce is fully alive to the objections which can be made against his preliminary account and concludes the first phase of his argument by summing up the difficulties to which it gives rise. 'To sum up then, our apparent difficulties,' he says, 'they are these. Loyalty is a good for the loyal man but it may be mischievous for those whom its cause assails. Conflicting loyalties may mean general social disturbances; and the fact that loyalty is good for the loyal does not of itself define whose cause is right when various causes stand opposed to one other. And if, in accordance with our own argument in a foregoing lecture, we declare that the best form of loyalty for the loyal individual is the one that he freely chooses for himself, so much the greater seems to be the complication of the moral world and so much the more numerous become the chances that the loyalties of various people will conflict with one another.'[8]

3.   Royce's next step is to point out that a clue to a deeper and

more adequate conception of loyalty is to be found in the difficulties to which his preliminary conception of it has given rise. The clue to a deeper conception of loyalty lies in the fact that it is the conflict of loyalties which appears to weaken the moral significance of the preliminary conception. Why is it that a conflict between different loyalties is judged to be morally bad? Royce answers that it is because the conflict results in the destruction of loyalty. He writes: 'If loyalty is a supreme good, the mutually destructive conflict of loyalties is in general a supreme evil. If loyalty is a good for all sorts and conditions of men, the war of man against man has been especially mischievous, not so much because it has hurt, maimed, impoverished or slain men, as because it has so often robbed the defeated of their causes, of their opportunities to be loyal, and sometimes of their very spirit of loyalty.'[1]

Loyalty, according to Royce's preliminary account of it, is inconsistent with itself when regarded as identical with morality. It is inconsistent with itself because it cannot be universally practised without bringing about its own destruction. But, according to Royce, it is just here that the clue to the nature of morality is to be found. The conception of loyalty must be made consistent with itself. It must be revised so as to make the universal practice of loyalty possible. This revision is accomplished by including, in the conception, the principle of loyalty to loyalty. This principle is the criterion by which causes deserving of loyalty are to be distinguished from those which are not. Royce writes: 'And so a cause is good not merely for me but for mankind, in so far as it is essentially a loyalty to loyalty, i.e. is an aid and a furtherance of loyalty in my fellows. It is an evil cause in so far as, despite the loyalty that it arouses in me, it is destructive of loyalty in the world of my fellows.'[2]

Now in his preliminary account of the conception of loyalty, Royce said that there was an element of autonomous choice in the devotion of a loyal man to a cause. This autonomous choice, according to the revised account, must be guided by the principle of loyalty to loyalty. The missing element of positive moral significance has now been introduced. In the following passage Royce emphasizes the responsibility of the loyal man for his choice of a cause and sums up the revised conception of loyalty.

He writes: 'However much the cause may seem to be assigned to me by my social station, I must co-operate in the choice of the cause before the act of loyalty is complete. Since this is the case, since my loyalty is never my mere fate, but is always also my choice, I can of course determine my loyalty, at least to some extent, by the consideration of the actual good or ill which my proposed cause does to mankind. And since I now have the main criterion of the good and ill of causes before me, I can define a principle of choice which may so guide me that my loyalty shall become a good not merely for myself but for mankind. This principle is now obvious. I may state it thus: "In so far as it lies in your power, so choose your cause and so serve it, that, by reason of your choice and your service, there shall be more loyalty in the world rather than less. And in fact, so choose and so serve your individual cause as to secure thereby the greatest possible increase of loyalty amongst men. More briefly, in choosing and in serving the cause to which you are to be loyal, be in any case loyal to loyalty".'[3]

Royce goes on to maintain that the principle of loyalty to loyalty is implicit in the every-day recognition of virtues and is the standard by which qualities of character are to be judged. 'My thesis is,' he writes, 'that all the common-place virtues, in so far as they are indeed defensible and effective, are special forms of loyalty to loyalty, and are to be justified, centralized, inspired, by the one supreme effort to do good, namely the effort to make loyalty triumphant in the lives of all men.'[4] And the same holds also in the case of duties and in that of rules of conduct. 'My thesis is,' he writes a few pages later, 'that all those duties which we have learned to recognize as the fundamental duties of the civilized man, the duties that every man owes to every man, are to be rightly interpreted as special instances of loyalty to loyalty. In other words, all the recognized virtues can be defined in terms of our conception of loyalty and this is why I assert that, when rightly interpreted, loyalty is the whole duty of man.'[5]

4.   Having stated his revised conception of loyalty, Royce then

considers its implications for the life of the individual moral agent. The attempt to live in accordance with the principle of loyalty to loyalty will inevitably give rise to problems. The agent must decide for himself to which of the various possible causes confronting him he is to give his loyalty. He may find that two causes, each apparently equally deserving of his loyalty, are mutually exclusive. How is he to decide between them? Royce recognizes that such choices constitute genuine moral problems. 'Our question still remains however this:' he writes, 'since the only loyal life that we can undertake to live is so complex, since the one cause of universal loyalty can only be served by each of us in a personal life wherein we have to try to unify various special loyalties, and since in many cases these special loyalties seem to us to conflict with one another, how shall we decide as between two apparently conflicting loyalties, which one to follow? Does our principle tell us what to do when loyalties seem to us to be in conflict with one another?'[1]

In answering his own question, Royce begins by emphasizing that in morality, as in everything else, human judgement is fallible and human beings liable to error. 'Now my special choice of my personal cause is always fallible,' he writes, 'for I can never know with certainty but that if I were wiser, I should better see my way to serving universal loyalty than I now see it.'[2] But this inevitable fallibility does not justify inaction. Moral problems cannot be solved by default. There is always a duty to make a positive decision. 'Now what does this my highest cause, loyalty to loyalty, command?' Royce asks and he answers: 'It commands simply but imperatively that, since I must serve and since at this critical moment my only service must take the form of a choice between loyalties, I shall choose even in my ignorance what form my service is henceforth to take. The point where I am to make this choice is determined by the obvious fact that, after a certain waiting to find out whatever I can find out, I always reach the moment when further indecision would of itself constitute a sort of decision, a decision namely to do nothing and so not to serve at all. Such a decision to do nothing my loyalty to loyalty forbids and therefore my principle clearly says to me: "after fair consideration of the facts, decide knowingly if you can, ignorantly if you must, but in any case decide and have no fear".[3]

Thus the moral agent who finds himself confronted by a clash of loyalties, e.g. between the claims of family or friendship on the one side and profession or nation on the other, cannot put off deciding which to serve on the grounds that he is not sure which will make the greater contribution to universal loyalty. He must ask himself, in the light of his present limited knowledge, which of the two presents him with the chance of contributing most to universal loyalty in the situation in which he is placed, or alternatively, which will do the least harm to universal loyalty if he failed to serve it. Having answered his question, he must go ahead and act. Once the moral decision has been taken, he must go through with it. Only fresh knowledge leading to the recognition of error justifies the abandoning of a loyalty once given. 'Fidelity to the cause once chosen,' Royce writes, 'is as obvious an aspect of the thorough devotion of the self to the cause of universal loyalty as is decisiveness. Only a growth in knowledge which makes it evident that the special cause once chosen is an unworthy cause, disloyal to universal loyalty, only such a growth in knowledge can absolve from fidelity to the cause once chosen.'[4] It may be added that, according to the logic of Royce's argument, the moral agent is not only justified in abandoning a cause when he discovers it to be disloyal to universal loyalty, he has a positive duty to do so. To continue in the service of the cause knowing it to be undeserving of loyalty would be immorality.

5.   In his introductory lecture, Royce said: 'You can truthfully centre your entire moral world about a rational conception of loyalty.' The subsequent lectures were devoted to developing a rational conception and it is as a rational conception that his general doctrine must be judged. From the standpoint of the theory of rational activity developed in this book, each level of rationality above that of private self-satisfaction may be regarded as embodying a rational conception of loyalty. At the level of moral rules and customs, rational loyalty is loyalty to the established institutions and conventions of one's society. It is in terms of this primary loyalty that

all special claims to loyalty must be evaluated. At the level of spheres of rational activity, rational loyalty is conceived in terms of the responsibilities of work, leisure, personal relations and citizenship. Claims upon the rational agents' loyalty will arise in each sphere. These he must evaluate by thinking out his responsibilities in each sphere and assessing their relative importance. Since citizenship embodies the highest level of rationality and incorporates the other spheres within itself, his primary loyalty must be to his responsibilities as a citizen and it is in terms of this primary loyalty that all special claims must ultimately be judged. Finally, at the level of self-consistent human achievement, rational loyalty is conceived in terms of the rational agent's responsibilities as a human being. All special claims to loyalty must be evaluated not merely from the standpoint of citizenship but from that of self-consistent human achievement. The rational agent's primary loyalty is to those causes and those activities which he thinks in a given situation will foster rather than diminish self-consistent human achievement.

Thus the scale of levels of rationality, so far as the levels above private self-satisfaction are concerned, may be regarded as a scale of rational conceptions of loyalty. The relation between these conceptions is the same as the relation between the corresponding levels of rationality. The conception of loyalty embodied in the level of spheres of rational activity is more rational than that embodied in the level of moral rule and custom but less rational than that embodied in the level of self-consistent human achievement. The primary loyalty of a lower level becomes at a higher level one more special claim to loyalty. Thus the loyalty to established institutions and conventions, which at the level of moral rules and customs is primary, becomes, at the level of spheres of rational activity, just one more special claim to loyalty. The same is true of loyalty to citizenship at the level of self-consistent human achievement.

I have said that the levels of rationality above that of private self-satisfaction may be regarded as embodying rational conceptions of loyalty. But loyalty may also be significant at the level of private self-satisfaction. Many loyalties are given to persons and to causes on purely emotional grounds. They are given, that is to say, not on the basis of whether the person or cause is in some way deserving of loyalty but simply because the agent feels himself drawn to them and finds personal satisfaction in serving them. From the standpoint of the moral levels of rationality, the persons or causes may or may not be deserving of loyalty. The point is that, so far as the agent whose loyalty is given is concerned, whether they are so deserving or not is irrelevant. The loyalty is given capriciously. The agent who gives his loyalty capriciously is acting at the level of private self-satisfaction even if in the service of his loyalty he sacrifices himself. I said just now that such loyalties are given on purely emotional grounds. I do not mean by this to deny the importance, indeed the necessity, of emotion in all loyalty whether rational or capricious. No one can be loyal to anything without being emotionally drawn to it. Perhaps the most valuable feature of loyalty as a moral conception is that it includes, as duty and obligation do not, the emotional aspect of all morality. But while admitting all this, it remains true that emotion by itself can never be the ground of a rational loyalty.

Let us now return to Royce. His principle of loyalty to loyalty is fundamentally the same as the rational conception of loyalty embodied in the level of self-consistent human achievement. Only those causes, persons and activities are deserving of loyalty which respect the capacity for loyalty in all who have it. This amounts to saying that only self-consistent human achievements are ultimately deserving of loyalty, only those achievements, that is to say, which respect human personality and moral autonomy wherever it is found. This in turn amounts to saying that the ultimate moral community, the responsibilities of which take priority over all others, is the human community. Royce's doctrine here is fundamentally the same as Green's. Moreover he is in fundamental agreement with Green that the responsibilities of the human community for the most part must be identified and fulfilled through the responsibilities of limited communities. The agent must choose his loyalties in the situation in which he finds himself. He must be loyal to loyalty by supporting those causes and activities going on around him which, to the best of his knowledge, deserve loyalty.

The account which Royce gives in his early lectures of a preliminary conception of loyalty, with its emphasis on the voluntary choice by the individual of his cause, suggests that he may have had in mind something along the lines of the level of spheres of rational activity. He explicitly rejects adherence to routine as a case of loyalty and says that: 'the loyal man may have to be as inventive of his duties as he is faithful to them'. It may also be recalled that the examples he gives of possible causes of loyalty are friendship, a family and a state. But while he may have had something like the level of spheres of rational activity as distinct from the level of moral rules and customs in mind, he does not explicitly develop a rational conception of loyalty in terms of citizenship. He poses the problem of the man who is trying to evaluate the various special claims to his loyalty on rational grounds, but then goes straight to the rational conception embodied in the highest level of rationality. He has perhaps done less than justice to the rational conception of loyalty embodied in the level of moral rules and customs. The point here is that without at least this minimum loyalty no social life can last. Loyalty to established institutions and conventions, although uncritical and sometimes obscurantist from the standpoint of the higher levels of rationality, is nevertheless solid and enduring by comparison with the capricious loyalties of the level of private self-satisfaction. It is a necessary step to a more rational conception of loyalty and Royce in his preliminary conception of loyalty has not brought out its significance.

These however are only minor points. Royce's general theory can be amended to incorporate them. What is important to notice is that his central thesis about morality is fundamentally the same as Green's. He also agrees with Green about the relation between the theory of morality and its practice. It will be recalled that Bradley in *Ethical Studies* held that the theory of morality, apart from exhibiting the general character of moral problems, namely in a collision of duties, had nothing to say about moral practice. Green, on the other hand, argued in *Prolegomena to Ethics* that the theory of morality is indirectly of practical significance. It can help the moral agent not only to understand what constitutes a moral problem but also what considerations are relevant to its solution. Royce thinks that moral problems arise from a conflict of loyalties and his principle of loyalty to loyalty is intended to help the moral agent in his attempts to think out where his duty lies. It will not solve his problems for him but it will make clear what sort of solution he must try to find.

But Royce is not content with a theory of morality by itself. He still retains the point of view of the introduction to *Religious Aspects of Philosophy*. Near the end of *The Philosophy of Loyalty*, he writes: 'One wants a doctrine of the real world or a religion to help out one's ethics.'[1] On the next page, he says: 'So far we have defined the moral life as loyalty and have shown why the moral life is for us men the best life. But now we want to know what truth is behind and beyond the moral life.'[2] To this he adds: 'We want to see the relation of loyalty to the real universe.'[3] His thought seems to be that unless it is rooted in metaphysics, no theory of morality will ultimately carry conviction. To his metaphysics then let us go.

B : THE NATURE OF BEING

1. Royce's first attempt to expound a metaphysical theory was made in Book II of *Religious Aspects of Philosophy* where it was intended to provide a foundation for the theory of morality developed in Book I. The attempt was repeated in several later works, and although there were changes in emphasis and in statement, the basic doctrine underwent no fundamental change. His most thorough and comprehensive attempt was made in his two series of Gifford Lectures which were delivered in 1901 and 1902, and were subsequently published under the title of *The World and the Individual*. The theory expounded in these lectures is the theory of 'the real universe' to which he refers at the end of *The Philosophy of Loyalty*. In this section and the next I shall state the central thesis of his argument and will then attempt to estimate its validity and significance.

In the first volume of *The World and the Individual*, Royce maintains that cognition and volition are not separate but inseparable. Every cognition involves volition and every volition involves cognition. 'Facts are never known,' he writes, 'except with reference to some value that they possess for our present or intended activities.'[1] Intellectual activities are as much matters of will as are those which are usually thought of as practical. 'Volition is as manifest in counting objects,' he writes, 'as in singing tunes; in conceiving physical laws as in directing the destinies of nations; in laboratory experiments as in artistic productions; in contemplating as in fighting.'[2] But without cognition, we could not formulate our volitions to ourselves. Royce argues that: 'our voluntary activities are never known to us except as referring to facts to which we attribute in one way or another, an intellectually significant being, a reality other than what is present to us at the moment.'[3]

Cognition and volition, knowledge and will, are two aspects of human consciousness which can be distinguished from each other but not separated. Summing up his contention, Royce writes: 'From this point of view then, the contrast between knowledge and will within our own conscious field is so far this: namely, that we speak of our conscious process as a knowing, in so far as all data are woven into one unity of consciousness, while we speak of this same process as will, in so far as this unity of consciousness involves the fulfilment or embodiment of a purpose.'[4] These two aspects of human consciousness are brought together, according to Royce, under the head of 'meaning'.

He continues: 'The word "meaning" very properly lays stress upon both of these aspects at once, for what we call a "meaning" is at once something observed with clearness as a unity of many facts, and something also intended as the result which fulfils a purpose.'[5] Royce's point here is that what gives meaning to a proposition is not merely that it propounds a relation, e.g. that A is to the left of B, or that X is an attribute of Y, but that it is the answer to a question; and a question which has been asked, not at random, but for the sake of implementing a purpose. Elsewhere in *The World and the Individual*, Royce distinguishes between what he calls 'external' and 'internal' meanings. An external meaning is the import of a proposition, that which it propounds. An internal meaning is the purpose for the sake of which particular questions are asked and particular actions done. All external meanings are ultimately dependent upon internal meanings. Taken by themselves, apart from any purpose, external meanings lose their significance and become meaningless.

K

2.   Thus for Royce, there are no facts which are independent of human purposes and no human purposes which are formulated without reference to facts. His next step is to argue that human consciousness has its being in the effort to formulate and fulfil purposes, an effort which is at once volitional and cognitive. Every centre of human consciousness is a centre of self-determining activity. The self-determination is achieved through the effort to formulate and fulfil purposes, or to make the same point from the other side, the formulation of every human purpose and the attempt by the agent whose purpose it is to implement it, is the activity through which the agent determines himself. Apart from this determination of himself through autonomous self-criticizing activity, he is not a human agent at all. What we call 'ideas' are nothing but integral elements in the process of self-determination. They are purposes which we present to ourselves and which lead us on to implement them in determinate activities. 'In all cases every idea,'' Royce writes, 'whether mathematical or scientific, seeks its own further determination. In every case it is true that such further determination is also to be given only in terms of experience.'[1]

By 'experience' Royce does not mean only sensations but every form which human consciousness can take. He goes on to illustrate : 'Sometimes it is a definite group of sense experiences that we mean in advance;' he writes, 'then we are said to be observant in the physical world, and then in physical nature only do we find the desired determination of our will. Sometimes, as in the mathematician's world, we deal with objects that appear more directly under our control than do physical objects.'[2] He admits that from one point of view, all ideas are themselves facts. They are psychical events, or, as he puts it, 'masses of experience'. But he points out that they are facts only for an observer who finds knowledge of such facts necessary for the fulfilment of the purposes through which he is trying to achieve his own self-determination. Royce continues : 'But there are no ideas which have not an aspect in which they are masses of experience : and masses of experience are never objective facts except in so far as they present the answers to specific questions about facts : and the answer to a question is merely the more precise determination of the will that asks the question.'[3]

To sum up Royce's central thesis so far : he is making a criticism of our ordinary, common sense notion of existence. What common sense takes to be hard facts, independent realities existing in their own right, turn out to be something different. They are members of worlds of ideas which we are obliged to present to ourselves and to develop in detail, in order to be able to formulate and fulfil our purposes. The common sense notion of existence therefore calls for revision. The revised notion may be put in Royce's own words: 'for, according to our central thesis,' he writes, 'except as consciously fulfilling a purpose, nothing can, logically speaking, exist at all.'⁴ The qualification 'logically speaking' emphasizes that this is the implicit rationale of the notion of existence, i.e. how we are obliged to think of it when it is fully worked out. The assertion that only what 'consciously fulfils a purpose' can exist, emphasizes that to exist is to be found necessary for the achievement of self-determination.

3. Royce's general argument as we have seen it so far does not differ in essentials from that developed by Green in *Prolegomena to Ethics* in the course of expounding his general theory of the character and structure of human experience. Royce, that is to say, agrees with Green that there is nothing given ready-made in human experience prior to and independent of the work of thought. His doctrine about the interdependence of cognition and volition also recalls what was said in Chapter VI of this book about knowledge as an integral part of rational activity and to this point I shall return later. For the moment, however, let us continue to follow Royce's own exposition. His position is clearly untenable as it stands. If 'to exist' is 'consciously to fulfil a human purpose', then it seems that things must be called into existence when somebody has need of them and disappear when they are no longer needed. But things do not appear and disappear in this convenient way. They frequently force themselves upon us when they are not wanted and frustrate the fulfilment of our purposes. Moreover, one man's purpose may conflict with another's. It seems to follow therefore that something which fulfills A's purpose and at the same time frustrate B's, simultaneously both exists and does not exist. Royce is however fully alive to these difficulties

and meets them by further revising and developing the notion of existence. 'Our concept of being implies that whatever is,' he writes, 'is consciously known as the fulfilment of some idea and is so known either by ourselves at this moment or by some consciouness inclusive of our own.'[1]

The objection is met by introducing the conception of a supra-human consciousness which is clearly recognizable as a restatement of Green's conception of an eternal consciousness. 'What is,' Royce writes, 'is present to the insight of a single, self-conscious knower whose life includes all that he knows, whose meaning is wholly fulfilled in his facts and whose self-consciousness is complete.'[2] This 'single knower' or eternal consciousness, is a single, infinite act of self-determination, achieved through the formulation of a single, infinite purpose. The world, or what exists, is what fulfils this purpose. The self-determination which we manage to achieve through our efforts to formulate and fulfil our human purposes is possible because in it we are participating in the infinite purpose. Our human finite purposes are fragments of the absolute, infinite purpose. It is what our innumerable finite human purposes would be if they could all be consistently developed and worked out. The world, or what exists, is therefore what would fulfil our fragmentary human purposes if we were able to work out fully all that they imply.

'What our view asserts,' Royce writes, 'is that the world is and can be real only as the object expressing in final, in individual form, the whole meaning which our finite will, imperfectly embodied in fleeting instants, seeks and attempts to define as its own other, and also precisely as its own ultimate expression. In other words, the world, from our point of view, becomes real only as such an ultimate expression of our ideas.'[3] Royce maintains that this notion of a single, infinite act of self-determination is the real significance of the conception of God. In the following passage where he speaks of 'meanings' he is referring to inner meanings or purposes.

He writes: 'All meanings, if completely developed, unite in one meaning, and this it is which the real world expresses. Every idea, if fully developed, is of universal application. Since this one world of expression is a life of experience fulfilling ideas, it possesses precisely the attributes which the ages have most associated with the name of God. God is the absolute being, the perfect fulfilment of life. Only God, when thus viewed, is not other than his world, but is the very life of the world taken in its wholeness as a single conscious and self-possessed life. In God we live and move and have our being.'[4] And a few pages later, speaking of the complete and all-embracing nature of the divine insight which is the self-consciousness of the infinite act of self-determination, he says: 'This final view for which the realm of being possesses the unity of a single conscious whole, indeed ignores no fragment of finite consciousness, but it sees all at once as the realm of truth in its entirety.'[5]

4. To the question: if the world as the fulfilment of an infinite purpose is eternal, how are we to understand time? Royce makes the following reply. 'In brief, only in terms of will, and only by virtue of the significant relations of the stages of a teleological process, has time, whether in our inner experience, or in the conceived world order as a whole, any meaning.'[1] He maintains that the distinctions between before and after, between earlier and later, between past and future, are distinctions which are necessary for the formulation and fulfilment of finite purposes. 'Time is the form of the will,' he writes, 'and the real world is a temporal world in so far as, in various regions of that world, seeking differs from attainment, pursuit is external to its own goal, the imperfect tends towards its own perfection, or in brief, the internal meanings of finite life win, in successive stages, their union with their own external meanings.'[2]

From the point of view of human agents, striving to determine themselves through the formulation and fulfilment of finite purposes, the world appears as a world of temporal events. But 'these same events however, in so far as they are viewed at once by the Absolute, are for such a view all equally present and this, their presence, is the presence of all time as a "totum simul" to the Absolute.' And Royce continues: 'And the presence in this sense of all time to the Absolute constitutes the eternal order of the world: eternal, because it is inclusive of all distinctions of temporal past and temporal future: eternal, because, for this very reason, the totality of temporal

events at once to the Absolute, has no events that precede or
follow it, but contains all sequences within it: eternal because,
finally, this view of the world does not, like our partial glimpses
of this or of that relative whole or sequence, pass away and
give place to some other view but includes an observation of
every passing away, of every sequence, of every event and of
whatever in time succeeds that event, and includes all the views
that are taken by the various finite selves.'[3] By 'the Absolute'
in this passage, Royce means of course the infinite act of self-
determination, of divine, all-embracing insight.

Some light may be thrown on Royce's central thesis if we
try to think of it in terms of the notion of the concrete universal
expounded in Chapter I of this book. That notion is somehow
bound up with his argument, although, as I shall argue in a
later section, much of the difficulty of his position is due to a
failure to appreciate its full significance. The infinite act of
self-determination which Royce understands by God, may be
thought of as a complete individual achievement of rationality,
an achievement which is at once all-embracing, including all
lesser achievements within itself, and completely successful. It
may thus be regarded as an absolute concrete universal but,
unlike the Absolute of Bradley and Bosanquet, it is not even in
some metaphorical sense an organism. Its individuality and
unity are the individuality and unity of an individual achievement of rationality but of an individual achievement of rationality raised to a super-human level. Like the Absolute of Bradley
and Bosanquet, it is a self-maintaining, all-embracing system
with nothing outside it. But unlike their Absolute, it is not indifferent to the finite centres of experience which it includes.
They, or rather we and all other finite centres of experience, in
so far as we manage to determine ourselves, contribute to the
fulfilment of the absolute purpose, the purpose by expressing
and fulfilling which the infinite act of self-determination is
achieved.

But owing to the limitations of our finitude, we can never
see in detail how all this is so. We are in the midst of the expression and fulfilment of the absolute purpose which therefore appears to us as a temporal process. But the eternal consciousness takes it all in, as it were, at a stroke. Just as we are
able to take in the unity of a picture or the meaning of a sen-

tence at a glance, or to appreciate the unity of a tune, even though all these things can be broken down by analysis into sequences and relations, so that eternal consciousness appreciates the whole universe. The universe is created and appreciated all at once in a single act of self-determination. This is the central thesis in Royce's theory of being or reality. Certain difficulties at once come to mind, especially when we remember that it is a theory which is supposed to provide a foundation for morality. How does it do this and how is evil to be explained if everything contributes to the fulfilment of the absolute purpose? What becomes of human freedom? How are we to understand nature, the world of events which, in our efforts to achieve self-determination, we are obliged to present to ourselves and study in detail? Somehow the fact that we are obliged to do this must contribute to the fulfilment of the absolute purpose. But Royce is well aware of these difficulties and he devotes the greater part of the second volume of *The World and the Individual* to developing and expanding his central thesis in an attempt to meet them. Before embarking on any criticism of his argument, therefore, let us briefly see how he does it.

C: THE PLACE OF NATURE AND HUMANITY IN BEING

1. Let us begin with the philosophy of nature which Royce believes is implied in his general theory of being. His first step is to acknowledge the limited validity of the view of nature implied in the human activities of empirical science and technology. For each of these activities, what exists or the facts, are what is found necessary in the fulfilment of their purposes. Royce holds that both empirical science and technology originated in the effort to develop human social life. 'It is our interest in social organization,' he writes, 'that has given us both industrial art and empirical science. As industrial art regards its facts as mere contrivances that have no life of their own but which merely express their human artificers' intents, so a philosophy of nature founded solely on our special sciences tends to treat the facts of nature, regarded in the light of our cunningly con-

trived conceptions, as having no inner meaning, and as being mere embodiments of our formulas.'[1]

Royce admits that such conceptions of nature, those implied in industrial art and empirical science, are justified from the standpoint of human activity. 'Those doctrines,' he says, 'are perfectly justified as expressions of the perspective view of nature which we men naturally take.'[2] He maintains however that 'neither view can stand against any deeper reason that we may have for interpreting our experiences of nature as a hint of a vaster realm of life and of meaning, of which we men form a part, and of which the final unity is in God's life.'[3] And he believes that he has already shown good reasons for believing that what ultimately exists is not what consciously fulfils merely human purposes, but what fulfils an absolute purpose through the expression and fulfilment of which God determines himself. So what is essentially a humanistic conception of nature must be revised to conform to this deeper conception. The reference to a vaster realm of life and of meaning foreshadows the direction of the revision.

2.   Royce holds that: 'We have no right whatever to speak of merely unconscious nature, but only of uncommunicative nature, or of nature whose mental processes go on at such a different time-rate from ours that we cannot adjust ourselves to a live appreciation of their inward fluency, although our consciousness does make us aware of their presence.'[1] Now this is a difficult, not to say strange, doctrine. The central thought may perhaps be summarized as follows. The absolute concrete universal, the expression and fulfilment of the absolute purpose through which God determines himself, is a vast system of conscious activity. It is achieved through what must be supposed to be an infinite number of finite centres of consciousness. There are different types of finite centre; each type has its own special contribution to make to the fulfilment of the absolute purpose and accordingly determines itself in its own way. One type is differentiated from another by, among other things, the fact that each has its own rate of self-determination, and so a different appreciation of temporal succession. What seems like a year to us, may be no more than a fraction of a second to another type of consciousness, e.g. the type

which determines itself through the formulation and fulfilment of purposes embodied in what we take to be the phenomena of inorganic nature.

On this view, what we think of as nature is our human experience of types of finite consciousness different from our own. Both they and we are elements in a vast system of consciousness; both they and we exist in the activity of self-determination, through which each type of finite consciousness contributes to the fulfilment of the absolute purpose. Royce sums up his contention thus: 'My hypothesis is that, in the case of nature in general, as in the case of the particular portions of nature known as our fellow men, we are dealing with phenomenal signs of a vast conscious process whose relation to time varies vastly, but whose general characters are throughout the same. From this point of view evolution would be a series of processes suggesting to us various degrees and types of conscious processes. These processes, in case of so-called inorganic matter, are very remote from us, while in case of the processes which appear to us as the expressive movements of the bodies of our human fellows, they are so near to our own inner processes that we understand what they mean. Just suppose then that, when you deal with nature, you deal with a vast realm of finite consciousness of which your own is at once a part and an example.'[2]

Royce thinks that the evolution of new natural species may be understood as stages in the successive fulfilment of the purposes through which various types of finite consciousness determine themselves. It is a process fundamentally the same as that in which we human agents develop and expand our own personalities in the conduct of our lives. 'I now make the wholly tentative hypothesis,' he writes, 'that the process of the evolution of new forms of consciousness in nature is throughout of the same general type as that which we observe when we follow the evolution of new sorts of plans, of ideas and of self-hood in our own lives.'[3] He calls this a 'wholly tentative hypothesis' and is prepared to admit that all that he has to say about the detailed working out of the central thought underlying his conception of nature is tentative, but about the central thought itself, he feels quite sure. He further insists that new species, new types of finite consciousness, when they are developed, may become at least relatively autonomous. All of them have their existence in their contribution to the fulfilment of the absolute purpose, but some which achieve self-consciousness break away, as it were, from the parent type which first produced them and directly function in the absolute system. Others, which do not achieve self-consciousness, or only achieve it to a limited extent, have their being in fulfilling the finite purposes of their parent consciousness. In the following passage, which is not free from obscurity, Royce attempts to expound this notion which he believes will reconcile the theory of evolution with his own general theory of being.

He writes: 'But now these new creations, if they survive, are not the mere contents of another and larger consciousness. They are all processes occupying time and embodying will. They are themselves finite, conscious purposes, having an inner meaning, a relation to the Absolute of which they are also, ipso facto, partial expressions, and a tendency to adjust themselves to the goal in their own way. If, as in case of the conscious self of any one of us, they become aware of this, their own relation to the Absolute, then they no longer survive or pass away merely so far as they serve the larger purpose that originally invented them as tentative devices of its own. They then, like all finite purposes of self-conscious grade, define their own lives as individually significant, conceive their goal as the Absolute, and their relation to their natural sources as relations that mean something to themselves also. Their destiny thus becomes relatively free from that of the finite self within which they first grew up.'[4] Perhaps much, if not all, organic life, other than human, is a case of types of finite consciousness which do not become self-conscious, or only to a very slight extent; and so have their being in the fulfilment of the purposes of the larger types of finite consciousness which produced them. They do not consciously serve the Absolute purpose, but do so through the part they play in fulfilling larger finite purposes.

3. Space does not permit a more thorough investigation of Royce's philosophy of nature and of the many questions to which it gives rise. Indeed in *The World and the Individual*, Royce himself does no more than sketch, on a somewhat larger

scale and with a wealth of imagery and illustration, the central thought which I have condensed into the preceding paragraphs. He does not attempt to work systematically through all its implications; nor does he do so elsewhere. We need not however try to repair this omission. What is important is to decide whether or not there are good reasons for accepting his general metaphysical doctrine, and to this I shall turn in the next section. But we must not forget that Royce believed that his theory of morality required his theory of being as a foundation without which it would fail to carry conviction. We have yet to see how he thought that this foundation was provided.

We may recall once more the central thesis of Royce's argument. Whatever exists does so through the contribution which it makes to the fulfilment of the absolute purpose. Human agents, in attempting to formulate and fulfil their own purposes and so determine themselves, are thereby contributing to the fulfilment of the absolute purpose. 'That it is true that God here also wills in me,' Royce writes, 'is unquestionably the result of the unity of the divine consciousness.'[1] But he goes on to point out that, through his actions, the human agent is contributing to the unity of the divine consciousness. Each centre of human consciousness, like every other type of finite consciousness, has a unique contribution to make. 'But it is equally true,' he goes on, 'that this divine unity is here and now realized in me and by me, only through my unique acts. My act then is part of the divine life that, however fragmentary, is not elsewhere repeated in the divine consciousness. When I thus consciously and uniquely will, it is I then who just here am God's will, or just here consciously act for the whole.'[2] We, that is to say, as finite centres of consciousness, are not annihilated in the eternal consciousness, but have an essential function to perform. God is necessary to us but we are also necessary to God. 'Despite God's absolute unity,' Royce writes, 'we, as individuals, preserve and attain our unique lives and meanings, and are not lost in the life that sustains us and that needs us as its own expression. This life is real through us all and we are real through our unity with that life.'[3]

Royce maintains that human self-determination is achieved through morality. It is through morality that human agents make their contribution to the fulfilment of the divine purpose.

Our human self-consciousness, which has its being in our efforts to achieve self-determination, is a moral consciousness. Its essence lies in the awareness by each of us of our own personal responsibility for our conduct: it is our consciousness that, whatever our private wishes, there is something which, as men, we ought to be trying to do. 'For now, however you define your moral philosophy,' Royce writes, it is indeed true that by the "ought" you mean at any temporal instant, the rule that, if followed, would guide you so to express at that instant your will, that you should thereby be made nearer to union with the divine, nearer to a consciousness of the oneness of your will with the absolute will, than you would become if you acted counter to this "ought".'[4] And in support of this, he appeals to the common experience of mankind. 'It is enough for us here,' he writes, 'that this consciousness of the "ought" can and does arise, while the essence of it is that the self is to accomplish the object of its search through obedience to an order which is not of its own momentary creation.'[5]

Thus Royce tries to bring his theory of morality into line with his metaphysics, the theory of morality being that which he first expounded in Book I of *Religious Aspects of Philosophy* and which a few years later he was to restate in *The Philosophy of Loyalty*. The universal standard of morality, summed up in the principle of loyalty to loyalty, has been given metaphysical roots. It is only by acting on the principle of loyalty to loyalty that men can contribute to the fulfilment of the absolute purpose and achieve their own self-determination as men. It is through morality that mankind becomes real, morality being the form of being which is appropriate to the human type of finite consciousness. So Royce believes that he has been able to show 'something in the nature of things' which supports his theory of morality. He thinks that he has shown 'what truth is behind and beyond the moral life and that we can now see' the relation of loyalty to the rest of the universe. This relation is summed up in his central thesis: 'Only in so far as a man is moral is he real. Morality is not a noble but impractical ideal. On the contrary, it is the only reality for man.'[6]

4.   But the matter cannot be left here; for a little reflection discloses a serious difficulty. If morality and self-determination

are equivalent, if a man exists only to the extent that he acts morally, what becomes of immorality? Can there be such a thing at all? Must it not amount merely to error in the achievement of self-determination, and is this not at variance with the facts of ordinary moral experience? But Royce is perfectly aware of this difficulty and recognizes that unless he can overcome it, his metaphysical doctrine will not provide a foundation for his theory of morality but will undermine it. He does not deny that immorality, or as he calls it 'sin', exists, and he explains its essential character thus. 'To sin is consciously to choose to forget, through a narrowing of the field of attention, an "ought" that one already recognizes.'[1] And a little later, he writes: 'All sin then is sin against the light, by free choice to be inattentive to the light already seen.'[2]

In other words, the heart of immorality is perversity: the deliberate refusal to admit and do what one already knows to be right. It is conscious irrationality, the deliberate attempt to achieve self-determination in a way in which one knows that it cannot be achieved. In so far as he is immoral, a man is destroying himself. No man could be absolutely and completely immoral without ceasing to exist as a man. Absolute immorality would be absolute caprice: total and utter irresponsibility. Immorality is a deliberate turning one's back on morality, the adopting of a purpose which is known to be in conflict with the system of purposes through which self-determination is being achieved. Royce's account of evil is indeed substantially the same as that given in various parts of their work by Bradley, Green and Bosanquet.

But if immorality is a fact, if men can and do formulate and fulfil immoral purposes, purposes which to their knowledge contravene the principle of loyalty to loyalty, then evil must somehow contribute to the fulfilment of the absolute purpose. Everything which exists does so through the contribution which it makes to the fulfilment of the absolute purpose, and, since evil cannot be an illusion, it can be no exception. Now Royce accepts this implication of his position. 'For us, evil is certainly not an unreality,' he writes; 'It is a temporal reality and, as such, is included within and present to the eternal insight.'[3] But he insists that, although the fulfilment of the absolute purpose includes evil, the absolute purpose is not as such evil.

'What we have asserted throughout,' he writes, 'is that no evil is a whole or complete instance of a being. In other words, evil, for us, is something explicitly finite, and the absolute as such, in the individuality of its life, is not evil, while its life is unquestionably inclusive of evil which it experiences, overcomes and triumphantly transcends.'[4]

A few pages later, Royce restates the central thesis of his metaphysical position so as to give explicit recognition to the fact of evil. 'For us, God has and is a will:' he writes, 'and through all the struggles of the temporal order, just this will is winning its way, while on the other hand, in the eternal order, just this will is finally and triumphantly expressed. Meanwhile in the temporal order, there is, at every point and in every act, relative freedom. And for that very reason there is the possibility and the fact of a finite conscious resistance to the will of the world by the will of the individual. The consequences of such resistance are real evils, evils that all finite beings and the whole world suffer.'[5] To the question: why are such evils necessary for the conscious fulfilment of the absolute purpose? Royce has an answer. 'Such evils are justified,' he writes, 'only by the eternal worth of the life that endures and overcomes them, and they are temporally overcome through other finite wills and not without moral conflict. The right eternally triumphs and yet not without temporal warfare.'[6]

Royce's argument thus is that evils are necessary because they enable a richer purpose to be expressed and fulfilled than would be possible without them. Every sin creates the opportunity for its own conquest, either by the sinner or by someone else, and thus the opportunity for the realization of qualities which could not otherwise be developed. We can be sure that all evils will be overcome for otherwise the absolute purpose would be frustrated, which is inconceivable. Royce does not think that the presence of limited opposition within the world constitutes any tarnish on the perfection of the absolute purpose. He also thinks that ordinary human experience bears him out. 'For as a fact, we ourselves even in our finitude,' he writes, 'know that the most significant perfections include, as a part of themselves, struggles whereby opposing elements, set by this very struggle into contrast with one another, become clearly conscious.'[7]

He further thinks that all the suffering which befalls mankind, not as the result of human wickedness, but from natural disasters, disease and the like, can be explained in the same way. They are necessary because of the qualities which they summon forth in the effort to overcome them or to endure them, and these, the highest human qualities, are necessary for the fulfilment of the absolute purpose. 'Such perfections also include suffering,' he writes, 'because in the conquest over suffering all the nobler gifts of the world, all the richer experiences of life, consist. As there is no courage without a dread included and transcended, so in the life of endurance there is no conscious heroism without the presence of tribulations in whose overcoming heroism consists.'[8] Royce, in other words, is maintaining that all the vicissitudes of human life, whether the product of human wickedness or folly, or of apparently arbitrary natural events, ultimately contribute to the fulfilment of the absolute purpose, through the qualities whose achievement they make possible. 'These things are sent to try us' sums up his doctrine on this point. Even the eventual extinction of the human type of finite consciousness within the temporal order would mean only that humanity had made its contribution to the fulfilment of the absolute purpose. This final frustration of all human purposes, which the extinction of humanity would involve, is not ultimately different in significance from the thwarting of the purposes of an individual human being which occurs with his death.

As to the meaning of the death of human beings in early life, or before they have had the chance to formulate and fulfil any significant purposes, Royce has this to say. 'But now what purpose can be fulfilled by the ending of a life whose purpose is so far unfulfilled? I answer at once the purpose that can be fulfilled by the ending of such a life is necessarily a purpose that in the eternal world is consciously known and seen as continuous with, yet as inclusive of, the very purpose whose fulfilment temporal death seems to cut short.'[9] And he goes on : 'The thwarting of the lesser purpose is always included within the fulfilment of the larger and more integral purpose.'[10] His point seems to be that the grief and suffering of the parents caused by the death of a child summons forth in them qualities of fortitude and compassion which contribute to the fulfilment of the absolute purpose. So Royce believes that he has faced and overcome the apparent difficulties which stood in the way of his metaphysical theory and prevented it from providing a foundation for his theory of morality. He believes that, through his conception of the eternal consciousness, he has developed a philosophy of religion in which metaphysics and ethics are reconciled.

D : ROYCE AND HUMANISTIC IDEALISM

1.   In the last section I said that the important thing about Royce's metaphysics is to decide whether there are good reasons for accepting his central thesis. With the argument of the last few paragraphs fresh in mind, it may be convenient to approach this problem with some remarks about the adequacy of his metaphysics as a foundation for his theory of morality, supposing for the moment that his central thesis is accepted. We must not, I may add, allow ourselves to be put off by his contention that evil and suffering are justified because they contribute to the fulfilment of the absolute purpose by making it richer and deeper than would otherwise be possible. Royce is not condoning immorality; nor is he indifferent to human suffering. Rightly rejecting all facile arguments which pretend that these things are somehow illusory, he accepts their existence and is trying to understand and explain them. His appeal to every-day experience in this connection is surely not without force. A world devoid of hardship, of pain, of frustration and of grief, while it might be a more comfortable place than the world we know, would be one in which endurance, fortitude, compassion and sympathy would be irrelevant.

But does Royce's metaphysical doctrine really strengthen his theory of morality? It claims to show that morality is an integral element in the universe. Immorality is also admitted to have its place, but it is subordinate to morality. We are told that in the temporal order, although there is immorality, it never predominates, but is overcome through the struggle and effort of moral agents. Presumably if humanity one day disappears from the temporal order, this will not be owing to self-destruction as the result of the predominance of immorality, but will come about through the process of evolution. Humanity will be superseded by other types of finite consciousness more suited to contribute to the fulfilment of the absolute purpose in the stage now reached. From the point of view of God, of course, nothing disappears and nothing comes into being. His absolute purpose is expressed and fulfilled in a single act of self-determination which is also one of insight and appreciation. The world is a temporal process only for us who are in the midst of it. But taking account of all this, does the claim that, within human life, morality will always triumph over immorality add anything to our understanding of morality? On the contrary, it seems to me to take the heart out of morality. If the possibility of the triumph of immorality is denied, if we can be sure that, no matter how bad things may seem, no matter how feeble and irresolute current behaviour appears, nevertheless all will come right in the end, our own human responsibility becomes a hollow sham. Unless there is a real possibility of failure, success is worthless.

Royce tells us that within the temporal order there is relative freedom, that there 'is the possibility and the fact of resistance to the will of the world by the will of the individual'. But he also maintains that everything contributes to the fulfilment of the absolute purpose. In other words, the resistance is not serious, and when properly understood is no resistance at all, since it, too, contributes to the fulfilment of the absolute purpose through the qualities which are summoned forth in overcoming it. Our freedom and responsibility are, as he says, only relative. We cannot do any serious damage and even our resistance is, after all, a negative contribution. Royce might have preserved genuine human responsibility at the cost of admitting that the absolute purpose may be frustrated. But this would mean that God fails to determine himself, which would call for a wholesale revision of the metaphysical doctrine. Alternatively, he might have argued that if immorality does triumph in the temporal order, if humanity destroys itself through its own wickedness, then this must be for the sake of fulfilling the absolute purpose. Whichever triumphed, morality or immorality, it would not really matter, because in either case the absolute's purpose is being fulfilled. This alternative would preserve his metaphysical doctrine, but at the cost of failing to provide, in that doctrine, any foundation for his theory of morality.

We have seen what Royce's theory of morality is, independently of metaphysical considerations. In essentials, it is the same as Green's and implies, if it does not explicitly set forth, a theory of rational activity along the lines of that expounded in this book. The notion of human responsibility is an integral part of it. The individual moral agent is responsible for deciding which of the various possible causes of loyalty he ought to serve and how best to serve them. Each moral agent, that is to say, must implement the principle of loyalty to loyalty for himself; nobody else can do it for him. There is nothing except his own moral decision to prevent him from ignoring his responsibilities and surrendering himself to a life of caprice. Now in demanding a theory of morality founded on metaphysics, by which he means not only a theory of human experience but of ultimate reality, Royce is revealing himself unwilling to accept the implications for human responsibility which his theory of morality involves. He is unwilling, that is to say, to leave it to us. Morality must be shown to be not merely our responsibility, dependent on our capacity and resolution, but must be shown to be in wiser and more powerful hands. He is, in other words, going back on his theory of morality although he does not seem to realize that he is doing so. The fact that he does not realize that he is doing so suggests that his own grasp of his theory, and of the theory of rational activity implied in it, is imperfect.

2.   As a result of the foregoing discussion, I conclude that Royce cannot have it both ways. He must choose between his theory of morality and his metaphysics. If he wishes to retain the theory of morality first propounded in Book I of *Religious Aspects of Philosophy* and later restated in *The Philosophy of Loyalty*, then he must give up the metaphysical theory of *The World and the Individual*. If he wishes to retain the latter, then he must give up the former. I shall not argue that he ought to give up his metaphysical theory, that there are no good reasons for accepting it and that his theory of morality really implies a position along the lines of that sketched in Chapter VI of this book under the title of Humanistic Idealism.

Let us recall Royce's first step in the exposition of his central thesis. It was to criticize and revise the common sense notion of existence. Royce argued that what exists, the facts, is whatever is found necessary for the formulation and fulfilment of purposes. But he then went on to argue that these purposes cannot be merely human purposes because human purposes frequently clash and their fulfilment is often frustrated. His next step therefore was to argue that what exists is what is found necessary not for the formulation and fulfilment of merely human purposes but for an absolute purpose. This absolute purpose is expressed and fulfilled in a single infinite act of self-determination. It is an infinite all-embracing completely successful achievement of rationality, an absolute concrete universal. Everything that exists does so by virtue of the fact that it contributes in some way to the expression and fulfilment of the absolute purpose. To exist is to be an element, a phase or a moment in the infinite, all-embracing, completely successful, individual achievement of rationality.

But is Royce justified in abandoning the humanistic standpoint after his first step? He thought that he was because of the difficulty involved in maintaining that what exists is what is found necessary for the formulation and fulfilment of human purposes. But is this difficulty insuperable? At the levels of ends and means and private self-satisfaction, the purposes of different agents will undoubtedly conflict. At the level of moral rules and customs, however, so far as the members of the same society are concerned, conflict between purposes will be less frequent. It will not be wholly absent because no set of rules and customs is fully consistent and because rules and customs are always susceptible to varying interpretations. At the level of spheres of rational activity the limitations of rules and customs no longer apply. Among the members of the same society, who have reached this level of rationality, purposes will not normally be in conflict. But the purposes of members of different societies may still conflict even at this level and there may also be conflict between purposes formulated in terms of the responsibilities of citizenship and those formulated in terms of some activity belonging to the level of self-consistent human achievement. It is only at the level of self-consistent human achievement, where purposes are formulated and fulfilled in terms of the responsibilities of the human community or, what comes to the same thing, in terms of the principle of loyalty to loyalty, that the possibility of conflict is in principle removed. The significance of this, so far as Royce's argument is concerned, is that the conflict between human purposes is not ineradicable. In so far as they are formulated in terms of the highest level of rationality there will be no basic conflict.

Royce's difficulty over the conflict of human purposes can be avoided if his revised notion of existence is reformulated thus. What exists is what is found necessary for the fulfilment of those human purposes which are formulated in terms of rational activity at the level of self-consistent human achievement. Such purposes do not in principle conflict. But as it stands, this will not do. The humanistic aspect is not properly brought out. A better formulation, which takes account of this aspect, would be: what exists is whatever we find ourselves obliged to acknowledge as present in the situation confronting us in our efforts to fulfil those purposes which we have formulated in terms of rational activity at the level of self-consistent human achievement. This avoids any suggestion that we know what exists independently of or apart from human experience and at the same time takes account of the 'given' or de facto character of whatever exists. It does not deny that something exists over and beyond our experience: it only asserts that we cannot have knowledge of it.

Here it is important to recall the distinction between the knowledge which is an integral part of rational activity and the knowledge the pursuit of which may be the purpose of rational activity. To say that what exists is whatever we are obliged to acknowledge as present in rational activity at the level of self-consistent human achievement, is to say that what exists is whatever we may come to know as an integral part of rational activity at this level. There remains the knowledge of what exists which we gain through the systematic pursuit of knowledge, this systematic pursuit being itself an instance of rational activity at the level of self-consistent human achievement. Moreover this systematic knowledge, e.g. in natural science and history, is a development of the knowledge on its theoretical side which is an integral part of rational activity. For a more developed and sophisticated notion of existence, therefore, we must turn from the knowledge which is an integral part of rational activity at the highest level of rationality to natural science and history. But we must turn to these forms of knowledge not as scientists and historians but as philosophers. Our task must be, that is to say, to elicit and examine the notions of existence implicit in natural science and history and to work out a theory of the character and structure of human experience in which the significance of these notions becomes intelligible. All this is to say that, if we are serious in our attempt to revise the common sense notion of existence, what we are in search of is a philosophical notion of existence, a notion which must be developed through a critical study of the significance of the notion in human experience.

Now when Royce expounded his revised notion of existence, he was already committed to just such a philosophical enterprise. The revised notion was based on his doctrine of the interdependence of cognition and volition and this doctrine in turn was the outcome of an examination of the role and significance of cognition and volition in human experience. What he should have done, when confronted by the difficulty of the conflict of human purposes, was to examine and elucidate the notion of purpose. This would have led him into the theory of rational activity and to the conclusions that, at the level of self-consistent human achievement, human purposes are not in conflict. It would have led him, in other words, to his own principle of loyalty to loyalty. From this, he would have been able to go on to a notion of existence along the lines of that sketched in the last two paragraphs. The logic of his own argument, that is to say, should have led him in the direction of the position sketched in Chapter VI of this book under the title of 'Humanistic Idealism' and not to the doctrine of an eternal consciousness. He was not justified, on the basis of his own argument, in abandoing the humanistic standpoint. What is strange is that, especially in view of his theory of morality, he did not see this for himself. Why did Royce find a humanistic position unsatisfactory? Why did he fail to see that his metaphysical theory does not support but rather undermines his theory of morality?

3. A clue to the reason why Royce's philosophical thought

took the course that it did may be found in his preoccupation with religion, a preoccupation which, as we saw at the beginning of this chapter, made itself evident in his first book. He seems to have been convinced that there is something greater than merely human experience which is also inclusive of human experience. He seems to have thought that religion is based on the human recognition of this fact and to have conceived it to be the business of philosophy to work out and theorize the insight embodied in religion, a task which involves developing a theory of morality and a metaphysical theory and showing the relation between them. This was a general presupposition of all Royce's philosophy and he does not seem ever to have subjected it to a serious critical scrutiny. Thus for him the question of whether a humanistic position was philosophically satisfactory did not arise. It was excluded from the start by his general presupposition according to which any position, to be philosophically satisfactory, must incorporate the insight of religion into a realm transcending but inclusive of human experience. It follows that the question of justifying his departure from the humanistic standpoint after his first step in *The World and the Individual* did not occur to him. From the beginning he was in search of more than a merely humanistic standpoint. This interpretation is borne out by Royce's procedure in expounding his philosophy of nature in *The World and the Individual*. We saw in section C, sub-section 1 of this chapter, that, having reviewed the conceptions of nature implied in empirical science and technology, he comments: 'Those doctrines are perfectly justified as expressions of the perspective view of nature which we men naturally take. Neither view can stand against any deeper reason that we may have for interpreting our experiences of nature as a hint of a vaster realm of life and of meaning of which we men form a part and of which the final unity is in God's life.' It is assumed without question that the insight of religion provides a 'deeper reason' than any drawn from 'the perspective view of nature which we men naturally take'.

In the same way, Royce is convinced from the outset that no theory of morality couched in merely human terms will do. It is not that he begins with a humanistic theory of morality and finds himself driven beyond it by its inherent defects. This is true of Bradley in *Ethical Studies* but it is not true of Royce. It is rather that he assumes without question that an adequate theory of morality must be a religious theory. It must make morality intelligible in terms of the insight of religion. That insight must itself be theorized and so a theory of morality must be linked to a metaphysical theory. It follows that Royce would not have been impressed by the criticism developed against him in the last sub-section. That the conflict of human purposes is not ineradicable, that in his own principle of loyalty to loyalty he has pointed out a level of rationality at which they do not conflict, would not have seemed to him reasons for abandoning his quest for a theistic rather than a humanistic metaphysical theory. No doubt he would have accepted my suggested reformulation of his revised notion of existence, but would still have insisted that it must be further revised so as to incorporate the insight of religion.

There is, however, the criticism made at the beginning of this section, that Royce's metaphysical theory undermines his theory of morality by taking away the substance of human responsibility. Whether he would have been impressed by this criticism I do not know. That success is hollow when there is no real possibility of failure is a point which does not seem to have occurred to him. He assumed from the outset that morality is conduct in the service of something greater than but inclusive of human interests and purposes, and from this stand-point the question of failure, its possibility and significance does not arise, or at least does not arise in a way which presents a serious problem. In this connection, the use which he makes of the notion of the concrete universal is significant. In section B of this chapter I said that Royce's conception of God is the conception of an infinite completely successful individual achievement of rationality. It is the conception, that is to say, of an absolute all-embracing concrete universal. It differs from the Absolute of Bradley and Bosanquet in that it is free from the ambiguity which pervades their conception. Royce does not confuse an individual achievement of rationality with an organic whole. Recognizing that the notion of the concrete universal is the notion of what is real in rational activity, he has raised it to a super-human level. He has in fact literally deified it.

That Royce should have developed the notion of the con-crete universal in this way is intelligible in the light of his general presupposition. He wanted to find a conception in terms of which he could theorize the insight of religion, namely the recognition that there is something greater than human ex-perience which is at the same time inclusive of it. In the notion of the concrete universal, it seemed to him that he had found what he was looking for. The rational agent who realizes him-self in an individual achievement of rationality at the level of self-consistent human achievement is participating in a system of activity which transcends but at the same time includes him. It is an open non-competitive system, a system in which all rational agents may participate and find the fulfilment of their rational natures. It represents a standpoint from which the limitations of lower levels of rationality are offset while what is positive in them is preserved, modified and adjusted so as to reconcile them. What Royce did was to extrapolate the scale of levels of rationality beyond the level of self-consistent human achievement to a superhuman level. He believed that he had found in the structure of rational activity a key to the structure of ultimate reality, of what was greater than but in-clusive of human experience. At the same time, he was aware that at the highest level, that of God, rational activity is some-thing fundamentally different from what it is at any of the human levels. God, the eternal consciousness, is self-creating, all-embracing and infinite. There is nothing beyond or outside him. The structure of rational activity is his structure as it appears to us who are part of it.

But is it legitimate to extrapolate the scale of levels of ration-ality to a super-human level? The scale exhibits the structure of human rational activity and its significance is confined to the context of human experience. As to ultimate reality, that which lies beyond and yet also includes our experience, all that we can say is that it must be of such a nature as to make pos-sible or at least not to prohibit the rational activity which we know. To say more than this is to claim to know what ex hypothesi we cannot know. Royce was misled by his general presupposition into two errors. The first was to try to gain knowledge of something which, because it lies outside human experience, cannot be known. The second was to misapply the notion of the concrete universal, to try to extend it beyond the context in which it is significant. Royce's general presupposition, that is to say, is one which he ought not to have made and his metaphysical theory is the outcome of his failure to realize that he ought not to have made it.

But, I shall be told, you are forgetting the insight of religion. Should it not count for something and was not Royce right to take it seriously? Moreover, is it not a defect of the humanistic standpoint that it excludes religion from its perspective and is therefore unable to take it seriously? Now in urging a humanistic standpoint against Royce and in criticizing his preoccupation with religion, I may seem to be denying any significance or value to religion. But this is not the case. I am denying only that religion has any special privilege so far as philosophy is concerned. G. R. G. Mure said of common sense that 'in the court of philosophy, its place is not on the bench but in the dock'.* The same may be said of religion and for that matter also of science, art and morality. No one form of human activity can claim exemption from philosophical scrutiny and criticism. What religion claims to be its special insight cannot therefore be accepted at its face value. If it professes to be an insight into what lies beyond human experience, I do not see how it can be taken literally as knowledge. But this does not mean that religion is without significance or interest. It has a rational as well as an emotional side and is a proper object for philosophical study. I cannot attempt this here but it may be worth remarking that the general position of Humanistic Idealism suggests that the roots of religion are to be found in the ultimate mystery surrounding the fact that there is human experience at all, and that religion is concerned with articulating human feelings about and responses to this mystery, and developing a way of life in which these may be adequately expressed. But religion is not metaphysics and it is perhaps the chief defect of Royce's philosophy that he failed to appreciate this fact.

At the beginning of this chapter I referred to Green's doctrine of the eternal consciousness and to my remarks about it in Chapter III. Those remarks were limited to pointing out that Green was mistaken in thinking that he needed the doctrine to

* See *The Retreat from Truth.*

help out his theory of human experience and in particular his theory of knowledge. I did not at that stage attempt to criticize the doctrine on its own merits. Now I have tried to do so, taking Royce's version of the doctrine as my target. I think that my criticisms are, in principle, equally applicable to Green's version. Green, in his published work, is more cautious about the eternal consciousness than Royce. He indicates the general form of the doctrine and affirms his belief in its necessity but does not systematically expound it. Whether he would have done so had he lived longer is an open question. It does not, however, affect the point I am making here which is that the doctrine of an eternal consciousness is not tenable. No more than the Absolute of Bradley and Bosanquet is it a necessary part of Idealism if we take Idealism to be a philosophical position based on the notion of the concrete universal.

In the introduction to this book, I said that its thesis was that there is a valid and significant form of Idealism to be found in the work of Bradley, Green, Bosanquet and Royce, but that they failed to develop it fully and consistently. They came nearest to doing so in their social philosophy and were least successful in their metaphysics. The discussion of Royce's work in the present chapter completes my attempt to develop this thesis. I shall not try to summarize my main arguments since to do so would only be to repeat in condensed and garbled form what has been said at length in the course of the book. My case rests upon the notion of the concrete universal together with the theory of rational activity with which it is integrally linked, and upon the doctrine that there is nothing given ready-made in human experience prior to and independent of the work of thought, together with certain corollary doctrines about the scope and limits of human knowledge. Whether, or to what extent, it is a convincing case, the reader must decide What is more important is whether I have managed to persuade him that there is something to be said for Idealism, that in particular its social philosophy is worth taking seriously. If I have been able to do this, the book will have served its purpose.

APPENDIX I

SOURCES OF QUOTATIONS IN TEXT

In the following table the numbers in brackets refer to those in the text after each quotation. The reader who follows up these quotations to their sources will find that here and there I have made minor alterations in punctuation. This has been done partly in order to incorporate a particular passage more smoothly into my own text and partly in the interests of greater intelligibility when the original punctuation has left something to be desired in this respect.

CHAPTER II. All quotations in this chapter are from F. H. Bradley's *Ethical Studies*, second edition.

A. sub-section 1. (1) p. 5 (2) p. 11. (3) p. 36. (4) p. 38. (5) p. 39.
2. (1) p. 65. (2) p. 65. (3) p. 65. (4) p. 69. (5) p. 69. (6) p. 70. (7) p. 77. (8) p. 78.

B. sub-section 1. (1) p. 163. (2) p. 166. (3) p. 166. (4) p. 166. (5) p. 174. (6) p. 187.
2. (1) p. 190. (2) p. 192. (3) p. 192
3. (1) p. 217. (2) p. 222. (3) p. 223. (4) p. 223.

C. sub-section 1. (1) p. 219. (2) p. 220. (3) p. 220. (4) p. 220. (5) p. 220. (6) p. 221.
2. (1) p. 224. (2) p. 225. (3) p. 225. (4) p. 225. (5) p. 226. (6) p. 226. (7) p. 226.
3. (1) p. 233. (2) p. 233. (3) p. 233. (4) p. 313. (5) p. 313.

D. sub-section 1. (1) p. 314. (2) p. 314. (3) p. 314. (4) p. 315. (5) p. 316. (6) p. 319. (7) p. 320. (8) p. 320. (9) p. 321. (10) p. 328.
2. (1) p. 333. (2) p. 333. (3) p. 333. (4) p. 334. (5) p. 334.

CHAPTER III. All quotations except those in section C, subsection 4, from T. H. Green's *Prolegomena to Ethics*.

A. sub-section 1. (1) p. 12. (2) p. 12.
2. (1) p. 50. (2) p. 52. (3) p. 52. (4) p. 37. (5) p. 21. (6) p. 74. (7) p. 74. (8) p. 58. (9) p. 59.

4.   (1) p. 80. (2) p. 80.
5.   (1) p. 98. (2) p. 98.
6.   (1) p. 151. (2) p. 151.

B. sub-section 1.   (1) p. 103. (2) p. 106. (3) p. 195. (4) p. 256.
2.   (1) p. 210. (2) p. 218. (3) p. 218. (4) p. 210. (5) p. 271.
3.   (1) p. 242. (2) p. 287.

C. sub-section 1.   (1) p. 346. (2) p. 346. (3) p. 346. (4) p. 350. (5) p. 351. (6) p. 351. (7) p. 351.
2.   (1) p. 352. (2) p. 352.
3.   (1) p. 373. (2) p. 373. (3) p 374. (4) p. 374. (5) p. 376. (6) p. 394.
4.   Quotations from T. H. Green's *Lectures on the Principles of Political Obligation*, 1941 edition. (1) p. 3. (2) p. 3. (3) p. 3. (4) p. 2.

CHAPTER IV.   All quotations in this chapter from T. H. Green's *Lectures on the Principles of Political Obligation*, 1941 edition.

A. sub-section 1.   (1) p. 29.
2.   (1) p. 34. (2) p. 34. (3) p. 37. (4) p. 37. (5) p. 38.
3.   (1) p. 41. (2) p. 41. (3) p. 41. (4) p. 41. (5) p. 44. (6) p. 48. (7) p. 45.

B. sub-section 1.   (1) p. 121. (2) p. 121. (3) p. 121. (4) p. 144. (5) p. 139.
2.   (1) p. 94. (2) p. 103. (3) p. 98. (4) p. 98. (5) p. 98. (6) p. 99. (7) p. 99. (8) p. 102.
3.   (1) p. 143. (2) p. 144. (3) p. 146. (4) p. 146. (5) p. 147.
4.   (1) p. 148. (2) p. 148. (3) p. 149. (4) p. 150. (5) p. 151. (6) p. 151. (7) p. 151.

C. sub-section 1.   (1) p. 155. (2) p. 155. (3) p. 158. (4) p. 159. (5) p. 164. (6) p. 164. (7) p. 170. (8) p. 173. (9) p. 173. (10) p. 173. (11) p. 173.
2.   (1) p. 186. (2) p. 186. (3) p. 186. (4) p. 190. (5) p. 188. (6) p. 189.
3.   (1) p. 186. (2) p. 195. (3) p. 195. (4) p. 202. (5) p. 203. (6) p. 204. (7) p. 205. (8) p. 204.
4.   (1) p. 208. (2) p. 209. (3) p. 159. (4) p. 209. (5) p. 220. (6) p. 220. (7) p. 220. (8) p. 220. (9) p. 221. (10) p. 221. (11) p. 221.

5. (1) p. 233. (2) p. 233. (3) p. 235. (4) p. 235. (5) p. 236. (6) p. 236. (7) p. 238. (8) p. 242. (9) p. 238. (10) p. 240.

CHAPTER V.

A. sub-section 1. (1) From F. H. Bradley's *Appearance and Reality* 2nd edition. p. 1. (2) From L. T. Hobhouse's *Metaphysical Theory of the State*. p. 116. (3) Ibid. p. 117.

2. (1) From Bradley's *Principles of Logic* 2nd edition, Vol. 1. p. 188. (2) Ibid. p. 190.

3. (1) From Bradley's *Appearance and Reality* p. 1. (2) Ibid p. 120. (3) Ibid. p. 123. (4) Ibid. p. 127. (5) Ibid. p. 127. (6) Ibid. p. 127. (7) Ibid. p. 127. (8) Ibid. p. 127. (9) Ibid. p. 128. (10) Ibid. p. 129.

4. (1) From Bradley's *Principles of Logic* Vol. 1. p. 10. (2) Ibid. p. 50. (3) Ibid. p. 50. (4) Ibid. p. 70. (5) Ibid. p. 94. (6) Ibid. p. 94. (7) From *Appearance and Reality* p. 148. (8) Ibid. p. 148. (9) Ibid. p. 140. (10) Ibid. p. 140.

5. (1) From *Appearance and Reality* p. 152. (2) Ibid. p. 152.

B. sub-section 1. (1) From B. Bosanquet's *Logic* Vol. 1. p. 3. (2) From Bosanquet's *The Principle of Individuality and Value* p. 37.

2. (1) From Bosanquet's *The Principle of Individuality and Value* p. 54. (2) Ibid. p. 68. (3) Ibid. p. 268. (4) Ibid. p. 51. (5) Ibid. p. 268.

3. (1) From Bosanquet's *The Value and Destiny of the Individual* p. 212. (2) Ibid. p. 212. (3) Ibid. p. 212. (4) Ibid. p. 214.

4. (1) From *The Value and Destiny of the Individual* p. 205. (2) Ibid. p. 205. (3) Ibid. p. 207. (4) Ibid. p. 207. (5) Ibid. p. 206. (6) Ibid. p. 215. (7) Ibid. p. 304. (8) Ibid. p. 304.

C. sub-section 2. (1) From Bradley's *Appearance and Reality* p. 1.

CHAPTER VII.

A. All quotations in this section are from Bernard Bosanquet's *Philosophical Theory of the State*, 2nd edition.

sub-section 1.   (1) p. 2. (2) p. 47.
         2.   (1) p. 90. (2) p. 52. (3) p. 52.
         3.   (1) p. 111. (2) p. 114. (3) p. 114.
         4.   (1) p. 66. (2) p. 166.

B. All quotations in this section from the *Philosophical Theory of the State.*

sub-section 1.   (1) p. 118. (2) p. 133. (3) p. 134. (4) p. 133.
         2.   (1) p. 140. (2) p. 140. (3) p. 140. (4) p. 172. (5) p. 141. (6) p. 142. (7) p. 172.
         3.   (1) p. 302. (2) p. 302. (3) p. 304. (4) p. 304.
         4.   (1) p. 306. (2) p. 307. (3) p. 308. (4) p. 308.

C. sub-section 1.   (1) From Bosanquet's *Social and International Ideals* p. 12. (2) Ibid. p. 14. (3) Ibid. p. 14. (4) Ibid. p. 312. (5) Ibid. p. 315. (6) Ibid. p. 315.
         2.   (1) From essays by Bosanquet in *Aspects of the Social Problem* p. 290. (2) Ibid. p. 309. (3) Ibid. p. 310. (4) Ibid. p. 311. (5) Ibid. p. 311. (6) Ibid. p. 311. (7) Ibid. p. 313. (8) Ibid. p. 313. (9) Ibid. p. 306. (10) Ibid. p. 313. (11) Ibid. p. 313.
         3.   (1) From *Philosophical Theory of the State* p. 178. (2) Ibid. p. 178. (3) Ibid. p. 179. (4) Ibid. p. 186. (5) Ibid. p. 187.
         4.   (1) From *Philosophical Theory of the State* p. 188. (2) Ibid. p. 195. (3) Ibid. p. 195. (4) Ibid. p. 192. (5) Ibid. p. 192. (6) Ibid. p. 188. (7) Ibid. p. 196. (8) Ibid. p. 197. (9) Ibid. p. 198. (10) Ibid. p. 198. (11) p. 197.

CHAPTER VIII.

A. All quotations in this section, except for sub-section 1, are from Royce's *Philosophy of Loyalty.*

sub-section 1.   (1) From Royce's *Religious Aspects of Philosophy* p. 3.
         2.   (1) p. 15. (2) p. 16. (3) p. 102. (4) p. 108. (5) p. 108. (6) p. 108. (7) p. 108. (8) p. 110.
         3.   (1) p. 116. (2) p. 118. (3) p. 120. (4) p. 129. (5) p. 139.
         4.   (1) p. 181. (2) p. 186. (3) p. 188. (4) p. 191.
         5.   (1) p. 305. (2) p. 306. (3) p. 307.

B. All quotations in this section are from Royce's *The World and the Individual* Vol. 1., except those in sub-section 4 which are from Vol. 2 of the same work.

sub-section 1.   (1) p. 436. (2) p. 311. (3) p. 436. (4) p. 437.
          2.   (1) p. 334. (2) p. 334. (3) p. 334. (4) p. 461.
          3.   (1) p. 396. (2) p. 400. (3) p. 391. (4) p. 394.
          4.   (1) p. 132. (2) p. 132. (3) p. 141.

c. All quotations in this section are from *The World and the In-dividual* Vol. 2., except where another reference is given.

sub-section 1.   (1) p. 203. (2) p. 203. (3) p. 203.
          2.   (1) p. 225. (2) p. 225. (3) p. 315. (4) p. 320.
          3.   (1) From Vol. 1. *The World and the Individual*. p. 468. (2) Ibid. p. 468. (3) p. 452. (4) p. 347. (5) p. 348.
          4.   (1) p. 359. (2) p. 359. (3) p. 395. (4) p. 395. (5) p. 398. (6) p. 398. (7) p. 409. (8) p. 409. (9) p. 440. (10) p. 440.

APPENDIX 2

SELECTED BIBLIOGRAPHY IN IDEALIST PHILOSOPHY

The following list of authors and titles may possibly be of use to any reader who wishes to study Idealist philosophy for himself. It begins with the philosophers with whom this book has been concerned and includes not only the works from which I have quoted but certain others which may also be of interest. It then continues with a list of some more recent works and authors. The latter is a purely personal selection and consists of books which in one way or another seem to me to indicate something of the Idealist standpoint and method. Anyone who wishes to learn more about Idealism may find them helpful but I should add that, in recommending them, I do not mean that I necessarily agree with them.

A.

F. H. BRADLEY: *Ethical Studies. The Principles of Logic. Appearance and Reality. Essays in Truth and Reality.*

T . H . G R E E N :   *Prolegomena to Ethics. Lectures on the Principles of Political Obligation.* A memoir to R. L. Nettleship in Green's *Collected Works.* Note : the latter do not include *Prolegomena to Ethics.*

B . B O S A N Q U E T :   *Logic, or the Morphology of Thought. The Essentials of Logic. Aspects of the Social Problem. The Philosophical Theory of the State. The Principle of Individuality and Value. The Value and Destiny of the Individual. Social and International Ideals.*

J O S I A H R O Y C E :   *The Religious Aspects of Philosophy. The Spirit of Modern Philosophy. The World and the Individual. The Philosophy of Loyalty.*

B.

G . P . A D A M S :   *Idealism and the Modern Age.*

B R A N D B L A N S H A R D :   *The Nature of Thought.*

R . G . C O L L I N G W O O D :   *Speculummentis. An Essay on Philosophical Method. The Principles of Art. The New Leviathan. The Idea of History.*

A . C . E W I N G :   *Idealism: a Critical Survey. The Idealist Tradition from Berkeley to Blanshard.*

M . B . F O S T E R :   *The Political Philosophies of Plato and Hegel.*

H . H . J O A C H I M :   *The Nature of Truth.*

J . H . M U I R H E A D :   *The Platonic Tradition in Anglo-Saxon Philosophy.*

G . R . G . M U R E :   *The Retreat from Truth.*

M . J . O A K E S H O T T :   *Experience and its Modes.*

H . A . R E Y B U R N :   *Hegel's Ethical Theory.*

R . H . W O L L H E I M :   *F. H. Bradley.*

THE END